DEC 0 7 2018

Best Hikes of the Appalachian Trail: South

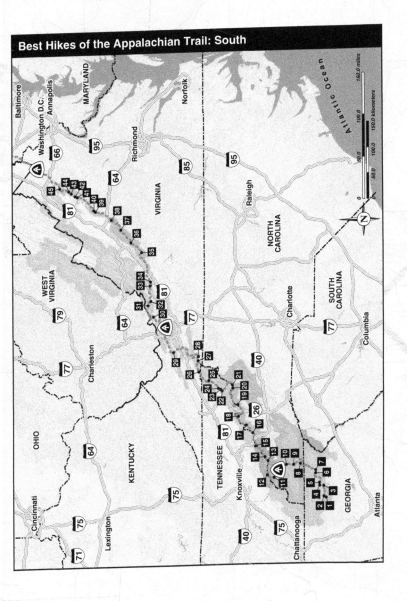

Overview Map Key

BEST HIKES OF THE
APPALACHIAN
TRAIL

APPALACHIAN TRAIL
MAINE TO GEORGIA

South

Georgia • North Carolina • Tennessee • Virginia

JOHNNY MOLLOY

MENASHA RIDGE PRESS
Your Guide to the Outdoors Since 1982

APPALACHIAN TRAIL
CONSERVANCY®

Best Hikes of the Appalachian Trail: South

First edition, first printing

Cover design by Scott McGrew
Text design by Annie Long
Cartography and elevation profiles by Scott McGrew
Cover photos (Clockwise from top): Hike 9, Silers Bald; Hike 20, Highlands of Roan;
Hike 13, Clingmans Dome; Hike 15, Mount Cammerer
Frontispiece: View of the Tye River Valley from The Priest (page 214)
All cover and interior photographs, unless otherwise noted, by Johnny Molloy
The Appalachian Trail symbol is a registered trademark of Appalachian Trail Conservancy.

Library of Congress Cataloging-in-Publication Data

Names: Molloy, Johnny, 1961- author.
Title: Best hikes of the Appalachian Trail. South / Johnny Molloy.
Other titles: South
Description: First edition. | Birmingham, AL : Menasha Ridge Press, 2016.
Identifiers: LCCN 2015051021 | ISBN 9780897324748 (paperback)
Subjects: LCSH: Hiking—Southern States—Guidebooks. | Hiking—Appalachian
   Trail—Guidebooks. | Southern States—Guidebooks. | Appalachian
   Trail—Guidebooks. | BISAC: TRAVEL / United States / South / General.
Classification: LCC GV199.42.S66 M65 2016 | DDC 796.510975—dc23
LC record available at http://lccn.loc.gov/2015051021

ISBN 9780897324748 (pbk.); ISBN 9780897324809 (ebook);
ISBN 9781634041812 (hardcover)

⊞ MENASHA RIDGE PRESS

An imprint of AdventureKEEN
2204 First Ave. S., Suite 102
Birmingham, AL 35233

⊞ APPALACHIAN TRAIL CONSERVANCY

799 Washington St.
Harpers Ferry, WV 25425
appalachiantrail.org

Visit **menasharidge.com** for a complete listing of our books and for ordering information. Contact us at our website, at **facebook.com/menasharidge,** or at **twitter.com/menasharidge** with questions or comments. To find out more about who we are and what we're doing, visit our blog, **trekalong.com.**

DISCLAIMER

This book is meant only as a guide to select routes along the Appalachian Trail. This book does not guarantee hiker safety in any way—you hike at your own risk. Neither Menasha Ridge Press nor Johnny Molloy is liable for property loss or damage, personal injury, or death that result in any way from accessing or hiking the trails described in the following pages. Please be especially cautious when walking in potentially hazardous terrains with, for example, steep inclines or drop-offs. Do not attempt to explore terrain that may be beyond your abilities. Please read carefully the introduction to this book as well as further safety information from other sources. Familiarize yourself with current weather reports and maps of the area you plan to visit (in addition to the maps provided in this guidebook). Be cognizant of park regulations and always follow them. Do not take chances.

Contents

Georgia   22

Tennessee and North Carolina   60

Dedication

This book is for Eve Sherwood.

Acknowledgments

THANKS TO ALL THE PEOPLE who have constructed, maintained, and advocated the Appalachian Trail through the decades. And a special thanks to my wife, Keri Anne.

Preface

DON'T WE ALL WISH we could thru-hike the Appalachian Trail? What an adventure that would be! Sooner or later some of us will. However, for most of us Appalachian Trail (A.T.) enthusiasts, walking the entire length of America's master path from Maine to Georgia will remain an elusive goal. However, we love the A.T. and want to explore and enjoy the trail when and where we can. That is where this book comes into play. *Best Hikes of the Appalachian Trail: South* details 45 hikes along the A.T. from the trail's southern terminus atop Springer Mountain in Georgia, north through North Carolina and Tennessee, and on into Virginia to the Maryland state line.

These hikes head to overlooks, waterfalls, and backcountries, as well as scenic, cultural, and historical sites, even trail towns. Some hikes exclusively use the Appalachian Trail, while others, such as loop hikes, use it in combination with other connecting paths to fashion a rewarding trek.

And there are rewarding treks aplenty, for the Southern Appalachians are an incredibly scenic land, a place where mountains tower thousands of feet above fertile valleys, where crashing cascades plunge into deep forests, where picturesque rivers cut deep gorges through majestic highlands. Along these Southern mountain ranges, the A.T. makes elevation changes in excess of 5,000 feet. This extreme elevation range and the north–south axis of the mountains create ecotones that replicate flora and fauna stretching from Dixie to New England. And the A.T. takes you through these biological wonderlands. Georgia's Blood Mountain proudly displays gardens of mountain laurel, while deep woodlands of birch and rhododendron rise astride Long Creek. In North Carolina, the open meadows of Silers Bald contrast with the lush forests of Standing Indian Mountain. In Tennessee, the spruce-fir evergreens on Roan Mountain juxtapose the great oak woodlands found on the shores of Watauga

THE A.T. TAKES YOU TO A VIEW OF NORTH MOUNTAIN FROM DEVILS SEAT. *(See page 194.)*

Lake. In Virginia, fern gardens line the A.T. on the slopes of Stony Man Mountain, while wind-stunted pine ridges flank the path near the Dragons Tooth. In this varied terrain and habitat, we follow the A.T. to our hiking destinations.

The Southern Appalachians are also blessed with abundant public lands through which the trail roams. Georgia's Chattahoochee National Forest, North Carolina's Pisgah and Nantahala National Forests, Tennessee's Cherokee National Forest, and Virginia's George Washington and Jefferson National Forests collectively avail millions of acres of untamed land, rich with flora and fauna. Then there are the national parks the A.T. explores—Great Smoky Mountains National Park and Shenandoah National Park—as well as the Blue Ridge Parkway. These preserves were set aside for a reason and offer opportunities to experience the best of the best.

These bountiful public lands are enhanced by the most heralded and hiked footpath in our country, the Appalachian Trail. Its 1,000-mile journey through highland Dixie links to a network of trails spreading through local wildlands that creates additional hiking opportunities. The proximity of the A.T. and the trail towns of Hot Springs, North Carolina; Erwin, Tennessee; and Damascus, Virginia, put the Appalachian Trail on the front burner of outdoor activities in the Southern highlands.

Using the A.T., its connecting trail network, and this guide, you can make a loop using the A.T. and Benton MacKaye Trail while visiting the southern terminus of the A.T. atop Springer Mountain in Georgia. Or trek from Dockery Lake to Preaching Rock. Venture into Tray Mountain Wilderness. Grab a 360-degree view from North Carolina's Wesser Bald Tower. Walk the highest point of the entire A.T. at Clingmans Dome. Overlook the magnificence of the Smokies from Charlies Bunion. Traverse the meadows of Roan Mountain, contemplating their origin, and view the mountain's world-famous wildflower gardens, where rhododendron blooms in concentrations unseen anywhere else on the planet. Soak in views from an old farm, where the A.T. travels atop a ridge known as Cross Mountain that links Holston and Iron Mountains. Enjoy a swim at Laurel Falls.

And more hiking possibilities are included in this guide. Follow the A.T. through the trail town of Damascus, Virginia, then to the backwoods and a view before returning to town. Head to Mount Rogers, Virginia's highest point, nestled in the rare spruce-fir ecosystem. Traverse open meadows of Chestnut Knob to visit a ranger cabin turned A.T. trail shelter. Stand at the narrow pinnacle of the Dragons Tooth. Hunt for the ghost of Ottie Powell atop Bluff Mountain. At Shenandoah National Park you can visit a streamside presidential retreat, view multiple waterfalls from Browns Gap, or capture the essence of the Blue Ridge Mountains and Shenandoah Valley from Marys Rock, all using the A.T. and connecting trails.

Still other A.T. hikes are water oriented, with waterfalls as destinations. These include Virginia's Apple Orchard Falls and Lewis Spring Falls. Waterside treks include more than just cataracts. Hikes in this book also visit swimming holes, sunning rocks, and even fishing hot spots.

And then there are A.T. hikes that explore the fascinating geology of our Southern highlands. Grab views from clearings on Georgia's Rocky Mountain. North Carolina's High Rocks present another window into the geology of the Appalachian Mountains, as do the crags of Lovers Leap above the French Broad River. Walk the stony spine of the A.T. on Firescald Ridge. Peer out from the rocky brow of Virginia's McAfee Knob. View adjacent talus slopes from the edge of The Priest.

Solitude can be found on the A.T. Walk from Rocky Gap near Blacksburg, Virginia, to grab a view from Kelly Knob. Explore the Laurel Branch Wilderness in Tennessee to find an outcrop near Vandeventer shelter delivering stellar panoramas. Hike with nature in Georgia's Tray Mountain Wilderness.

The A.T. hikes in this guide take both the long and the short ways. The jaunt at Cross Mountain is brief and wheelchair accessible, while the Mountain Lake Wilderness hike stretches a full 11 miles. The Spence Field–Russell Field Loop in the Smokies is an all-day endeavor, while the quick trip to Blackrock Summit is suitable for A.T. enthusiasts of all ages.

Therefore, the best hikes of the Appalachian Trail in the South can mean a ramble through the backcountry of the Great Smoky Mountains, a trek to a crashing cascade down Georgia way, or a quick escape to an eye-popping vista at Virginia's Wind Rock. It all depends on your mood, company, and desires. So not only is the "where to hike" component covered, but so is the "what type of hike." As far as when, you can hike year-round on the Appalachian Trail, but most of us will be walking the A.T. spring through fall. The important thing is getting out there and enjoying this fascinating footpath.

This guide is designed to help you explore the Appalachian Trail. The variety of hikes contained within its pages reflects the variety of opportunities along the master path of the East. I sought to include hikes covering routes of multiple lengths, ranging from easy to difficult. Trail configurations are diverse as well—including out-and-back hikes, loops, and balloon loops. Hike settings vary from the

LOWER DOYLES RIVER FALLS *(See page 229.)*

town of Damascus to secluded national forest hinterlands to mountain gorges and lakes.

The routes befit a range of athletic prowess and hiking experience. Simply scan through the table of contents, randomly flip through the book, or utilize the hiking recommendations list included. Find your hike, get out there, and enjoy it. And bring a friend too. Enjoying nature in the company of another is a great way to enhance your relationship as well as escape from television, e-mail, the Internet, and other electronic chains that bind us to the daily grind.

One last thing—there is a reason I live in the shadow of the Appalachian Trail. Having written outdoor guidebooks covering 26 states, I truly believe that the Southern Appalachians are the best part of the best country on God's green earth. May this book help you enjoy the wonderful, rewarding trails of highland Dixie.

Hiking Recommendations

Best for Scenery

Best for Wildlife

Best for Seclusion

Best for Kids

Best for Dogs

Best for Water Lovers

Best for Waterfalls

Best for History

Best for Geology

Best for Geology *(continued)*

Best for Wildflowers

Best for Views

Introduction

About This Book

BEST HIKES OF THE APPALACHIAN TRAIL: SOUTH details 45 great hikes using the Appalachian Trail and connecting paths within the states of Georgia, North Carolina, Tennessee, and Virginia. It presents the reader with an array of treks that reflect the magnificence of the mountain South, ranging from the peaks and waterfalls of northern Virginia and Shenandoah National Park down to the Appalachians of North Georgia. Of course, this includes the hundreds of miles of mountain lands in between.

For this guide, the author and Menasha Ridge Press have collaborated with the Appalachian Trail Conservancy, or A.T.C. as it is known in the hiking universe. The A.T.C.'s mission is to "preserve and manage the Appalachian Trail—ensuring that its vast natural beauty and priceless cultural heritage can be shared and enjoyed today, tomorrow, and for centuries to come." It is in that vein that we invite you to enjoy and immerse yourself in the Appalachian Trail and be a part of the Appalachian Trail community.

I believe the Southern Appalachians to be one of the best outdoor destinations in the United States. Proximity to seemingly endless outdoor opportunities—hiking, paddling, bicycling, camping, hunting, fishing, nature study, and more—vastly enhances the quality of life here. Millions of acres of mountains lie within national parks and forests here. Literally thousands of miles of trails lace these mountain lands. And the Appalachian Trail is the spine of this vast trail network.

This creates ample opportunities to hike the Appalachian Trail and link it with adjacent paths to create hikes that truly are among the best—hikes that lead through deep gorges, past wild waterfalls, and to unique rock features. Hikes in this book cover a mosaic of places and experiences from the untamed grandeur of Pond

Mountain Wilderness to lofty Mount Rogers National Recreation Area to sonorant Slaughter Creek above Lake Winfield Scott.

Moreover, the greater Southern Appalachian climate is ideal for hiking; we have four distinct and beautiful seasons. If you like winter, the mountains annually deliver more than 60 inches of snow above 5,000 feet! Yet many mild days occur that are perfect for trail trekkers. The elevation and terrain variations make spring exciting too, as the season of rebirth grows its way from the river valleys to the high country. Wildflowers follow. Summer finds many of us escaping to cool waters and to refreshing mountaintops, where heat-relieving breezes blow on A.T. hikers. During fall the Southern Appalachians' incredible variety of trees explode in their annual color display, brought on by warm, dry days and cool nights.

How do you get started? Peruse this book, pick out a hike, and strike out on the trail. The wide assortment of paths, distances, difficulties, and destinations will suit any hiker's mood and company. And try them all—the varied hikes will leave you appreciating the Appalachian Trail more than you ever imagined. Enjoy!

Appalachian Trail Divisions

The hikes in this book have been divided into three geographic divisions. Georgia covers about 79 miles of the Appalachian Trail through the Peach State, from Springer Mountain to the North Carolina state line. The hikes here include the famed Blood Mountain, a loop atop Rocky Mountain, and others, for a total of seven Georgia hikes.

The North Carolina–Tennessee section includes approximately 100 miles of the A.T. exclusively in North Carolina, about 200 miles of A.T. mileage straddling the Tennessee–North Carolina border, and about 85 miles exclusively in Tennessee. Among these miles you can experience outlooks from Standing Indian Mountain, as well as Shuckstack fire tower, Mount Cammerer, and high Big Hump Mountain. Don't forget Max Patch, with its open fields delivering 360-degree panoramas. This Volunteer State and Tar Heel State segment presents 18 hikes.

The Virginia segment covers 556 miles of the Appalachian Trail, the most mileage of any state in the footpath's entire length. This includes hiking to the Angels Rest near Pearisburg, seeing the homestead and view at Humpback Rocks, and enjoying the forests and vistas of Shenandoah's Sugarloaf Loop. The unique Mount Rogers High Country avails a trek to the Old Dominion's high point, as well as the mix of rock, meadows, and forests rising more than a mile high. Twenty hikes from Virginia are detailed in this guide.

Altogether, the four states of the Southern Appalachians through which the Appalachian Trail travels create a mosaic of natural splendidness that will please the most discriminating hiker.

How to Use This Guidebook

THE FOLLOWING SECTIONS will walk you through each of the organizational elements of the profiles as they're presented in this book. The goal is to make it as easy as possible for you to plan a hike you'll enjoy, a hike you'll remember, and a hike that matches whatever you're looking for on any given day.

Overview Map & Map Key

The overview map on the inside front cover shows the general location of each hike's primary trailhead. Each hike's number appears on the overview map, on the map key facing the overview map, and in the table of contents. Thus, if you know you will be traveling to a particular area, you can check that area on the overview map, find the appropriate hike numbers, and then flip through the book and easily find those hikes by looking for the hike numbers at the top of each profile page. Or if you find a specific hike on the overview map, you can locate the profile by following the number.

Trail Maps

In addition to the overview map, a detailed map of each hike's route appears with its profile. On this map, symbols indicate the complete route and topographic landmarks, such as creeks, overlooks, and peaks.

To produce the highly accurate maps in this book, the author used a handheld GPS unit to gather data while hiking each route, and then sent that data to the publisher's expert cartographers. However, your GPS is never a substitute for sound, sensible navigation that takes into account the conditions that you observe while hiking. The GPS is a remarkable tool, but it can't replace knowing how to use a map and compass. If you're interested in learning more about using a GPS for navigation, check out *Outdoor Navigation with GPS,* third edition, by Stephen W. Hinch. Be sure to check out books and articles, or even take a class at your local outdoor store, on using a map and compass as well.

Further, despite the high quality of the maps in this guidebook, the publisher and author strongly recommend that every time you venture out into the woods, you always carry an additional, accurate, up-to-date map of the area in which you're hiking, such as the ones noted in each entry opener's listing for "Maps."

Elevation Profile (Diagram)

This diagram represents the rises and falls of the trail as viewed from the side over the complete distance (expressed in miles) for that trail. From this, you should be able to judge where the steep sections will come during the hike. Don't underestimate the intensity of a hike that may be associated with these diagrams.

On the diagram's vertical axis, or height scale, the number of feet indicated between each tick mark lets you visualize the climb. Use these side-view profiles, along with contour markings on the additional maps you will carry, to determine the relative intensity of the hike. To avoid making flat hikes look steep and steep hikes appear flat, varying height scales provide an accurate image of each hike's climbing challenge. For example, one hike's scale might rise to 200 feet, while another goes to 2,000 feet.

The Hike Profile

Each hike profile opens with an information box that encapsulates all the details you'll need to know for that particular hike. The at-a-glance information includes the hike's star ratings (for hike difficulty, how appropriate the hike is for kids, scenery, trail condition, and solitude), GPS trailhead coordinates, the overall distance of the hike, trail configuration (out-and-back or point-to-point), facilities, and contacts for local information. Each profile also includes a listing of the appropriate maps to have on hand for the hike (see "Trail Maps," pages 3–4).

The text for each profile includes four sections: Overview, Route Details, Nearby Attractions, and Directions (for driving to the trailhead area). Below is an explanation of each of these elements.

★ **Overview** gives you a quick summary of what to expect on the trail.

★ **Route Details** takes you on a guided hike from start to finish, including landmarks, side trips, and possible alternate routes along the way.

★ **Nearby Attractions** mentions the nearest towns, as well as other trails or parks close by.

★ **Directions** will get you to the trailhead from a well-known road or highway.

STAR RATINGS

Here's a guide to interpreting the rating system of one to five stars in each of the five categories for each hike—scenery, trail condition, children, difficulty, and solitude.

SCENERY:

★★★★★ Unique, picturesque panoramas

★★★★ Diverse vistas

★★★ Pleasant views

★★ Unchanging landscape

★ Not selected for scenery

TRAIL CONDITION:

★ ★ ★ ★ ★   Consistently well maintained

★ ★ ★ ★   Stable, with no surprises

★ ★ ★   Average terrain to negotiate

★ ★   Inconsistent, with good and poor areas

★   Rocky, overgrown, or often muddy

CHILDREN:

★ ★ ★ ★ ★   Appropriate for babes in strollers

★ ★ ★ ★   Fun for any kid past the toddler stage

★ ★ ★   Good for young hikers with proven stamina

★ ★   Not enjoyable for children

★   Not advisable at all for children

DIFFICULTY:

★ ★ ★ ★ ★   Grueling

★ ★ ★ ★   Challenging, with stretches of ease

★ ★ ★   Exhilarating

★ ★   Pleasantly invigorating

★   Good for a relaxing stroll

SOLITUDE:

★ ★ ★ ★ ★   Positively tranquil

★ ★ ★ ★   Spurts of isolation

★ ★ ★   Moderately secluded

★ ★   Could be crowded on weekends and holidays

★   Steady stream of individuals/groups

GPS TRAILHEAD COORDINATES

As noted in the "Trail Maps" section on page 4, I used a handheld GPS unit to obtain geographic data. In the opener for each hike profile, I have provided the intersection of the latitude (north) and longitude (west) coordinates to orient you at the trailhead. Plug these into your own handheld GPS unit or your phone if you prefer to use that. And remember, a handheld GPS unit or GPS app in your phone does not replace having a map and compass and the knowledge to use them properly.

In some cases, you can drive within viewing distance of a trailhead. Other hikes require a short walk to reach the trailhead from a parking area. Either way, the trailhead coordinates are given from the trail's actual head—its point of origin.

You will also note that this guidebook uses the degree–decimal minute format for presenting the GPS coordinates. The latitude and longitude grid system is likely quite familiar to you, but here is a refresher, pertinent to visualizing the GPS coordinates: Imaginary lines of latitude—called parallels and approximately 69 miles apart from each other—run horizontally around the globe. The equator is established at 0°. Each parallel is indicated by degrees, increasing from the equator: up to 90°N at the North Pole and down to 90°S at the South Pole.

Imaginary lines of longitude—called meridians—run perpendicular to latitude lines and are likewise indicated by degrees. Starting from 0° at the Prime Meridian in Greenwich, England, they continue to the east and west until they meet 180° later at the International Date Line in the Pacific Ocean. At the equator, longitude lines also are approximately 69 miles apart, but that distance narrows as the meridians converge toward the North and South Poles.

The GPS coordinates map to latitude and longitude and are generated by a network of 24 geosynchronous satellites positioned such that they cover Earth's entire surface. A GPS unit locks onto at least three or four of those satellites to triangulate position. The system works well, but reception can be stymied by weather, dense forests, or deep canyons. To convert GPS coordinates given in degrees, minutes, and seconds to the format shown above in degrees–decimal minutes, the seconds are divided by 60. For more on GPS technology, visit **usgs.gov.**

DISTANCE & CONFIGURATION

The distance is the full, round-trip length of the hike from start to finish. If the hike description includes options for a shorter or longer hike, those round-trip distances will also be described here.

The configuration defines the trail as an out-and-back (taking you in and out via the same route, such as hiking to the summit of a mountain and then down the same way), point-to-point, or some other configuration.

HIKING TIME

In most mountainous regions, the general rule of thumb for the hiking times is 1 hour per 1 mile and 1,000 feet of elevation gain. Not all hikes even have that much elevation gain, and others are steep and rocky and would probably result in a slower pace. Check the summary information and the text of the hike profiles, which will provide as much detail as possible.

That pace also allows time for taking photos, for stopping to admire the views (of which there are many), and for alternating stretches of steep hills, rolling forest floors, and gentle descents. When you're deciding whether or not to follow a particular trail described in this guidebook, be flexible. Consider your own pace, the weather, your general physical condition, and your energy level on that day.

HIGHLIGHTS

Many of these hikes take you past spectacular highlights, which will be noted here. These may include waterfalls, massive cliffs, or particularly scenic views from the summit.

ELEVATION

In each hike's key information, you'll see the elevation at both the trailhead and the peak. The full hike profile also includes a complete elevation profile (see "Elevation Profile" on page 4).

ACCESS

No fees are required for any of these hikes. However, there may be park entrance fees, such as at Shenandoah National Park. Trailhead parking fees will sometimes be noted here. If there are any restrictions on hours to access the trail (such as sunrise–sunset), that will also be mentioned here. Overnight backpackers using these loops may be required to purchase a backcountry permit, such as at Great Smoky Mountains National Park.

MAPS

Maps of your hiking route and the surrounding area are essential. A GPS unit or GPS app on your phone is a useful tool, but it's no replacement for detailed, up-to-date maps. This section will list any additional maps you could and should carry with you for the hike being profiled. Maps can be purchased from the Appalachian Trail Conservancy at **atctrailstore.org.**

FACILITIES

This information includes restrooms, water, picnic areas, campgrounds, and other basics at or near the trailhead.

CONTACT

Listed here are phone numbers and websites for checking trail conditions and gleaning other day-to-day information.

Weather

EACH OF THE FOUR SEASONS distinctly lays its hands on the Southern Appalachians. Summer is generally mild—but humid—in the mountains of the South. Thunderstorms can pop up in the afternoons. Storm possibilities increase with elevation. Hikers get a little extra pep in their step when fall's first northerly fronts sweep cool, clear air across highland Dixie. Mountaintop vistas are best enjoyed during this time. Crisp mornings give way to warm afternoons. Fall is drier than summer and is the driest of all seasons. Winter can bring frigid, subfreezing days and chilling rains—and copious snow in the high country. We're talking more than 60 inches per year above 5,000 feet. However, a brisk hiking pace will keep you warm. Each cold month will have a few days of mild weather. However, be apprised that mild in the lowland may still be frigid along the spine of the Appalachians. Spring will be more variable. A warm day can be followed by a cold one. Extensive spring rains bring regrowth but also keep hikers indoors. Moreover, spring rains can mean spring snow in the highlands. On average, March dumps the most inches of snow upon the Smoky Mountains. Nevertheless, avid hikers will find more good hiking days than they will have time to hike in spring and every other season. For the best weather prediction for your chosen Appalachian Trail hike, visit **weather.gov,** the National Weather Service website. Enter the nearest town to your hike. Note that the temperatures given here are from stations in cities and towns; for higher elevations, subtract 3.5°F per 1,000 feet of elevation from the nearest recording station to get a better idea of the temperature.

In addition to predictions for that town, you will see an interactive map. Scroll the map for your exact trailhead position, and then click on the trailhead position for a pinpoint forecast. Then you will be prepared for the ensuing weather on your hike. For more detailed weather forecasting and historical data, check out the following sites:

★ **noaa.gov**   ★ **usclimatedata.com**   ★ **weatherbase.com**

Water

HOW MUCH IS ENOUGH? Here's a simple physiological fact that should convince you to err on the side of excess when deciding how much water to pack: A hiker walking steadily in 90°F heat needs approximately 10 quarts of fluid per day. That's 2.5 gallons.

A good rule of thumb is to hydrate prior to your hike, carry (and drink) 6 ounces of water for every mile you plan to hike, and hydrate again after the hike. For most people, the pleasures of hiking make carrying water a relatively minor price to pay to remain safe and healthy. So pack more water than you anticipate needing, even for short hikes.

If you are tempted to drink "found" water, do so with extreme caution. Many ponds and lakes encountered by hikers are fairly stagnant and taste terrible, plus they present inherent risks for thirsty trekkers. *Giardia* parasites contaminate many water sources and cause the dreaded intestinal giardiasis that can last for weeks after ingestion. For information, visit the Centers for Disease Control website at **cdc.gov/parasites/giardia.** In any case, effective treatment is essential before using any water source found along the trail. Boiling water for 2–3 minutes is always a safe measure for camping, but day hikers can consider iodine tablets, approved chemical mixes, filtration units rated for *Giardia*, and ultraviolet (UV) filtration. Some of these methods (for example, filtration with an added carbon filter) remove bad tastes typical in stagnant water, while others add their own taste. As a precaution, carry some means of water purification to help in a pinch. It's better to have some purified water that tastes a little off than to risk dehydration or an intestinal parasite.

Clothing

WEATHER, UNEXPECTED TRAIL CONDITIONS, fatigue, extended hiking duration, and wrong turns can individually or collectively turn a great outing into a very uncomfortable one at best—and a life-threatening one at worst. Thus, proper attire plays a key role in staying comfortable and, sometimes, staying alive. Here are some helpful guidelines:

★ *Choose silk, wool, or synthetics for maximum comfort* in all of your hiking attire—from hats to socks and in between. Cotton is fine if the weather remains dry and stable, but you won't be happy if it gets wet.

★ *Always wear a hat,* or at least tuck one into your day pack or hitch it to your belt. Hats offer all-weather sun and wind protection as well as warmth if it turns cold.

★ *Be ready to layer up or down* as the day progresses and the mercury rises or falls. Today's outdoor wear makes layering easy, with such designs as jackets that convert to vests and pants with zip-off or button-up legs.

★ *Wear hiking boots or sturdy hiking sandals with toe protection.* Flip-flopping on a paved path in an urban botanical garden is one thing, but never hike the Appalachian Trail in open sandals or casual sneakers. The A.T. can be very rocky. Your bones and arches need support, and your skin needs protection.

★ *Pair that footwear with good socks!* If you prefer not to sheathe your feet when wearing hiking sandals, tuck the socks into your day pack; you may need them if the temperature plummets or if you hit rocky turf and pebbles begin to irritate your feet. And, in an emergency, if you have lost your gloves, you can adapt the socks into mittens.

★ *Don't leave raingear behind,* even if the day dawns clear and sunny. Tuck into your day pack, or tie around your waist, a jacket that is breathable and either water resistant or waterproof. Investigate different choices at your local outdoors retailer. If you are a frequent hiker, ideally you'll have more than one raingear weight, material, and style in your closet to protect you in all seasons in your regional climate and hiking microclimates.

Essential Gear

TODAY YOU CAN BUY outdoor vests that have up to 20 pockets shaped and sized to carry everything from toothpicks to binoculars, or if you don't aspire to feeling like a burro, you can neatly stow all of these items in your day pack or backpack. The following list showcases never-hike-without-them items:

★ *Water* (As emphasized more than once in this book, bring more than you think you will drink. Depending on your destination, you may want to bring a container and iodine or a filter for purifying water in case you run out.)

★ *Maps and a high-quality compass* (Even if you know the terrain from previous hikes, don't leave home without these tools. And, as previously noted, bring maps in addition to those in this guidebook, and consult your maps prior to the hike. If you are versed in GPS usage, bring that as well. However, do not rely on it as your sole navigational tool. Your GPS battery can dwindle or fade completely, or you might not get a signal in mountainous terrain or dense forests. Be sure to compare its guidance with that of your maps. Furthermore, phones with GPS capability can lose signal or power as well.)

★ *Pocketknife/multitool*

★ *Flashlight or headlamp* with extra bulb and batteries

★ *Windproof matches/lighter,* as well as a fire starter

★ *Extra food* (trail mix, granola bars, or other high-energy foods)

★ *Extra clothes* (raingear, warm hat, gloves, and change of socks and shirt)

★ *Whistle* (This can be your best friend in an emergency if you're trying to help rescuers find you.)

★ *Insect repellent* (When you want it, you really want it. Bring a small bottle with DEET in it.)

★ *Sun protection, including sunglasses, lip balm, and sunscreen* (Note the expiration date on the tube or bottle; it's usually embossed on the top.)

★ *Space blanket or emergency blanket* (This can save someone who becomes hypothermic.)

Today's handheld devices not only have a phone that may help you contact help, but they also have built-in GPSs that can help with orientation. However, do not call for help unless you are truly in need, and remember your smartphone batteries can die too. In mountainous terrain of the Appalachian Trail, coverage can be spotty.

First-Aid Kit

IN ADDITION TO THE ITEMS ABOVE, those below may appear overwhelming for a day hike. But any paramedic will tell you that the products listed here, in alphabetical order, are just the basics. The reality of hiking is that you can be out for a week of backpacking and acquire only a mosquito bite—or you can hike for an hour, slip, and suffer a bleeding abrasion or broken bone. Fortunately, these items will collapse into a very small space, and convenient, prepackaged kits are available at your pharmacy and on the Internet.

★ Ace bandages or Spenco joint wraps

★ Antibiotic ointment (Neosporin or the generic equivalent)

★ Athletic tape

★ Band-Aids

★ Benadryl or the generic equivalent diphenhydramine (in case of allergic reactions)

★ Blister kit (such as Moleskin/Spenco Second Skin)

★ Butterfly-closure bandages

★ Epinephrine in a prefilled syringe (This is typically by prescription only for people known to have severe allergic reactions to hiking occurrences, such as bee stings.)

★ Gauze (one roll and a half dozen 4-by-4-inch compress pads)

★ Hydrogen peroxide or iodine

★ Ibuprofen or acetaminophen

★ Snakebite kit

Pack the items in a waterproof bag, such as a zip-top bag. Consider the nature of the terrain you intend to hike and the number of hikers in your party before you exclude any article cited above. When hiking alone, you should always be prepared for any medical need. If you are hiking with only one partner or with a group, one or more people in your party should be equipped with a complete first-aid kit.

General Safety

THE FOLLOWING TIPS may have the familiar ring of your mother's voice as you take note of them:

★ *Always let someone know where you will be hiking* and how long you expect to be gone. It's a good idea to give that person a copy of your route, particularly if you are headed into any isolated area. Let them know when you return.

★ *Always sign in and out of any trail registers provided.* Don't hesitate to comment on the trail condition if space is provided; that's your opportunity to alert others to any problems you encounter.

★ *Do not count on a smartphone for your safety.* Reception may be spotty or nonexistent on the trail.

★ *Always carry food and water,* even on a short hike. And bring more water than you think you will need. That's one point that can never be overemphasized.

★ *Stay on designated trails.* Even on the most clearly marked trails, there is usually a point where you have to stop and consider which direction you need to go. The Appalachian Trail is usually quite well marked and well-defined, but there are more remote areas where you may wonder where the trail is going. If you become disoriented, don't panic. As soon as you think you may be off track, stop, assess your current direction, and then retrace your steps to the point where you went astray. Using a map, a compass, GPS, and this book, and keeping in mind what you have passed thus far, reorient yourself, and trust your judgment on which way to continue. If you become absolutely unsure of how to continue, return to your vehicle the way you came in. Should you become completely lost and have no idea how to return to the trailhead, remaining in place along the trail and waiting for help is most often the best option for adults and always the best option for children.

★ *Always carry a whistle.* This is an exceptionally important precaution. It can be a lifesaver if you become lost or sustain an injury.

★ *Be especially careful when crossing streams.* Whether you are ford-ing the stream or crossing on a log, make every step count. If you have any doubt about maintaining your balance on a log, ford the stream instead. Use a trekking pole or stout stick for balance and face upstream as you cross. If a stream seems too deep to ford, turn back. Whatever is on the other side is not worth risking your life.

★ *Be careful at overlooks.* While these areas may provide spectacular views, they are potentially hazardous. Stay back from the edge of outcrops and be absolutely sure of your footing; a misstep can mean a nasty and possibly fatal fall.

★ *Standing dead trees and storm-damaged living trees pose a real haz-ard to hikers.* These trees may have loose or broken limbs that could fall at any time. While walking beneath trees, and when choosing a spot to rest or enjoy your snack, look up and look around. Also be extremely careful if you're reaching for a tree or limb to help you up a steep section. Test it with partial weight before committing to using it to help you move.

★ *Know the symptoms of hypothermia.* Shivering and forgetfulness are the two most common indicators of this stealthy killer. Hypothermia can occur at any elevation, even in the summer, especially when the hiker is wearing lightweight cotton clothing. If symptoms present themselves, get to shelter, hot liquids, and dry clothes ASAP.

★ *Know the symptoms of heat exhaustion* (hyperthermia). Two early indicators are light-headedness and loss of energy. If you feel either or both of these symptoms, find some shade, drink some water, remove as many layers of clothing as practical, and stay put until you cool down. Marching through heat exhaustion can lead to heat-stroke—which can be fatal. If you should be sweating and you're not, that's another classic warning sign. Your hike is over at that point. Heatstroke is a life-threatening condition that can cause seizures, convulsions, and eventually death. If you or a companion reaches that point, do whatever you can to cool the victim down and seek medical attention immediately.

★ *Ask questions.* National park, national forest, state park, and other land-management employees are there to help. It is a lot easier to ask advice beforehand, and it will help you avoid a mishap away from civilization when it's too late to amend an error. whistle

★ *Most important of all, take along your brain.* A cool, calculating mind is the single-most important asset on the trail. Think before you act.

★ *Watch your step.* Plan ahead. Avoiding accidents before they happen is the best way to ensure a rewarding and relaxing hike.

Animal, Insect, and Plant Hazards
Black Bears

Though attacks by black bears are very rare, they have happened in the Southern Appalachians. The sight or approach of a bear can give anyone a start. If you encounter a bear while hiking, remain calm and never run away. Make loud noises to scare off the bear and back away slowly. In primitive and remote areas, assume bears are present. In more developed sites, check on the current bear situation prior to hiking. Most encounters are food related, as bears have an exceptional sense of smell and not particularly discriminating tastes. While this is of greater concern to backpackers and campers, on a day hike you may have a lunchtime picnic or munch on a power bar or other snack from time to time. So remain aware and alert, especially at shelters along the A.T.

Snakes

Rattlesnakes and copperheads are among the most common venomous snakes in the United States, and hibernation season is typically October–April. In the Southern Appalachians, you will possibly encounter the timber rattler or copperhead. However, the snakes you most likely will see while hiking will be nonvenomous species and subspecies. The best rule is to leave all snakes alone, give them a wide berth as you hike past, and make sure any hiking companions (including dogs) do the same.

When hiking, stick to well-used trails and wear over-the-ankle boots and loose-fitting long pants. Rattlesnakes like to bask in the sun and won't bite unless threatened. Do not step or put your hands where you cannot see, and avoid wandering around in the dark. Step onto logs and rocks, never over them, and be especially careful when climbing rocks. Always avoid walking through dense brush or willow thickets. Copperheads are most often found along streams, also looking for a sunny spot atop a rock.

Mosquitoes

These little naggers are more often found in urban areas but sparingly in the hillier Southern Appalachians. Insect repellent and/or repellent-impregnated clothing are the only simple methods to ward off these pests. In some areas, mosquitoes are known to carry the West Nile virus, so all due caution should be taken to avoid their bites.

Ticks

Generally speaking, tick encounters are rare in the Southern Appalachians. Ticks are sometimes found on brush and tall grass, where they seem to be waiting to hitch a ride on a warm-blooded passerby. Adult ticks are most active April–May and again October–November. Among the varieties of ticks, the black-legged tick, commonly called the deer tick, is the primary carrier of Lyme disease. Wear light-colored clothing, making it easier for you to spot ticks before they migrate to your skin. At the end of the hike, visually check your hair, back of neck, armpits, and socks. During your post-hike shower, take a moment to do a more complete body check. For ticks that are already embedded, removal with tweezers is best. Use disinfectant solution on the wound.

Poison Ivy, Oak, & Sumac

Recognizing and avoiding poison ivy, oak, and sumac are the most effective ways to prevent the painful, itchy rashes associated with these plants. Poison ivy occurs as a vine or ground cover, 3 leaflets to a leaf; poison oak occurs as either a vine or shrub, also with 3 leaflets; and poison sumac flourishes in swampland, each leaf having 7–13 leaflets. Urushiol, the oil in the sap of these plants, is responsible for the rash. Within 14 hours of exposure, raised lines and/or blisters will appear on the affected area, accompanied by a terrible itch. Refrain from scratching because bacteria under your fingernails can cause an infection. Wash and dry the affected area thoroughly, applying a calamine lotion to help dry out the rash. If itching or blistering is severe, seek medical attention. If you do come into contact with one of these plants, remember that oil-contaminated clothes, pets, or hiking gear can easily cause an irritating rash on you or someone else, so wash not only any exposed parts of your body but also clothes, gear, and pets if applicable.

Hunting

SEPARATE RULES, regulations, and licenses govern the various hunting types and related seasons. Though there are generally no problems, hikers may wish to forgo their trips during the big-game seasons, usually in November and December, when the woods suddenly seem filled with orange and camouflage. Places you may encounter hunters will be the Chattahoochee, Cherokee, Nantahala, Pisgah, George Washington, and Jefferson National Forests. Hunters tend to approach the trail from the sides, not the trailheads, and may not know that they are in prohibited zones, so it is always best to exercise caution.

Trail Etiquette

ALWAYS TREAT THE TRAIL, wildlife, and fellow hikers with respect. Here are some reminders:

★ *Plan ahead* in order to be self-sufficient at all times. Carry all necessary supplies for changes in weather or other conditions. A well-executed trip is a satisfaction to you and to others.

★ *Hike on open trails only.*

★ *Respect trail and road closures* (ask if not sure), avoid possible trespassing on private land, and obtain all permits and authorization as required. Also, leave gates as you found them or as marked.

★ *Be courteous* to others you encounter on the trails.

★ *Never spook animals.* An unannounced approach, a sudden movement, or a loud noise startles most animals. A surprised animal can be dangerous to you, to others, and to itself. Give them plenty of space.

★ *Observe the yield signs* around the region's trailheads and backcountry. Be courteous to other trail users. Most sections of the Appalachian Trail are restricted to hikers, but you may encounter other trail users. Typically hikers should yield to horses, and bikers yield to both horses and hikers. By common courtesy on hills, hikers and bikers yield to any uphill traffic. When encountering mounted riders or horse packers, hikers should courteously step off the trail, on the downhill side if possible. Position yourself so the horse can see and hear you. Calmly greet the riders before they reach you and don't dart behind trees. Also resist the urge to pet horses unless you are invited to do so.

★ *Leave only footprints.* Be sensitive to the ground beneath you. This also means staying on the existing trail and not blazing any new trails.

★ *Be sure to pack out what you pack in.* No one likes to see the trash someone else has left behind.

Familiarize yourself with and adhere to the principles of Leave No Trace (**lnt.org**). You can find A.T.-specific guidelines at **appalachian trail.org/lnt**.

Tips on Enjoying Hiking the Appalachian Trail

BEFORE YOU GO, read the hike description in this book and visit the website of the land-management body. Call ahead if you have unanswered questions. This will help you get oriented to the forthcoming hike.

Investigate different destinations. The Appalachian Trail through the Southern Appalachians traverses terrain varying over 5,000 feet in elevation while exploring ridges, rivers, and geological and historic sites. Take a chance and make a new adventure instead of trying to re-create the same one over and over. You will be pleasantly surprised to see so many distinct landscapes along the A.T.

Take your time along the trails. Pace yourself. The landscape along the Appalachian Trail is filled with wonders both big and small. Don't rush past a tiny salamander to get to that overlook. Stop and smell the wildflowers. Go ahead and take a seat on a trailside rock. Peer into a stream to find secretive fish. Take pictures. Make memories. Don't miss the trees for the forest.

We can't always schedule our free time when we want, but try to hike during the week and avoid the traditional holidays if possible. Trails that are packed in the summer are often clear during the colder months. If you are hiking on a busy day, go early in the morning; it will enhance your chances of seeing wildlife. The trails really clear out during rainy times; however, avoid hiking during a thunderstorm.

OPPOSITE: THE KELLY KNOB HIKE OFFERS
SOLITUDE LEADING TO THIS VIEW. *(See page 189.)*

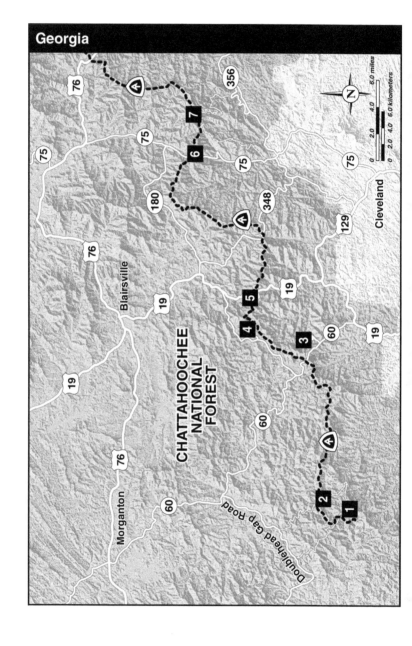

Georgia

GEORGIA HIKES INCLUDE THE TREK TO LONG CREEK FALLS. *(See page 29.)*

1

Springer Mountain Circuit

SCENERY: ★ ★ ★
TRAIL CONDITION: ★ ★ ★
CHILDREN: ★ ★
DIFFICULTY: ★ ★
SOLITUDE: ★

THIS VIEW CAN BE HAD AT THE A.T.'S SOUTHERN TERMINUS.

GPS TRAILHEAD COORDINATES: N34° 38.254' W84° 11.709'

DISTANCE & CONFIGURATION: 4.7-mile loop

HIKING TIME: 3 hours

HIGHLIGHTS: Southern terminus Appalachian Trail, views

ELEVATION: 3,370' at trailhead; 3,780' at high point

ACCESS: No fees or permits required

MAPS: Trails Illustrated #777 *Springer and Cohutta Mountains*; Appalachian Trail Conservancy *Chattahoochee National Forest*; USGS *Noontoola*

FACILITIES: None

CONTACT: Chattahoochee National Forest, Conasauga Ranger District: 706-695-6736, **www.fs.usda.gov/conf**

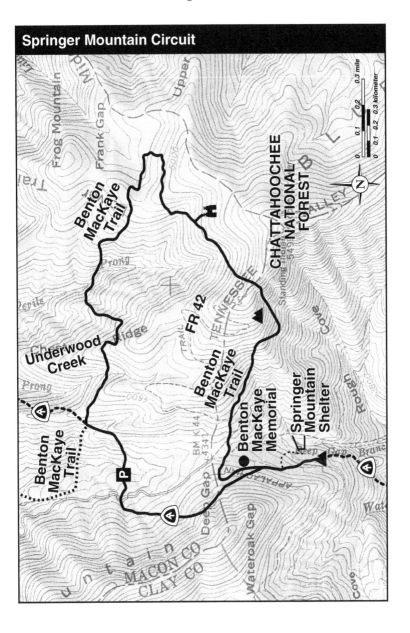

Overview

This hike takes you to famed Springer Mountain, the southern terminus of the entire Appalachian Trail (A.T.), then joins the trail named for the man who originated the idea of the Appalachian Trail, Benton MacKaye. Enjoy views from Springer Mountain and Ball Mountain. Finally, throw in a visit to a memorial to Benton MacKaye and you have a lot of A.T. history thrown into one loop hike.

Route Details

This trailhead is where most Appalachian Trail thru-hikers start their journey, even though it is 0.9 mile from the actual start of the trail atop foot-accessible-only Springer Mountain. Therefore, you begin the hike by crossing FR 42 and heading southbound on the Appalachian Trail. It is an exhilarating feeling working up Springer, clambering over open bedrock and smaller stones in oak-heavy woods. Partial views open right (west).

At 0.7 mile, reach a trail junction. Here, the white diamond–blazed Benton MacKaye Trail leaves left and is your future route. For now, go ahead and walk 0.2 mile farther on the A.T. to the top of Springer. En route, you will pass the side trail left leading to the Springer Mountain trail shelter and a spring. This shelter has a loft and picnic table. Other campsites are strung along this spur trail.

Open onto a rock slab at 0.9 mile. You are at the official southern terminus of the Appalachian Trail. This is where many hikers start or

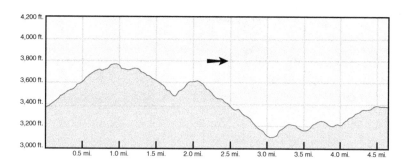

end their quest to hike the A.T. Two plaques are located up here. One, erected in 1934 by the Georgia Appalachian Trail Club, marks the exact A.T. terminus, with the words to all those who come here, "Appalachian Trail, Georgia to Maine, a footpath for those who seek fellowship with the wilderness." The Georgia Appalachian Trail Club was founded in 1930 in nearby Dahlonega, an official Appalachian Trail Community, and still promotes and maintains the A.T. in the Peach State.

A metal U.S. Forest Service marker maps the Appalachian Trail's pathway to Maine. Finally, the most southerly white blaze marking the route is painted on the rock slab here. This rock slab sports a view. Ironically, the vista opens to the west, the opposite direction the A.T. travels for the first several miles. Nevertheless, photos are taken by the dozen at this locale, making it one of the most photographed vistas on the Georgia A.T. You will notice a path leading south from here. The Appalachian Approach Trail winds 7.5 miles down to worth-a-visit Amicalola Falls State Park.

The Appalachian Trail extends around 2,100 miles to Maine. The precise mileage changes with yearly reroutes. You walk northbound from the top of Springer only 0.2 mile, backtracking to meet the Benton MacKaye Trail, also known as the B.M.T. The B.M.T. stretches 290 miles in length and was completed in 2005. It winds north through the Southern Appalachians, terminating at Davenport Gap on the Tennessee–North Carolina state line at the eastern end of Great Smoky Mountains National Park. Far fewer people have thruhiked the B.M.T., though it is much shorter. The B.M.T. is simply less known, less "glamorous," and seemingly less difficult. But mile for mile, the B.M.T. is every bit as challenging as the A.T., due to steeper ups and downs, fewer resupply locations, and no hiker hostels.

Turn right on the Benton MacKaye Trail, walking among young oaks growing over rock outcrops and ferns. Notice how much more slender and less used is the B.M.T. At 1.1 miles, on the right, a plaque commemorates Benton MacKaye and his contributions to the outdoor life. Drop off Springer Mountain, hitting a gap at 1.7 miles. The mountain drops off sharply to your right. It is a short climb over

Ball Mountain. Resume the easy but prolonged downgrade, bordered by grass and mountain laurel. At 2.5 miles, reach an intersection. Take the spur right to a view at the edge of a steep rock face, where you look east toward Little Sal Mountain and into the Etowah River headwaters—and beyond to flatter terrain. Locust, oak, and hickory frame the panorama.

Resume the B.M.T. and drop to reach FR 42 and Big Stamp Gap at 3 miles. Cross the forest road and enter ferny woods. The trail curves westward, crossing over a hill. Drop to cross a mountain laurel–choked tributary of Chester Creek at 3.5 miles. A small campsite lies just beyond the creek crossing. The B.M.T. joins an old roadbed and the walking becomes easier.

Ascend away from the stream to surmount another gap. Ahead, the shaded B.M.T. crosses Underwood Creek at 3.9 miles, then passes just above a slide cascade on a tributary at 4 miles. Meet the A.T. at 4.4 miles. Turn left (southbound) here on the A.T., again noticing the difference in the trail treads—the A.T. is much more heavily used. Reach the parking area on FR 42 and the end of your loop at 4.7 miles.

Nearby Attractions

Amicalola Falls State Park boasts the highest falls in the East at 729 feet. It also has a lodge, a campground, the Len Foote Hike Inn, and numerous hiking trails, including the Appalachian Approach Trail that links the park to Springer Mountain.

Directions

From Dahlonega, Georgia, take GA 52 West for 5 miles to the split of GA 52 and GA 9. Here, stay right on GA 52 West for 4.6 more miles to Nimblewill Church Road. Turn right onto Nimblewill Church Road and follow it 2.3 miles to Forest Road 28-1. Turn right onto FR 28-1 and follow it 2.1 miles to FR 77. Veer left onto FR 77. Follow FR 77 for 5.1 miles to Winding Stair Gap. At Winding Stair Gap, make a hard left onto FR 42, and follow it for 2.7 miles to the trailhead.

2

Long Creek Falls

SCENERY: ★ ★ ★ ★ ★
TRAIL CONDITION: ★ ★ ★ ★
CHILDREN: ★ ★ ★ ★ ★
DIFFICULTY: ★
SOLITUDE: ★ ★

LONG CREEK FALLS NOISILY CRASHES OVER A SHEER LEDGE.

GPS TRAILHEAD COORDINATES: N34° 39.814' W84° 11.046'

DISTANCE & CONFIGURATION: 2-mile out-and-back

HIKING TIME: 1.5 hours

HIGHLIGHTS: Long Creek Falls

ELEVATION: 2,520' at trailhead; 2,805' at high point

ACCESS: No fees or permits required

MAPS: Trails Illustrated #777 *Springer and Cohutta Mountains;* Appalachian Trail Conservancy *Chattahoochee National Forest;* USGS *Noontoola*

FACILITIES: None

CONTACT: Chattahoochee National Forest, Conasauga Ranger District: 706-695-6736, www.fs.usda.gov/conf

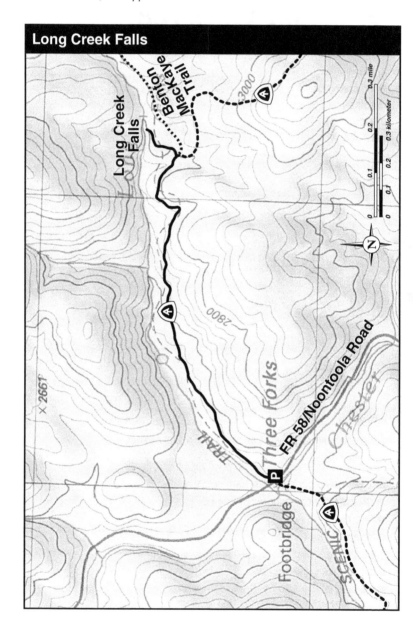

Long Creek Falls

Overview

Despite the Appalachian Trail (A.T.) being primarily a ridge-running high-country path, it does go along streams and by waterfalls. This Appalachian Trail hike cruises through the scenic Long Creek valley and then takes a short spur trail to Long Creek Falls, the most southerly cascade along the A.T. The short, easy hike gives A.T. hikers of all abilities a chance to experience some of the aquatic beauty found along this special path.

Route Details

Long Creek Falls is located on a short spur trail, 0.1 mile off the A.T., just a few miles north of the southern A.T. terminus atop Springer Mountain. This side trip to a feature is one of the first opportunities for a northbound thru-hiker to see something of beauty not *exactly* on the A.T. I cannot help but wonder how many thru-hikers arrive at the short spur trail to Long Creek Falls and pass it by, eager to get on with their journey. I also wonder if a southbound A.T. thru-hiker fewer than 5 miles from ending a 2,100-mile trip from Maine will take the spur trail to Long Creek Falls. If not, they should. And you should too. Hikers wanting to engage in the best hikes along the Appalachian Trail, and those determined to see the best of the Southern Appalachians, will stop to see Long Creek Falls. It is a great hike for kids or those of lesser abilities. The trail is foot friendly and wide for the most part, not steep, and presents a worthy reward at the end.

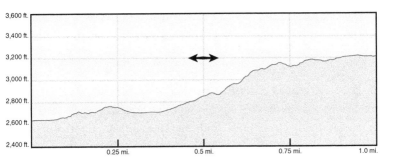

Start this hike at Three Forks, just a few miles north of Springer Mountain. Chester Fork, Stover Creek, and Long Creek meet to form Noontoola Creek, creating a name and a scenic spot to start your hike. At Three Forks, the Appalachian Trail runs conjunctively with the Benton MacKaye Trail. From the FR 58 trailhead, you will see a bridge spanning Chester Creek. Do not go that way, though it seems the proper direction for a waterfall hike; you will end up at Springer Mountain. Instead, head northbound, upstream along Long Creek, gurgling to your left. The rectangular diamond of the Benton MacKaye Trail and the standard white classic 2-by-6-inch rectangular blaze of the Appalachian Trail guides the way.

The wide, sandy track passes forest typical of a Georgia mountain hollow—rhododendron and mountain laurel coloring the forest floor green. Above that rise birch and tulip trees. Fragrant white pine towers over all. This layered biodiversity creates an eye-pleasing landscape.

Many campsites lie along the trail near Three Forks, as A.T. thru-hikers overnight here. The pathway begins to climb a bit. Listen for Long Creek tumbling, spilling, and crashing over falls scenic in their own right but overshadowed by the larger and more powerful Long Creek Falls. At 0.8 mile, a spur trail drops to one of these unnamed cataracts.

At 0.9 mile, reach a three-way trail junction. To your right, the Appalachian Trail heads north to Maine. Dead ahead the Benton MacKaye Trail aims for its endpoint in the Smokies. The spur trail to Long Creek Falls leaves left under tall white oaks and white pines, flanked by laurel. Take this blue-blazed spur trail back toward Long Creek. The roar of Long Creek Falls grows. At 1 mile, reach the first waterfall accessed from the Appalachian Trail.

Here, Long Creek Falls makes a two-tiered drop over moss-tinged rock, framed in thick vegetation. The upper drop is shorter and set back from the viewing area, but the lower drop spills 15–20 feet over a ledge, creating a froth of white, brightening the dark woods here above a shallow, sandy pool. Large repose rocks face the falls and will allow multiple perspectives and a good seat for lunch.

Nearby Attractions

Amicalola Falls State Park boasts the highest falls in the East at 729 feet. It also has a lodge, campground, the Len Foote Hike Inn, and numerous hiking trails, including the Appalachian Approach Trail that links the park to Springer Mountain.

Directions

From Dahlonega, Georgia, take GA 52 West for 5 miles to the split of GA 52 and GA 9. Here, stay right on GA 52 West for 4.6 more miles to Nimblewill Church Road. Turn right onto Nimblewill Church Road and follow it 2.3 miles to Forest Road 28-1. Turn right onto FR 28-1 and follow it 2.1 miles to FR 77. Veer left onto FR 77. Follow FR 77 for 5.1 miles to Winding Stair Gap. At Winding Stair Gap, veer slightly left onto FR 58, not the sharp left to FR 42. This is a confusing road junction. Descend along FR 58 for 2.6 miles to a signed spot where the Appalachian Trail and the Benton MacKaye Trail cross FR 58. Parking is on either side of the road.

3

Preaching Rock

THE VIEW FROM PREACHING ROCK IS SERMON WORTHY.

SCENERY: ★ ★ ★ ★
TRAIL CONDITION: ★ ★ ★
CHILDREN: ★ ★
DIFFICULTY: ★ ★ ★ ★
SOLITUDE: ★ ★ ★ ★

GPS TRAILHEAD COORDINATES: N34° 40.380' W83° 58.615'

DISTANCE & CONFIGURATION: 9.8-mile out-and-back

HIKING TIME: 6 hours

HIGHLIGHTS: Dockery Lake, views from Preaching Rock

ELEVATION: 2,415' at trailhead; 3,615' at high point

ACCESS: No fees or permits required

MAPS: Trails Illustrated *#777 Springer and Cohutta Mountains;* Appalachian Trail Conservancy *Chattahoochee National Forest;* USGS *Neels Gap*

FACILITIES: None

CONTACT: Chattahoochee National Forest, Blue Ridge Ranger District: 706-745-6928, www.fs.usda.gov/conf

Preaching Rock

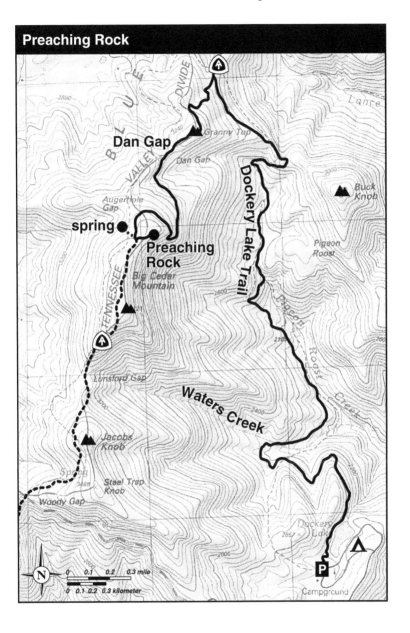

Dan Gap

BLUE VALLEY DIVIDE

Granny Top

Dan Gap

Augerhole Gap

spring

Preaching Rock

Big Cedar Mountain

TENNESSEE

Lunsford Gap

Jacobs Knob

Spring

Steel Trap Knob

Woody Gap

Buck Knob

Dockery Lake Trail

Pigeon Roost

Pigeon Roost Creek

Waters Creek

Dockery Lake

Campground

N

| 0 | 0.1 | 0.2 | 0.3 mile |
| 0 | 0.1 0.2 | 0.3 kilometer |

Overview

This variety-filled hike starts at a quiet mountain lake then leads through remote woods to reach the Appalachian Trail (A.T.). A trek over knobs and through gaps leads to Preaching Rock, a stone slab on the slope of Big Cedar Mountain, opening to highlands in the near distance and southeast to the Piedmont.

Route Details

This hike presents a mountain lake, formerly settled valleys now reverted to backcountry, highland ridges, and a rocky view to top it off. The hike starts at Dockery Lake, a popular trout-fishing and camping spot, with a neat little walking trail around it. From the parking area, join the Dockery Lake Trail, descending through a pretty picnic area. Reach the lakeshore, then veer left along the thickly wooded shore of Dockery Lake. Short spur paths lead to the water's edge, where you can angle for trout or simply admire the translucent waters of the 3-acre impoundment.

Reach the lake dam after 0.2 mile. A short trail continues across the dam to the camping area. Take the Dockery Lake left, away from the still water. A waterfall tumbles below the dam. The singletrack path curves left around a knob. Partial views open of Waters Creek valley to the right. Tributaries of Waters Creek crash toward the valley below. Rock outcrops and boulders add to an already rugged forest of oak, pine, and mountain laurel. Curve from the steep mountainside into secluded coves and the headwaters of Waters Creek. At 1.2 miles, you rock hop Waters Creek. Rock piles and low rock fences in this relatively level cove reveal the work of a long-ago farmer who used this cleared land for pasture or field. The trees have since risen again and are part of the Chattahoochee National Forest.

Turn downstream along Waters Creek. You begin to wonder how a downhill path is going to reach the ridge-running A.T. At 1.4 miles, the hike reaches a low point. Here, Dockery Lake Trail turns left, away from Waters Creek and up Pigeon Roost Branch. Officially enter Blood Mountain Wilderness.

Pigeon Roost Branch crashes to your right. Here, the old wagon track is quite rocky, despite the removal of stones and boulders that line the way. On the ascent, you will step over small branches and keep climbing. At 2.1 miles, the path makes a hard right and passes near a loud but difficult-to-access waterfall below. At 2.2 miles, the path enters the now-perched valley of Pigeon Roost Branch and passes near a visible and accessible slide cascade.

Keep uphill along the stream, crossing it at 2.5 miles. Just ahead, Dockery Lake Trail leaves the old wagon track for higher ground, as the wagon track is mired in mud. Briefly return to the creek, joining the wagon track as it turns to leave Pigeon Roost Branch for good at 2.8 miles on a hard right switchback. Ascend under oaks to reach a gap at 3 miles. Buck Knob rises to your right. At this point, the path turns left and joins a long-abandoned logging road. A gentle upgrade makes the walking easy. Granny Top and Big Cedar Mountain rise to your left. At 3.3 miles, a trickling spring branch flows over the trail. At 3.5 miles, the Dockery Lake Trail meets the Appalachian Trail near Miller Gap. This hike turns left (southbound) on the A.T. and works its way toward Granny Top. Climb to a second gap and a campsite at 3.7 miles. Top out on Granny Top at 3.9 miles. Relax and enjoy your first downgrade in more than two miles. Reach Dan Gap at 4 miles. Head uphill again, working up the south side of Big Cedar Mountain on a graded path. Cross the headwaters of Pigeon Roost Branch at 4.2

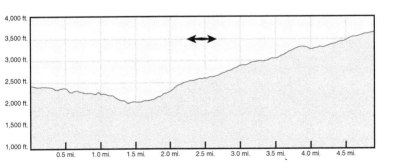

miles. A sharp switchback to the right at 4.5 miles takes you through a little boulder garden. You are 200 feet below Preaching Rock at this point but would never know it without a map. The A.T. circles around the north side of Big Cedar Mountain, still keeping a mild grade.

At 4.9 miles, a spur trail leads right and downhill to a spring and campsite. Walk just a bit farther and look for a well-used spur trail leading acutely left. Follow it through wind-stunted oaks to reach Preaching Rock. Here, at 3,600 feet, oaks and grasses open to southeasterly views. A long, sloping rock face clears the mountainside of trees, availing this panorama. Hardy lichens and mosses cling to the massive slab. The greater Chestatee River valley forms a series of valleys between which ridges stand. Though the origin of Preaching Rock's name is lost to time, such views as this have been known to inspire people to look both to the heavens and to the earth.

Nearby Attractions

The trailhead is located at Dockery Lake Recreation Area, a Chattahoochee National Forest destination that includes a fine tent campground and trout-fishing opportunities at the mountain-rimmed tarn. Each site has a tent pad, fire ring, picnic table, and lantern post. The campground is open mid-March–December.

Directions

From Dahlonega, Georgia, take GA 60 North for 12 miles. Turn right at the sign for Dockery Lake on FS 654, and go 1 mile. Pass through the campground; then stay right to reach the day-use parking area. Dockery Lake Trail starts on the right side of the parking area.

4

Slaughter Creek Loop

SCENERY: ★ ★ ★
TRAIL CONDITION: ★ ★ ★ ★
CHILDREN: ★ ★ ★
DIFFICULTY: ★ ★
SOLITUDE: ★ ★ ★

THIS HIKE STARTS AT SCENIC LAKE WINFIELD SCOTT.

GPS TRAILHEAD COORDINATES: N34° 44.256' W83° 58.375'

DISTANCE & CONFIGURATION: 5.7-mile loop

HIKING TIME: 3 hours

HIGHLIGHTS: Lake Winfield Scott, big woods

ELEVATION: 2,885' at trailhead; 3,800' at high point

ACCESS: No fees or permits required

MAPS: Trails Illustrated #777 *Springer and Cohutta Mountains;* Appalachian Trail Conservancy *Chattahoochee National Forest;* USGS *Neels Gap*

FACILITIES: None

CONTACT: Chattahoochee National Forest, Blue Ridge Ranger District: 706-745-6928, **www.fs.usda.gov/conf**

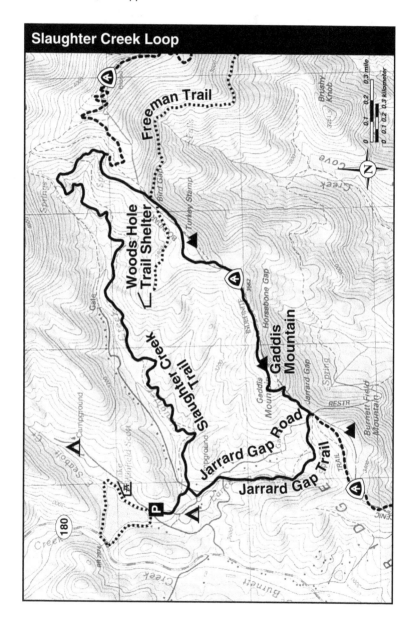

Overview

This is a classic North Georgia Appalachian Trail loop hike, and gives a good representation of the mountains and valleys of these most southerly Appalachian Mountains. Start at fun and attractive Lake Winfield Scott, then head up Slaughter Creek valley to reach the Appalachian Trail (A.T.). Make an archetypal forest cruise over knobs and gaps in noble hardwoods. Eventually leave the A.T. from Jarrard Gap, enjoying an intimate stream valley back to Lake Winfield Scott.

Route Details

Leave the trailhead parking area and cross the road bridge over Slaughter Creek. Scenic Lake Winfield Scott stretches to your left. The Slaughter Creek Trail starts on your right. Hike a grass-lined track to reach a hiker bridge over Slaughter Creek. Do not take the hiker bridge; instead veer left into thick woods. The hiker bridge leads to the south loop of the Lake Winfield Scott campground. Walk among rhododendron and Fraser magnolia trees, then cross Slaughter Creek on a different hiker bridge to emerge onto Slaughter Creek Road after 0.25 mile. Keep forward, crossing the gravel road near private inhold-ings, and begin the loop portion of your hike. Gaddis Mountain rises to your right. Cross the first of several branches of Slaughter Creek emanating from the ridgeline to your right, where the A.T. rises and falls. From here, the well-marked and maintained Slaughter Creek Trail leaves and joins logging grades with regularity. Gently rise in

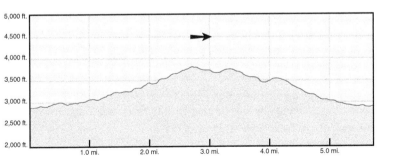

thickets of rhododendron and mountain laurel. Slaughter Creek crashes below, eventually to feed Lake Winfield Scott.

At 1.7 miles, a spur trail leads down to a campsite by the water. Enter the signed Blood Mountain Wilderness. The rocky path maintains a moderate ascent, crossing ever-smaller branches. Judging by the crossings, it seems Slaughter Creek has more tributaries than any other stream in Georgia. Finally, step over Slaughter Creek itself at 2.2 miles, and another tributary, to enter oak woods, a sign of a drier forest.

Reach the reroute of the Appalachian Trail at 2.4 miles. A keen eye will spot the old path heading up toward Slaughter Gap, formerly a trail junction and camping spot. Slaughter Gap is now left to nature, with nary a trail on it. Instead, you follow a steep hillside through a rugged boulder field seamed with small streambeds. Meet the Appalachian Trail at 2.7 miles. The headwaters of Slaughter Creek flow astride this intersection. Here, you can see the old A.T. coming in. If you are interested in camping, head left, up stone steps, northbound on the A.T. to a camping area about 100 yards distant. Tent sites have been leveled and are situated on a little loop off the A.T.

This loop hike keeps forward, southbound on the A.T. You have done most of your climbing by now. The walking is pleasant among oak, hickory, and white pine, along with locust and birch, representing both moist and dry forest flora, a reflection of the rich biodiversity of the Southern Appalachians, an overlapping of ecotones.

Descend to Bird Gap, meeting the Freeman Trail here, at 3.1 miles. Pass a couple of campsites. Just ahead is a spur trail leading right about 0.5 mile to the Woods Hole trail shelter. This is a three-sided Adirondack-style shelter, with a picnic table and bear-proof food storage cables. Water can be had from a spring on the way to the shelter.

The A.T. keeps a gentle track, slightly ascending from Bird Gap, but curving around the side of Turkey Stamp, a small knob. Rich, widely dispersed hardwoods, primarily tulip trees, stand regally over the trail. The A.T. eases downhill to meet Horsebone Gap at 3.9 miles. A benchmark stands in the gap. Curve around Gaddis Mountain, making a big downward switchback. This segment is fun whether you are day hiking or trekking the entire A.T.

Roll into Jarrard Gap at 4.5 miles. Here, the A.T. continues forward and gravel Jarrard Gap Road crosses the gap. Our loop turns right on the gravel road. Walk a short distance then pick up the blue-blazed Jarrard Gap Trail leaving left. The singletrack Jarrard Gap Trail drops to a spring used by A.T. hikers then drifts downward through the Lance Branch valley among rhododendron-filled coves. Bridge Lance Branch on a span at 4.9 miles. Ahead, small seeps cross the path. Pass around vehicle barrier boulders to reach Slaughter Creek Road at 5.2 miles. Here, keep forward, following Slaughter Creek Road around a curve to the left, then to the right. Pass a hiker bridge leading left at 5.4 miles. Just ahead, come to the Slaughter Creek Trail. You have been here before. Turn left, backtracking to reach the trailhead at 5.7 miles.

Nearby Attractions

Consider combining this Appalachian Trail trek with a campout at Lake Winfield Scott Recreation Area. This ideal, woodsy campground has a serene lake with fishing, hand-propelled and electric-motors-only boating, and a swim beach. The landward side presents a quality campground with two loops, parts of which are open year-round, in addition to a lakefront picnic area.

Directions

From Dahlonega, Georgia, take US 19 North for 9 miles to Stone Pile Gap and GA 60. Veer left onto GA 60 and follow it 7.3 miles to GA 180/Wolf Pen Gap Road. Turn right onto GA 180 and follow it 4.4 miles to Lake Winfield Scott Recreation Area, on your right. Enter the recreation area and follow the road 0.4 mile to a signed trail parking area on your left, just before the bridge over Slaughter Creek, where Slaughter Creek enters Lake Winfield Scott.

Blood Mountain Loop

SCENERY: ★ ★ ★ ★ ★
TRAIL CONDITION: ★ ★ ★
CHILDREN: ★ ★
DIFFICULTY: ★ ★ ★
SOLITUDE: ★ ★

A SULLEN SKY AND WAVES OF MOUNTAINS ARE VISIBLE FROM THE BLOOD.

GPS TRAILHEAD COORDINATES: N34° 44.492' W83° 55.365'

DISTANCE & CONFIGURATION: 5.9-mile loop

HIKING TIME: 3.5 hours

HIGHLIGHTS: Views, Blood Mountain Wilderness, geology

ELEVATION: 3,010' at trailhead; 4,458' at high point

ACCESS: No fees or permits required

MAPS: Trails Illustrated #777 *Springer and Cohutta Mountains;* Appalachian Trail Conservancy *Chattahoochee National Forest;* USGS *Neels Gap*

FACILITIES: None

CONTACT: Chattahoochee National Forest, Blue Ridge Ranger District: 706-745-6928, **www.fs.usda.gov/conf**

Blood Mountain Loop

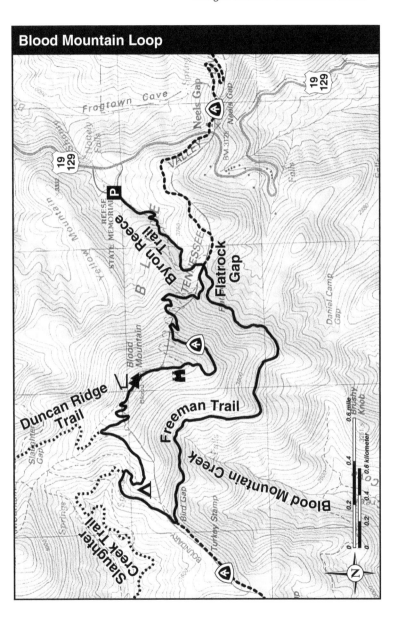

Overview

This is one of Georgia's finest circuit hikes. Enter Blood Mountain Wilderness on the Byron Reece Trail and climb to the Appalachian Trail (A.T.), soaking in panoramas from large, open rock faces on the shoulder of Blood Mountain. Pass a stone shelter before descending to meet the Freeman Trail at Bird Gap. Make a rocky return on the south slope of Blood Mountain, where travel is slow but scenic.

Route Details

Blood Mountain is Georgia's contribution to great mountains of the world—and the Appalachian Trail. This loop demonstrates such. You will start at the Byron Reece trailhead, built because of too many cars and not enough parking spots at nearby Neels Gap, where the A.T. crosses US 129. Plus, the Mountain Crossings store in the gap created additional problems. Therefore, this parking area was built.

Leave the trailhead on the wide Byron Reece Trail to enter the Blood Mountain Wilderness, then head up rhododendron-blanketed Shanty Branch, an all-time great Southern Appalachian name. The path ascends from Shanty Branch by switchbacks on well-placed steps, passing by a small waterfall. Return to a tributary of Shanty Branch and enter a fern-floored cove before meeting the A.T. and Freeman Trail at 0.7 mile. Freeman Trail is your return route. You stand at Flatrock Gap. Turn right (southbound) on the A.T., where you will pass over pine-bordered rock slabs. Come near

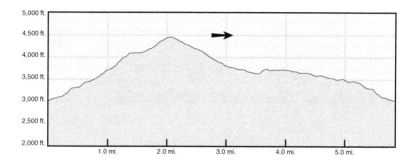

a rock overhang at 1.1 mile. Rise as the Blood rises. Be watchful when seeps flow over some rock faces the trail crosses. In other places, stone steps have been added to make the ascent easier. The strenuous labor required to install the stone steps makes hiking up the mountain seem a breeze.

Curve around the south slope of Blood Mountain. At 1.6 miles, come to the first major view from an open rock face. This mosaic of open rock and forest are part of what makes Blood Mountain special. Another view comes at 1.8 miles. Here, a host of hills sweeps across the southern horizon framed by the expansive rock face below and the Dixie sky above. From this point, the A.T. weaves in and out of stunted oaks, pines, and mountain laurel.

The A.T. levels off at a wide, vista-enriched rock slab at 2 miles. More sporadic outcrops open as you climb, including those with views to the north, before reaching the tiptop of Blood Mountain, elevation 4,458 feet, at 2.1 miles. Here, a U.S. Geological Survey marker is embedded into the rock. This is the highest point of the A.T. in Georgia. The path leads just a few feet more to reach the stone Blood Mountain shelter, erected in 1931 by the Civilian Conservation Corps. It is fully enclosed and the fireplace has been rocked shut.

Picnic Rock rises next to the shelter. It harbors good views too. Blood Mountain received its moniker after a particularly deadly battle between Cherokee and Creek tribesmen atop the peak. Legend had it the mountain ran red with blood after the clash, also giving name to nearby Slaughter Creek. The A.T. descends Blood Mountain by switchbacks through azalea-rich hardwood forest. Meet the Duncan Ridge Trail at 2.5 miles. It heads toward Springer Mountain.

The A.T. continues downhill to reach a spur camping loop at 2.9 miles. Just ahead, beside the gurgling headwaters of Slaughter Creek, meet the Slaughter Creek Trail, rising from Lake Winfield Scott. The A.T. turns left here. Continue heading downhill on an easy track under widely dispersed hardwoods with a brushy understory to reach Bird Gap at 3.4 miles. Turn left here on the narrow and brush-lined Freeman Trail.

The sporadic tree cover on the Freeman Trail is partly caused by an abundance of rocks and rock slabs embedded in the soil. This allows partial views to the south, but not quite as open as higher up on Blood Mountain. A warm summer sun can cook a hiker on this slow-moving rocky path. Pass a few rocky rills, the upper branches of Blood Mountain Creek, starting at 3.8 miles. These streams may or may not be flowing, depending on the time of year. The tree cover thickens around the streams. The Freeman Trail is more level than not, running generally around 3,500 feet. It roughly parallels the A.T. atop Blood Mountain. More rock slabs and rocky streambeds lie ahead. Pass a last pair of open rock slabs and then return to Flat-rock Gap and the Appalachian Trail at 5.2 miles. The loop portion of the hike is complete. From here, backtrack 0.7 mile down the Byron Reece Trail to reach the trailhead.

Nearby Attractions

Mountain Crossings outfitter is located in nearby Neels Gap in a historic rock structure built by the Civilian Conservation Corps. The A.T. actually passes through the building, the only place where the A.T. passes under a roof. For more information, visit **mountain crossings.com.**

Directions

From Cleveland, Georgia, head north on US 129 for 19.1 miles to the Byron Reece Trail and the Neels Gap trailhead parking. Coming from Cleveland, you will actually pass through Neels Gap and begin a downgrade, reaching the left turn into the parking area 0.4 mile beyond Neels Gap.

6

Rocky Mountain

SCENERY: ★ ★ ★ ★
TRAIL CONDITION: ★ ★ ★ ★
CHILDREN: ★ ★ ★
DIFFICULTY: ★ ★
SOLITUDE: ★ ★ ★

THIS SOUTHWARD VIEW FROM ROCKY MOUNTAIN ENCOMPASSES A HOST OF RIDGES EXTENDING INTO THE YON.

GPS TRAILHEAD COORDINATES: N34° 48.082' W83° 44.575'

DISTANCE & CONFIGURATION: 5-mile loop

HIKING TIME: 2.5 hours

HIGHLIGHTS: Views, solitude

ELEVATION: 2,940' at trailhead; 3,950' at high point

ACCESS: No fees or permits required

MAPS: Trails Illustrated *#778 Brasstown Bald and Chattooga River;* Appalachian Trail Conservancy *Chattahoochee National Forest;* USGS *Tray Mountain*

FACILITIES: None

CONTACT: Chattahoochee National Forest, Blue Ridge Ranger District: 706-745-6928, **www.fs.usda.gov/conf**

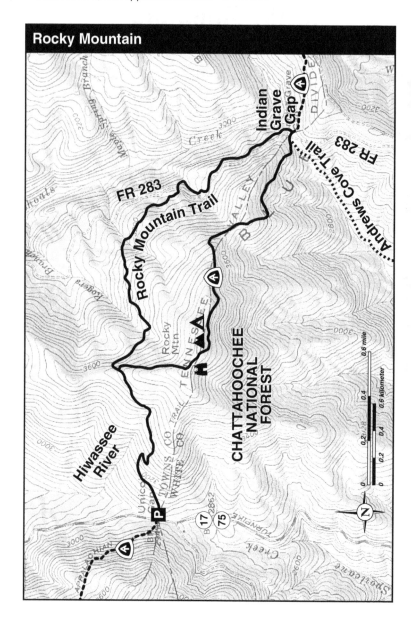

Rocky Mountain

Overview

This Appalachian Trail (A.T.) loop hike offers more solitude than many trail sections with views. Be apprised there is some climbing involved as you rise from Unicoi Gap to the crest of Rocky Mountain, where bare stone faces present panoramas. However, what goes up must come down. Therefore, you make a prolonged descent to Indian Grave Gap to join the Rocky Mountain Trail. Here, cruise the rich north slope of Rocky Mountain on old logging roads, easing the footing and allowing you to appreciate the scenery as the trail meanders the mountainside back to Unicoi Gap.

Route Details

At the trailhead, note the big stone embedded with a plaque commemorating the Georgia Appalachian Trail Club. From the plaque, head northbound on the Appalachian Trail, away from Unicoi Gap. Climb steps into rocky woods. The ascent will make you sweat in summer and warm your bones in winter. Ahead, a stream sings down the mountainside. The A.T. leads you near the moving water, then takes you away on a switchback, climbing more. Return to the waterway, then parallel it, climbing. The A.T. turns left to cross it at 0.6 mile. This is the uppermost portion of the mighty Hiwassee River. This tiny stream, most often more rock than water, bears little resemblance to our mental image of a river. From here at 3,400 feet, the Hiwassee descends to gain tributaries and is dammed as big Lake

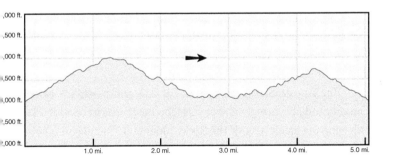

Chatuge at the North Carolina state line. From there it flows westerly through North Carolina, is dammed twice more, then meets the Tennessee River on the west side of the Appalachians. And the journey begins here.

Your trail journey continues up the shoulder of Rocky Mountain to reach an intersection at 0.8 mile. Your return route, the Rocky Mountain Trail, leaves left. The A.T. curves right (south), up the nose of the ridgeline, aiming for the crest of Rocky Mountain.

At 1.2 miles, the trail finally levels out atop Rocky Mountain. You are just below 4,000 feet. Catch your breath as the A.T. turns back east and opens onto a rock face similar to those scattered along the A.T. in Georgia. These stone faces are responsible for many views along the path. And this rock face has given Rocky Mountain its name. At 1.3 miles, a short spur trail leads to a designated campsite. Another view opens at 1.5 miles. These outcrops adorn the south side of Rocky Mountain. Here, you can gaze south into the Smith Creek drainage, across at Smith Mountain and Crumbly Knob. Popular Anna Ruby Falls is down there under the trees.

The A.T. passes several more rock faces, and actually travels directly over some of them, opening more southward vistas. Oak woods cover segments of this south slope as you drop off Rocky Mountain, losing your hard-earned elevation.

At 1.9 miles, the trail reaches a gap, but instead of climbing over the knob ahead, the A.T. swings around the right side of it, avoiding a *pud*, the term A.T. hikers define as a "pointless up and down." Instead, the A.T. uses stone steps galore to wind through white pine, laurel, black gum, and young chestnuts, declining further to reach Indian Grave Gap and Forest Road 283 at 2.5 miles. The Andrews Cove Trail comes in from your right, having climbed 2 miles from Andrews Cove Campground.

The Appalachian Trail crosses FR 283 and heads for North Carolina and points beyond, but this loop hike turns left on FR 283, following the blue blazes of the Rocky Mountain Trail. Begin following the blue blazes that are painted on the roadside trees of FR 283.

Make an easy walk on the shaded gravel forest road. At 3.1 miles, as FR 283 curves left, look for the Rocky Mountain Trail leaving the forest road and climbing woods to the left.

The Rocky Mountain Trail now joins an old logging grade, passing beneath young woods. Tributaries of High Shoals Creek flow across the trail. High Shoals is a fine waterfall at the north base of Rocky Mountain. Notice how tulip and maple trees thrive on this cooler, moister north slope of the mountain, along with ferns and mosses. At 3.4 miles, the path suddenly drops right from the wide grade to become a singletrack hiking trail. At 3.5 miles, cross a last stream, then climb Rocky Mountain one last time, a 500-foot pull.

At 4.2 miles, you intersect the A.T., happy there is nothing but a downhill cruise ahead. Backtrack toward Unicoi Gap, stepping over the Hiwassee River again. Your easy downhill backtrack allows more sightseeing than the climb did. Reach Unicoi Gap and complete your hike at 5 miles.

Nearby Attractions

Consider using Andrews Cove Campground as your Appalachian Trail–hiker base camp. It is located but a few miles from this hike's beginning. If coming from Helen, a designated Appalachian Trail Community, you will pass it on the way to the trailhead. Set in a richly wooded cove on Andrews Creek, flanked by Rocky Mountain to the north and Crumbly Knob to the south, "the little campground that could" provides a waterside getaway in the shadow of the Appalachian Trail, where trout fishing is the cast of a line away and the mountain town of Helen is accessible—but not too close.

Directions

From the bridge over the Chattahoochee River in Helen, Georgia, take GA 75 North for 9.2 miles to Unicoi Gap. The parking area is on the east side of the gap and is where you pick up the A.T.

7

Tray Mountain Wilderness

SCENERY: ★ ★ ★ ★
TRAIL CONDITION: ★ ★ ★ ★
CHILDREN: ★ ★ ★ ★ ★
DIFFICULTY: ★
SOLITUDE: ★ ★ ★

THE A.T. VIEW EXTENDS NORTH ACROSS THE HIWASSEE RIVER VALLEY INTO MOUNTAIN-RUMPLED WESTERN NORTH CAROLINA.

GPS TRAILHEAD COORDINATES: N34° 47.958' W83° 41.456'

DISTANCE & CONFIGURATION: 2.6 mile out-and-back

HIKING TIME: 1.5 hours

HIGHLIGHTS: Views, historic trail shelter site, backcountry

ELEVATION: 3,850' at trailhead; 4,390' at high point

ACCESS: No fees or permits required

MAPS: Trails Illustrated #778 Brasstown Bald and Chattooga River; Appalachian Trail Conservancy Chattahoochee National Forest; USGS Tray Mountain

FACILITIES: None

CONTACT: Chattahoochee National Forest, Blue Ridge Ranger District: 706-745-6928, www.fs.usda.gov/conf

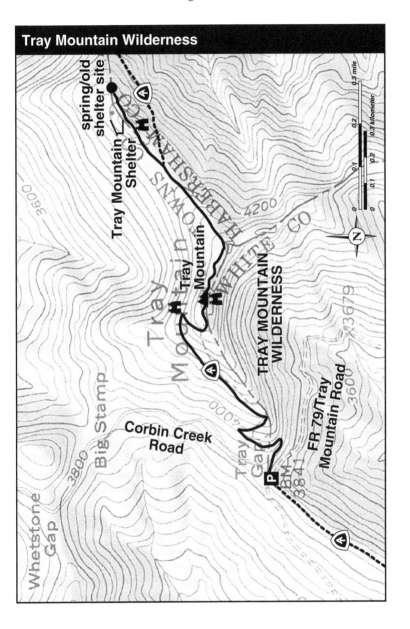

Tray Mountain Wilderness

Overview

This highland hike explores Tray Mountain—its views, trail shelter, spring, and historic shelter site from the early days of the master path of the East. Start high on the shoulder of Tray Mountain, then make your way past multiple panoramas stretching in multiple directions. Take the spur trail to the Tray Mountain shelter and another view. Finally, view the shelter spring and foundations of an original shelter. The hike is good for families who want to experience a high-country wilderness.

Route Details

Tray Mountain is the second-highest point on the Appalachian Trail (A.T.) in Georgia, 31 feet lower than Blood Mountain. The peak lies within Tray Mountain Wilderness, 9,702 acres in size. The preserve was established in 1986 and contains more than 16 miles of Appalachian Trail, which draws in most visitors. However, the wilderness is rich in trout streams as well, including the upper drainages of Left Fork Goshen Branch and Wildcat Creek, along with other streams, totaling 41 miles of trout waters. The actual Tray Mountain is the centerpiece of it all, and you can make an easy hike to its crown.

Leave Tray Gap, 3,850 feet, and begin walking northbound on the white-blazed Appalachian Trail. The path heads uphill in hardwoods to immediately enter the Tray Mountain Wilderness. Ahead, switchback to the left and continue climbing. You have already broken

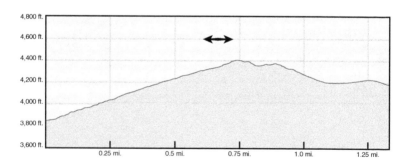

the 4,000-foot barrier. Look for high-elevation flora of yellow birch, only found in the highest peaks and coolest upper elevation valleys in the Peach State. Rhododendron flanks the path in places.

At 0.6 mile, the Appalachian Trail makes a sharp switchback to the right. Look for an outcrop extending left from the turn. Step onto a boulder and gaze north across the Hiwassee River valley to the high peaks of North Carolina's Nantahala National Forest, where the Appalachian Trail heads next. The trail curves south under a canopy of wind-sculpted yellow birch. Winter winds force the trees to bow to the blow. Reach the rocky crest of Tray Mountain at 0.7 mile, flanked by gnarled brush and trees, affording broken and slightly obscured views of the valleys below.

At 0.8 mile, near the crest of the mountain, fewer than 500 feet shy of Georgia's highest peak of Brasstown Bald, better views open. A pair of U.S. Geological Survey markers are embedded into the stone. To the north, you can see the waters of big Lake Chatuge, at the Georgia–North Carolina state line. Myriad peaks and valleys rise and fall in its wake. To the south, the Chattahoochee River valley opens a swath seemingly all the way to Atlanta.

The Appalachian Trail drops off the apex and courses between jagged rock and scraggly vegetation. Make the next knob, more wooded than the official peak. There is a campsite here. Begin descending the east shoulder of Tray Mountain. At 1.1 miles, reach a trail junction. Here, the A.T. splits right and downward, while a blue-blazed spur trail leads left toward the Tray Mountain shelter. Take the blue-blazed trail, staying atop the mountain crest under a shortish forest. At 1.2 miles, on your right, is a grassy clearing and campsite located next to a sizable sloping rock outcrop. Another view! This one extends easterly into the Soque River valley. You cannot have a mountain without a valley. This outcrop offers ample seating and beckons a stop.

The trail shelter lies a little beyond the outcrop. It is a three-sided bunkhouse, open on the front, with built-in benches on its sides. Tent pegs around back hold packs on those rainy nights when it can get crowded in spring. Beyond the shelter, follow the trail down to the shelter spring. The water flows from a concrete box and drips into a small pool before following gravity and delivering its gushes to the Hiwassee River. Directly by the spring, notice the stone foundation of an older, smaller shelter from the early days of the Appalachian Trail. The very first shelter on Tray Mountain was built in 1931. Known as the Montray shelter, it was all wood and lasted two decades. Others followed until the one we see today. Time changes, shelters change, yet Tray Mountain stands tall, weathering invisibly slowly through time.

Nearby Attractions

Make Andrews Cove Campground your Appalachian Trail–hiker base camp. It is located within striking distance from this hike's beginning. If coming from Helen, keep north on GA 17/75 past the right turn onto Forest Road 79 to access this hike. Set in a richly wooded cove on Andrews Creek, the camp provides a waterside getaway in the shadow of the Appalachian Trail, where trout fishing is the cast of a line away and the mountain town of Helen is accessible—but not too close.

Directions

From the Chattahoochee River bridge in downtown Helen, Georgia, head north on GA 17/GA 75 for 2 miles to Forest Road 79/Tray Mountain Road. This right turn onto FR 79 is easily missed. It occurs as GA 17/GA 75 is curving left. Be careful here. After turning right onto FR 79, follow the gravel road mostly uphill for 8.1 miles to Tray Gap. This is where FR 698 leaves left. The northbound Appalachian Trail begins on the north side of Tray Gap. *Note:* You will cross the A.T. on FR 79 en route to Tray Gap, but that road crossing is not the proper access for this hike.

OPPOSITE: THIS SHELTER ATOP BLOOD MOUNTAIN WAS BUILT IN 1931 BY THE CIVILIAN CONSERVATION CORPS, THE SAME YEAR AS TRAY MOUNTAIN'S NOW-VANISHED MONTRAY SHELTER. *(See page 44.)*

Tennessee and North Carolina

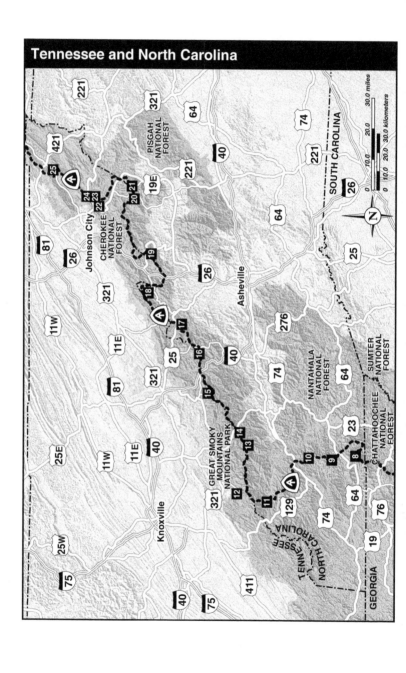

Tennessee
and North Carolina

THE VIEW OF GRASSY RIDGE STRETCHES FORTH FROM THE MONUMENT
HONORING CORNELIUS REX PEAKE. *(See page 124.)*

8

Standing Indian Mountain

SCENERY: ★ ★ ★ ★
TRAIL CONDITION: ★ ★ ★
CHILDREN: ★ ★
DIFFICULTY: ★ ★
SOLITUDE: ★ ★ ★

LOOKING SOUTH FROM STANDING INDIAN, THE SOUTHERNMOST MILE-HIGH MOUNTAIN ON THE APPALACHIAN TRAIL

GPS TRAILHEAD COORDINATES: N35° 2.379' W83° 33.150'

DISTANCE & CONFIGURATION: 5-mile out-and-back

HIKING TIME: 3 hours

HIGHLIGHTS: Great views, most southerly mile-high mountain on the A.T.

ELEVATION: 4,340' at trailhead; 5,499' at high point

ACCESS: No fees or permits required

MAPS: Trails Illustrated #785 *Nantahala and Cullasaja Gorges;* Appalachian Trail Conservancy *Nantahala National Forest;* USGS *Rainbow Springs*

FACILITIES: None

CONTACT: Nantahala National Forest, Nantahala Ranger District: 828-524-6441, www.fs.usda.gov/nfsnc

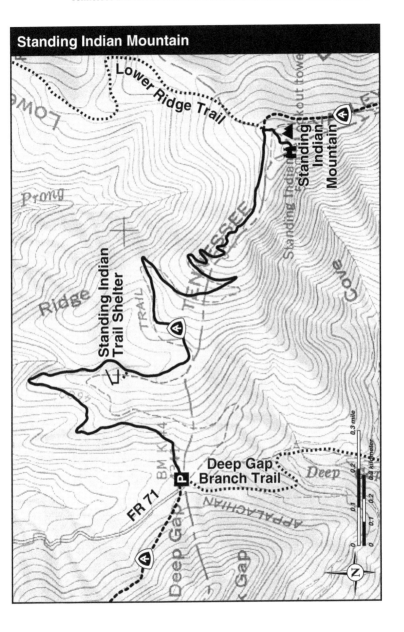

Overview

The Southern Nantahala Wilderness is the setting for this trek. Grab a rewarding view into Georgia and the adjacent Carolina highlands from the most southerly mile-high mountain on the Appalachian Trail (A.T.). Gently climb from Deep Gap to pass the Standing Indian trail shelter. Lots of switchbacks moderate your ascent. A spur trail takes you to the top of Standing Indian Mountain. Here, steep cliffs open onto a sky sweep of Georgia seemingly all the way to Valdosta.

Route Details

At Deep Gap, take the Appalachian Trail northbound under a canopy of buckeye, sugar maple, and yellow birch. Work your way up the west shoulder of Standing Indian Mountain. The trail is rocky and rooty. At 0.5 mile, the path circles around the point of a rib ridge, turning sharply south. Shortly pass a sign indicating entry into 23,000-plus-acre Southern Nantahala Wilderness, shared by North Carolina and Georgia. At 0.7 mile, the A.T. saddles alongside a little stream, then joins an old logging grade on a wider path. At 0.8 mile, a spur trail leads right to the Standing Indian trail shelter. The three-sided, open-fronted wooden structure stands atop a small knob covered in hickory and oak, one of hundreds of shelters strung out along the Appalachian Trail for its entire 2,100-plus miles. They serve as a refuge for day hikers in storms but are primarily used by backpackers

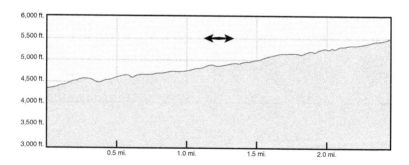

overnighting it, whether for a weekend or the customary five or six months people take to thru-hike the entire Appalachian Trail.

The old roadbed, mostly cleared of rocks, leads up to Standing Indian's crest. The A.T. is overlain on the road. This bed was originally constructed to build a fire tower that once sat atop Standing Indian. The tower was removed when the tower on nearby Albert Mountain was constructed. Loping switchbacks among rhododendron patches take you ever higher, yet Standing Indian looms above, despite your elevation gains. Looking west, you can grab a few views through the gap of Deep Gap. The switchbacks tighten until you make the spine of Standing Indian at 2.1 miles. The climb eases. Saunter beneath yellow birches in a carpet of ferns.

At 2.3 miles, the Lower Ridge Trail leaves left for Standing Indian Campground. Stay with the A.T. just a short distance and then pick up a wide trail heading right and uphill. This is the trail leading to Standing Indian's summit. Leave the A.T. and begin rising again. Pass a few campsites. Keep climbing and reach the level, grassy apex at 2.5 miles. The outcrop to your right opens. Below, the Tallulah River valley forms a maw extending south, down Georgia way. The Blue Ridge expands to your right. Lake Chatuge is that way too. It truly seems on a clear day—with binoculars—you can see all the way to Valdosta. Notice how sheer is the south slope of Standing Indian. Walk around to discover more rocky perches with other views. But be careful; it's a long, steep way down. Looking south, the next mile-high peak is in the Caribbean.

If you are thru-hiking the A.T. from Georgia to Maine, Standing Indian, elevation 5,499 feet, is the first mile-high mountain you encounter and the first noteworthy mountain after entering North Carolina. Standing Indian is more than that, however; it is also part of the Tennessee Valley Divide. Waters flowing from its south slope make their way to the Gulf of Mexico via Georgia, while its north side drains through North Carolina into the Tennessee River and beyond to the Mississippi River and thence to the Gulf. Same mountain, different routes to the same destination. The south side of Standing

Indian is very precipitous and steep, clad in open rock faces where wind-sculpted trees and weather-beaten brushes cleave to cracks.

Any mention of Standing Indian necessitates the following: the retelling of a Cherokee legend as old as Standing Indian Mountain. A great winged monster carried off a village child. The stunned Cherokee villagers prayed for the recovery of the child and the slaying of the monster. Subsequently, a giant lightning bolt struck the mountaintop, killing the winged monster, clearing the peak of vegetation, and simultaneously transforming a Cherokee sentry posted atop the peak into stone—the "Standing Indian." To this day, the very crest of the summit is grassy and a rock slab opens to a gratifying scene.

Nearby Attractions

Standing Indian Campground lies at the northern base of the mountain. It offers a multitude of streamside campsites along the upper Nantahala River. The A.T. cruises directly by the area, which has a multitude of other paths good for making loops with the A.T.

Directions

From the intersection of US 23/US 441 and US 64 in Franklin, North Carolina (a designated Appalachian Trail Community), take US 64 West 14.5 miles to Forest Road 71 (Deep Gap Road—there will be a sign for Deep Gap). Turn left onto FR 71. It starts out paved and then turns to gravel as it turns away from US 64. Stay with FR 71, driving a total of 5.9 miles to dead-end at Deep Gap.

9

Silers Bald

SCENERY: ★ ★ ★ ★ ★
TRAIL CONDITION: ★ ★ ★ ★
CHILDREN: ★ ★ ★
DIFFICULTY: ★ ★
SOLITUDE: ★ ★

SILERS BALD IS ONE OF THE SOUTHERN APPALACHIAN'S GRASSY SUMMITS WHOSE ORIGIN REMAINS UNEXPLAINED.

GPS TRAILHEAD COORDINATES: N35° 9.244' W83° 34.803'

DISTANCE & CONFIGURATION: 3.6-mile out-and-back

HIKING TIME: 2 hours

HIGHLIGHTS: Views from restored mountain meadow

ELEVATION: 4,155' at trailhead; 5,210' at high point

ACCESS: No fees or permits required

MAPS: Trails Illustrated #785 *Nantahala and Cullasaja Gorges*; Appalachian Trail Conservancy *Nantahala National Forest*; USGS *Wayah Bald*

FACILITIES: None

CONTACT: Nantahala National Forest, Nantahala Ranger District: 828-524-6441, www.fs.usda.gov/nfsnc

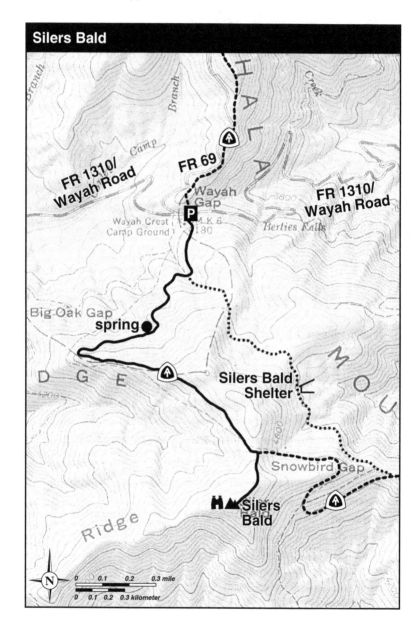

Silers Bald

Overview

This hike visits one of the most distinctive mountaintop meadows in the Southern Appalachians. Known as balds, these fields of unknown origins present incredible vistas of the encircling Carolina highlands. The climb to the high point is steady but moderate—and worth it for enjoying the spectacular vistas in the yon.

Route Details

Your rewards on this hike increase with the clarity of the sky. Silers Bald stretches nearly a mile high in elevation. Balds, or open meadows, such as Silers Bald are a botanical mystery of the Southern Appalachians. These meadows stretch from Georgia to Virginia along the Appalachian Trail (A.T.) and other high ridges. The balds you see today have almost all been restored or maintained in some way. Most historic balds have grown over with trees, and only the name remains. The origin of these fields has not been satisfactorily explained, although natural fires, clearing by American Indians, and grazing cattle possibly kept the fields clear. In summer, residents of the nearby lowlands would drive their cattle upon the meadows to graze for the summer while using valley fields to grow winter hay. Grazing certainly helped keep the balds open, for when the practice ceased, trees began reclaiming the meadows. Silers Bald is being kept open by mowing. A closed forest road links the bald to Wayah Gap. Yearly cuttings keep the trees and bushes at bay. Other efforts to

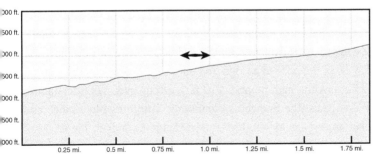

keep these Southern Appalachian balds open have included goat and cow grazing, burning, and old-fashioned hand cutting. A combination of the above seems to work best.

Those who want to restore the Southern Appalachians to their "original" state find the question as to preserving the balds a vexing one. Are the historic vistas worth keeping or should they keep the balds for their natural qualities? Or allow them to disappear? Since we don't know how they appeared in the first place, it is a tough call. I am in favor of preserving all the balds we have and restoring even more. Hikers are lured to places like Silers Bald. On a clear day, its views are astonishing.

Take the Appalachian Trail southbound from Wayah Gap. Wood and earth steps lead into a rich hardwood forest dominated by maple trees. Quickly cross the closed road the U.S. Forest Service uses to mow Silers Bald. The singletrack A.T. edges over to the west side of a ridge spurring from Silers Bald. Turn into a prototype mountain cove, then reach a spring at 0.5 mile. A.T. thru-hikers and section hikers rely on springs such as this for drinking water. Most treat the highland water by either filtering, using ultraviolet waves, or chemically making it free of parasites such as *Giardia* and thus drinkable. I am in a small minority and drink it straight from the source without treating it, and I haven't gotten sick in three decades of backpacking. Though I don't treat my water, I highly recommend you treat yours, and so does just about everyone else.

The A.T. reaches the crest of the ridge at 0.9 mile. Oaks shade the path. The path slides over to the west side of Silers Bald and levels out. At 1.6 miles, the Appalachian Trail opens onto the lower end of Silers Bald and meets the Silers Bald Vista Trail. Turn right here, leaving the A.T., and turn up the middle of the mown meadow, rising along the nose of a ridge. Top out at 1.8 miles. A marble marker delineates the high point, 5,210 feet, a little over 1,000 feet above Wayah Gap. The Snowbird Mountains, Tusquitee Mountains, and Nantahala Lake extend to the west. Standing Indian, the tower of Albert Mountain, and the Blue Ridge form southern ramparts. Still farther south—into Georgia—is Brasstown Bald, the Peach State's high point. The stone-faced Fishhawk Mountains stand to the east. The transmission towers on Wine Spring Bald roll north. On a clear day, you can see northwest into Tennessee and the western edge of the Great Smoky Mountains. The main crest of the Smokies stretches still farther north. Without Silers Bald being kept open, this view would be lost. . . .

Nearby Attractions

From the trailhead, take Forest Road 69 4.5 miles from Wayah Gap up to the restored Wayah Bald tower. The stone structure not only provides great views, it is a scenic spot where you can picnic and hike more of the A.T.

Directions

From the intersection of US 23/US 441 and US 64 in Franklin, North Carolina, take US 64 West 3.8 miles to turn right onto Patton Road. Drive 0.2 mile; then turn left onto NC 1310/Wayah Road. Follow NC 1310 9.2 miles to Wayah Gap. There are parking spots on both sides of the road. FR 69 leaves right from the gap, and you can also park along its shoulder.

SCENERY: ★ ★ ★ ★ ★
TRAIL CONDITION: ★ ★ ★ ★
CHILDREN: ★ ★ ★ ★
DIFFICULTY: ★ ★
SOLITUDE: ★ ★ ★

THIS CAPTURES BUT ONE DIRECTION OF THE 360-DEGREE VIEWS THAT CAN BE HAD FROM THE TOWER ATOP WESSER BALD.

GPS TRAILHEAD COORDINATES: N35° 16.070' W83° 34.288'

DISTANCE & CONFIGURATION: 2.2-mile loop

HIKING TIME: 1.5 hours

HIGHLIGHTS: 360-degree views from restored fire tower

ELEVATION: 3,870' at trailhead; 4,606' at high point

ACCESS: No fees or permits required

MAPS: Trails Illustrated #785 Nantahala and Cullasaja Gorges; Appalachian Trail Conservancy Nantahala National Forest; USGS Wesser

FACILITIES: None

CONTACT: Nantahala National Forest, Nantahala Ranger District: 828-524-6441, www.fs.usda.gov/nfsnc

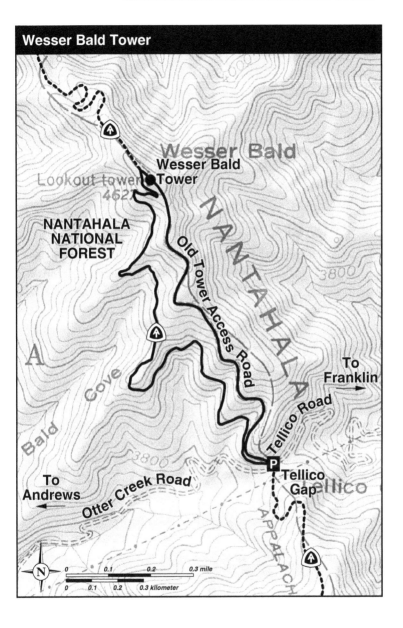

Overview

The 360-degree view from Wesser Bald is a Carolina Appalachian Trail (A.T.) highlight. Though Wesser Bald is bald no more, an observation tower keeps the views coming. This reconfigured lookout was formerly a ranger-manned fire tower. The observation deck replaced the fire watcher's box. From Tellico Gap, trace the Appalachian Trail gently to the tower. Return via an old road, also an easy walk, once used to build the original fire tower, making for a short and easy return trip.

Route Details

A.T. hikers from 4 to 84 can reap big rewards on this hike to an eye-popping panorama. An open observation tower leaves no obstructions. Moreover, if you get the sky to cooperate, your vistas will be horizon to horizon. To the north, the dark balsam-covered crest of the Great Smoky Mountains forms a backdrop. The A.T. runs along its mantle. Scan the crest for the tower on Clingmans Dome, the highest point in the Smokies and the highest point on the entire Appalachian Trail. Tennessee's Mount LeConte rises beyond the crest of the Smokies. The winding embayment of the Nantahala River is the snakelike arm of Fontana Lake to the north under the Smokies. The east–west portion of Fontana Lake delineates the southern edge of Great Smoky Mountains National Park. Cheoah Bald rises to the west, on the far side of the Nantahala Gorge. Now turn south. See the transmission towers of Wine Spring Bald? The Cowee Mountains, among other ranges, rise in the east.

From the parking area, hike northbound on the Appalachian Trail, leaving Tellico Gap. Briefly follow your return route, the gated road leading directly to Wesser Bald Tower. Split left on the A.T., a singletrack trail shaded by birch, maple, and rhododendron. Curve into a cove. And with a little change of exposure, you are walking among oaks, sourwood, and mountain laurel. The uptick is mild as you reach a rib ridge at 0.7 mile. Turn back northeast and repeat the cove-ridge pattern. A pair of switchbacks leads to the narrow summit of Wesser Bald and a trail junction at 1.4 miles. The Appalachian Trail leaves left for the deep Nantahala River gorge and points beyond. We go right on a short spur trail to the tower.

Soon take the steps up to the observation platform, opening to Southern Appalachian splendor. Savor the views; take your time, for the return route is a breeze. Trace the old tower road south from the tower. The path you take was not once but twice where trucks and men built the tower during the 1930s, then in 1995, when the tower was reconfigured to what you see today.

For four decades, from the 1930s to the 1970s, fire towers were manned by rangers throughout the United States to prevent wildfires from spreading. This system of wildfire watching followed the establishment of the American national forest system. A.T. hikers in this area see both metal towers, such as this one, and stone towers, such as the one atop nearby Wayah Bald or historic Mount Cammerer in Great Smoky Mountains National Park. Hired rangers lived on site at these towers. They quartered in adjacent outbuildings. In the 1970s, forestry officials shifted to fire watching from the air during times of high fire danger. Most towers were dismantled or fenced in, and some were reconfigured, like here at Wesser Bald.

Wesser Bald Tower was built in 1936 and included living quarters down at the base of the lookout. The live-in quarters were destroyed by fire in 1979. Though today's tower is lower, the views still stun—and the climb to the wide observation area is a lot less

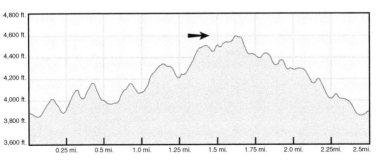

frightening for those with a fear of heights. Have you ever climbed an old-fashioned metal tower, rising up on ever-narrowing, slender aluminum structures, flight after flight, step after step? Here at Wesser Bald Tower, you get the view without the fear.

Nearby Attractions

During the warm season, the forest road to Wayah Bald is open, allowing an easy visit of that tower.

Directions

From Franklin, North Carolina, take NC 28 North 12 miles to Tellico Road. Turn left onto Tellico Road and follow it 8.2 miles to Tellico Gap.

ALTERNATE DIRECTIONS: From the intersection of US 19 Business and US 19/US 129 in Andrews, North Carolina, take US 19/US 129 North 6.9 miles to the point where US 129 turns left toward Robbinsville. At this point, keep straight on US 19 2.1 miles to NC 1310/Wayah Road. Turn right onto NC 1310 and follow it 5 miles to Otter Creek Road. Turn left onto Otter Creek Road and follow it 4 miles to Tellico Gap, situated under a transmission line clearing. There are several parking spots here.

11

Shuckstack Loop

SCENERY: ★ ★ ★ ★ ★
TRAIL CONDITION: ★ ★ ★ ★
CHILDREN: ★
DIFFICULTY: ★ ★ ★ ★
SOLITUDE: ★ ★ ★ ★

YOU WILL SPOT THIS OLD JALOPY EN ROUTE TO SHUCKSTACK ON LAKESHORE TRAIL.

GPS TRAILHEAD COORDINATES: N35° 27.643' W83° 48.663'

DISTANCE & CONFIGURATION: 11.5-mile loop

HIKING TIME: 6–8 hours

HIGHLIGHTS: Great views, swimming, historic, streams

ELEVATION: 1,955' at trailhead; 4,020' at high point

ACCESS: Fee and permit required if backpacking

MAPS: Great Smoky Mountains National Park map; Trails Illustrated #229 Great Smoky Mountains National Park; USGS Fontana Dam

FACILITIES: Picnic area, restrooms at Fontana Dam area, small store at nearby Fontana Marina

CONTACT: Great Smoky Mountains National Park: 865-436-1200, **nps.gov/grsm**

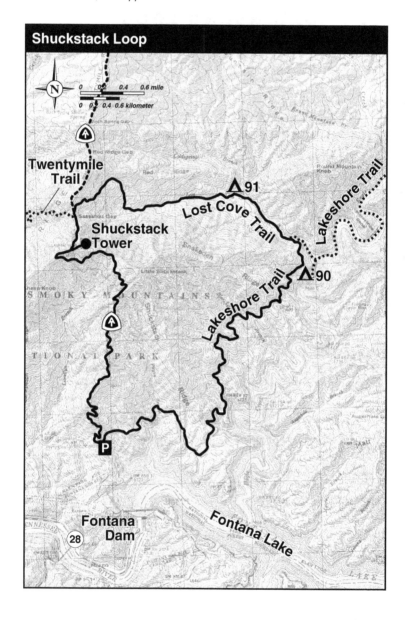

Shuckstack Loop

Overview

This is a rewarding but long day hike or good backpack. Travel the history-sprinkled Lakeshore Trail with many pre-park relics. Enjoy views of Fontana Lake. Climb along secluded Lost Cove Creek to the Appalachian Trail (A.T.). Reach astonishing vistas from atop Shuckstack fire tower. Trace the A.T. back down to the trailhead and Fontana Lake.

Route Details

This Appalachian Trail circuit can be a full day's hike or easily can be stretched into an overnight backpack. Its loop is also a great Smokies sampler hike. It presents pre-park history, lake views, mountain streams, old homesites, and ridge running and is capped off with a great view from a fire tower accessed via the A.T.

Start at Fontana Dam, near the designated Appalachian Trail Community of the same name, following a former highway reverted to backcountry due to the construction of the dam in the 1940s. Roller coaster over rib ridges divided by streams flowing into Fontana Lake. Reach Lost Cove Creek. You have the option of walking downstream to meet the Eagle Creek arm of Fontana Lake before traveling up secluded Lost Cove. A steep final ascent brings you to Sassafras Gap and the Appalachian Trail. One last uptick reaches Shuckstack fire tower and a panorama that will reward every uphill step you took. Views stretch as far as the clarity of the sky allows. From the top of

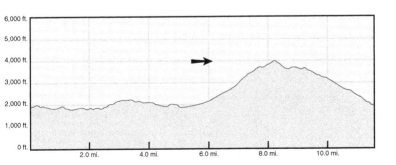

the tower, it's all downhill. Pass a natural vista from a rock face. The A.T. switchbacks down a dry ridge, leveling off at occasional gaps, before returning to the lowlands near Fontana Dam.

Pick up the Lakeshore Trail as it follows the wide bed of old NC 288. This area wasn't originally slated to be part of the Smoky Mountains National Park. It was added only after Fontana Lake was to be built to furnish power for the Alcoa aluminum plant in Maryville, Tennessee, for the World War II effort. The land around the dam and Fontana Lake was condemned and purchased by the federal government. The land on the north side of the impoundment was then deeded over to the park, making the boundary at Fontana Lake's edge. This was all hastily done before World War II. That is why this area has more "modern" relics and evidence, such as this wide highway grade and even roadside jalopies.

Oaks dominate the forest, along with plentiful tulip trees regenerating, even atop the roadbed. Creek bottoms are clothed in rhododendron and birch. Step over Payne Branch at 0.8 mile, then ascend to surmount a gap. Descend along a trickling tributary. Watch for some big holly trees here. Pass the ruins of an old car near a fast-disappearing farm clearing. Walnut trees are reclaiming the field. Rejoin the old auto highway at 1.5 miles. Ahead, more rusty hulks of vehicles lie abandoned along the old road. Views of the Eagle Creek embayment open to your right through the pines. Leave the road for the final time at 2.4 miles. Stay left here, traveling straight up a rhododendron-shaded branch, crossing the stream then climbing to a gap. This pattern is soon to repeat itself many times over.

Cross streams at 3.0, 3.1, and 3.5 miles, the last being Birch-field Branch. More stream-ridge undulations occur. The lake seems but an illusion at this point. Eventually Lost Cove Creek is audibly rushing below. A few switchbacks deliver you to Lost Cove Trail at 5.1 miles. At this point, you can take the Lost Cove Trail downhill 0.5 mile to reach Fontana Lake and backcountry campsite 90, Lost Cove. Here you can explore Lost Cove Creek, Fontana Lake, and Eagle Creek and overnight on the lake.

This loop turns left up the Lost Cove Trail. The dark hollow is tight here, and Lost Cove Creek plummets over mossy boulders into pools. Rock-hop the creek three times in the next 0.2 mile. The valley widens and you enter the Lost Cove, where several homes once were. Watch for a partial stone chimney to the right of the trail at 5.6 miles. More crossings lie ahead—if the water is high, you will get your feet wet. Reach Upper Lost Cove backcountry campsite 91 at 5.8 miles. The site is sloped but offers seclusion in a vale of spring wildflower profusion.

The slender footpath steepens beyond the campsite. Stream crossings ease up until you are stepping over more rock than water. The path turns away from what is left of Lost Cove Creek at 6.9 miles and ascends steeply. A few switchbacks ease the climb. Huff and puff your way into Sassafras Gap at 7.8 miles. The small gap beckons a rest.

Turn left (southbound) on the Appalachian Trail. It shows much more use than Lost Cove Trail. A brief level stretch is followed by an assault on the bouldery north flank of Shuckstack. Reach the spur trail to the fire tower at 8.2 miles. Stay left and switchback up the rocky summit to reach the fire tower and old lookout cabin site at 8.3 miles. Rangers, manning these fire towers, lived up here full time during the spring and fall fire seasons. The chimney and water cistern mark the site of what was a job offering a lot of solitude and no commute! Climb the metal tower. Undulating panoramas open in all directions. You can see Fontana Lake, the Lost Cove Valley, the main chain of the Smokies, Twentymile Creek valley, and the wall of Gregory Bald in the background. Maybe that fire watcher job did come with a few perks!

Return to the narrow hiker-only Appalachian Trail, continuing southbound. Make a sharp switchback, then pass an open stone face offering natural southbound vistas. Drop to a gap betwixt Shuckstack and Little Shuckstack at 9.2 miles. Continue the downgrade, briefly entering a hollow to step over a trickling stream at 10 miles. Occasional westerly views of Fontana Lake open. The switchbacks continue under the hickories and oaks. Emerge at the Fontana Dam trailhead at 11.5 miles, completing the loop.

Nearby Attractions

Fontana Dam is an amazing concrete structure you cross on the way to the trailhead. It stands 480 feet high and the Appalachian Trail travels directly on it.

Directions

From Townsend, Tennessee, take US 321 South 6.2 miles to the Foothills Parkway. Turn left and follow the Foothills Parkway 16.8 miles to US 129. Turn left (south) onto US 129 into North Carolina, and go 15 miles. Turn left onto NC 28 South, and go 9 miles, passing Fontana Village. Go 1.5 miles past the Fontana Village entrance and turn left at the sign to Fontana Dam. Follow the signs to Fontana Dam, crossing the dam, and then stay right just beyond the dam to dead-end at the trailhead, 2.2 miles from NC 28.

ALTERNATE DIRECTIONS: From Bryson City, North Carolina, take US 19/US 74 West 8.3 miles to NC 28. Follow NC 28 North 11.3 miles to the intersection with NC 143. Hit your odometer here and continue on NC 28 North. It is 9.9 miles on NC 28 to the right turn to Fontana Dam. Follow the signs to Fontana Dam, crossing the dam, and then stay right just beyond the dam to dead-end at the trailhead, 2.2 miles from NC 28.

12

Spence Field–
Russell Field Loop

SCENERY: ★ ★ ★ ★ ★
TRAIL CONDITION: ★ ★ ★ ★
CHILDREN: ★
DIFFICULTY: ★ ★ ★ ★ ★
SOLITUDE: ★ ★

SNOW HANGS ON TO WHAT'S LEFT OF SPENCE FIELD, WHILE THUNDERHEAD AND
ROCKY TOP (OF UNIVERSITY OF TENNESSEE FAME) RISE IN THE BACKGROUND.

GPS TRAILHEAD COORDINATES: N35° 36.298' W83° 46.214'

DISTANCE & CONFIGURATION: 13-mile loop

HIKING TIME: 6–8 hours

HIGHLIGHTS: Views, old growth trees, national park–level scenery

ELEVATION: 1,955' at trailhead; 5,050' at high point

ACCESS: Fee and permit required if backpacking

MAPS: Great Smoky Mountains National Park map; Trails Illustrated *#229 Great Smoky Mountains National Park;* USGS *Cades Cove* and USGS *Thunderhead Mountain*

FACILITIES: Picnic area, restrooms at trailhead, campground, camp store nearby

CONTACT: Great Smoky Mountains National Park: 865-436-1200, **nps.gov/grsm**

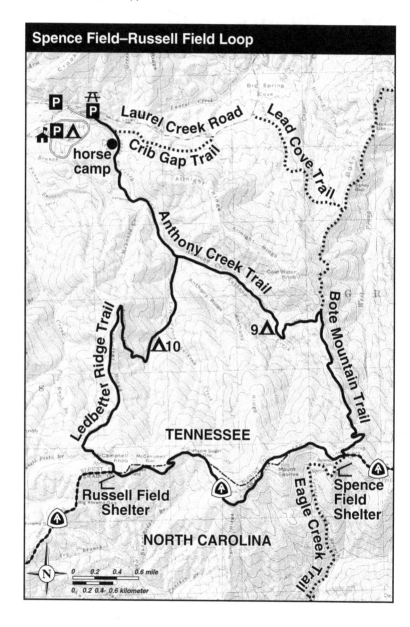

Spence Field–Russell Field Loop

horse camp

Laurel Creek Road

Lead Cove Trail

Crib Gap Trail

Anthony Creek Trail

Ledbetter Ridge Trail

Bote Mountain Trail

△10

9△

TENNESSEE

Russell Field Shelter

Spence Field Shelter

Eagle Creek Trail

NORTH CAROLINA

N

0   0.2   0.4   0.6 mile

0   0.2 0.4 0.6 kilometer

Overview

This strenuous all-day hike—or satisfying overnight backpack—provides ample reward to those who want to see the Smokies from bottom to top. Starting in Cades Cove, you will climb along a deeply forested crashing mountain stream. Intersect the Appalachian Trail (A.T.) at the Smokies crest. Once on the A.T., outstanding views open at Spence Field. Return to Cades Cove via Russell Field Trail with its section of old-growth trees. Backpackers will pass four backpack camping options along the way.

Route Details

Pick up the doubletrack Anthony Creek Trail, leaving the picnic area in preserved hemlock, tulip trees, sycamore, and rhododendron. Upper Abrams Creek crashes to your right. At 0.2 mile, the Crib Gap Trail leaves left for Turkeypen Ridge. Continue straight and dip to pass through Anthony Creek Horse Camp. The trail narrows beyond the camp. Bridge Abrams Creek at 0.6 mile, in a once-settled area. Look for leveled areas and old roadbeds. At 0.9 mile, span Abrams Creek on a foot log. Bridge it again at 1.1 miles. Note the rock walls on trail right at 1.4 miles, indicating another settled area, now returned to the bears. Bridge Left Prong Anthony Creek at 1.6 miles, then come to a trail junction. Stay left with the Anthony Creek Trail. Ledbetter Ridge Trail leaves right and is your return route.

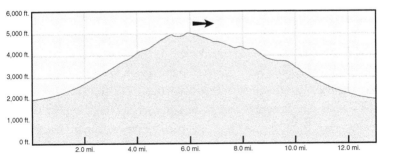

Watch for an old chimney on trail left at 1.7 miles. At 2 miles, bridge Anthony Creek. Keep ascending on a rocky tread. Tulip trees comprise a significant part of a majestic hardwood forest towering overhead. At 2.6 miles, step over a tributary of Anthony Creek. Continuing to climb, the trail passes the Anthony Creek backcountry campsite 9, on your right, at 2.8 miles. It is set in a series of semi-tiered flats. Turn away from the campsite, leaving Anthony Creek for Bote Mountain, rising in viny cove hardwoods nestled on a north-facing slope.

Intersect the Bote Mountain Trail at 3.5 miles. Turn right on the former Cherokee-built toll road. When building the turnpike from the lowlands to the Smokies' crest, the Cherokee chose the route that should be taken, "voting" for this ridge, which ended up being called Bote Mountain, because the natives had a hard time with the letter *v*. The next ridge east, not chosen, became known as Defeat Ridge.

The wide track was later used by herders driving their cattle to Spence Field for the summer. Reach an old jeep turnaround at 3.8 miles. This is where the trail narrows and becomes a deeply rutted rocky path, bordered by moss, galax, and rhododendron. Occasional short, level sections allow a breather. Watch for a hollowed out rock on trail right at 4.6 miles. Settlers would set out salt licks for their cattle using hollowed rocks or logs. The path can be rocky or muddy. Step over a spring branch, then make your final assault on Spence Field using switchbacks that take you through buckeye, beech, and yellow birch forest. Pass a piped spring at 5 miles. A final push takes you up to the lower reaches of Spence Field and the Appalachian Trail at 5.2 miles.

Explore this former pasture that still has broken fields, continually shrinking as tree cover advances. It is an ideal spot to have a snack and rest before you turn west on the Appalachian Trail toward Russell Field. Before leaving Spence Field, the A.T. passes Eagle Creek Trail, where a backcountry shelter and spring are located 0.2 mile distant. As you climb Spence Field, look back for views of Thunderhead Mountain and Rocky Top, *the* Rocky Top that inspired the University of Tennessee Volunteers' signature fight song. Leave what is left of Spence Field and reenter beech woods. Dip to a gap at 5.6 miles, then skirt around the north side of Mount Squires. Reach the high point of your hike, breaking the 5,000-foot mark at 5.9 miles. It is mostly downhill from here.

Slip over to the south side of the state-line ridge, passing through sporadic rhododendron thickets amid hardwoods. Step over a spring branch at 6.6 miles. Pass through Maple Sugar Gap at 7 miles, and continue a downgrade. A pair of switchbacks at 7.3 miles takes you lower still.

Reach McCampbell Gap at 7.7 miles, and then make a brief ascent around McCampbell Knob. At 8 miles, reach Russell Field trail shelter, a trail junction and your departure from the A.T. Turn right (northbound) on Russell Field Trail. Pass an evergreen-bordered spring, the headwaters of Russell Field Branch, before coming beside Russell Field at 8.4 miles. Spur trails lead right to a small relic meadow bordered in white pines.

Descend a north-facing slope, joining slender Ledbetter Ridge at 8.9 miles. The path runs nearly level in pines, oaks, mountain laurel, and maples. Make a sharp turn at 9.7 miles, descending for a tributary of Left Prong Anthony Creek. Between the ridge and Ledbetter Ridge backcountry campsite 10, at mile 10.6, look for sizable tulip trees. Ledbetter Ridge Trail crosses the tributary just below the campsite. Span Left Prong Anthony Creek on a footbridge at 10.8 miles. At 11.4 miles, come again to the Anthony Creek Trail, completing the loop portion of the hike. Retrace your steps down Anthony Creek Trail to arrive at the Cades Cove picnic area at 13 miles.

Nearby Attractions

Cades Cove presents a 10-mile scenic loop for driving or bicycling, historic preserved pioneer homes, a fine campground, and a picnic area at the trailhead.

Directions

From Townsend, Tennessee, take US 321 North/TN 73 3.5 miles into the Townsend Wye entrance to Great Smoky Mountains National Park. Quickly split right onto Laurel Creek Road and go 7.7 miles to reach Cades Cove. Just before the beginning of Cades Cove Loop Road, turn left toward Cades Cove Campground, and then immediately turn left into Cades Cove Picnic Area. Anthony Creek Trail is on your right at the back of the picnic area. Parking can be limited in the picnic area. If you are backpacking, be apprised that no overnight parking is allowed in the picnic area. Instead, park in the long parking strip at the beginning of Cades Cove Loop Road or return toward the campground and park in the lot beside the campground office and camp store.

13

Clingmans Dome Vistas

SCENERY: ★ ★ ★ ★ ★
TRAIL CONDITION: ★ ★ ★ ★
CHILDREN: ★ ★ ★ ★ ★
DIFFICULTY: ★ ★
SOLITUDE: ★

BACKPACKERS CRUISE THE A.T. JUST WEST OF CLINGMANS DOME, AS SPRUCE-FIR FOREST SPREADS BEFORE THEM.

GPS TRAILHEAD COORDINATES: N35° 33.408' W83° 29.766'

DISTANCE & CONFIGURATION: 2-mile loop with spur

HIKING TIME: 1.5 hours

HIGHLIGHTS: Highest point on A.T., views

ELEVATION: 6,300' at trailhead; 6,643' at high point

ACCESS: No fees or permits required; Clingmans Dome Access Road open only April–November

MAPS: Great Smoky Mountains National Park map; Trails Illustrated #229 *Great Smoky Mountains National Park;* USGS *Clingmans Dome* and USGS *Silers Bald*

FACILITIES: Restroom at trailhead

CONTACT: Great Smoky Mountains National Park: 865-436-1200, **nps.gov/grsm**

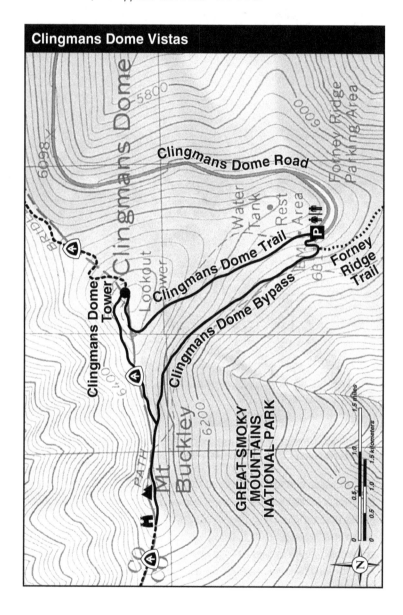

Overview

Begin at the Appalachian Trail's highest trailhead, near Clingmans Dome, and cruise spruce-fir forest. Then follow the Appalachian Trail (A.T.) along a knife-edge ridge, presenting stellar views. Head to the west side of Mount Buckley for a comprehensive vista and then backtrack, taking the A.T. to Clingmans Dome, with its views. Finish the circuit on the all-access (including wheelchairs) trail from the tower to the parking area.

Route Details

This hike fairly exudes the aura of the high country, as you traverse in and out of the spruce-fir forest that cloaks only the highest mantles of the Southern Appalachians. Start your hike at the highest trailhead in the park, 6,300 feet, just below Clingmans Dome. Straddle the very spine of the state-line ridge, joining the A.T. southbound. Walk a rocky ridge. Enjoy all-encompassing windswept vistas into both states that comprise the Smoky Mountains. Your return trip takes you over Clingmans Dome, the highest point on the entire Appalachian Trail, the highest point in Tennessee, and the highest point in the Smokies.

Start your hike at the Clingmans Dome parking area, leaving on the Forney Ridge Trail. Crowds will be milling about in summer, mostly taking the paved path up to the viewing tower atop Clingmans Dome, your return route. At 0.1 mile, leave Forney Ridge Trail to veer right on the Clingmans Dome Bypass Trail. The evergreen

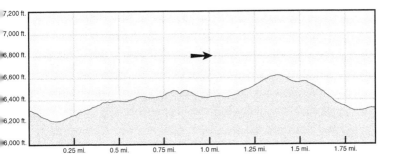

smells of the spruce-fir forest waft into your nostrils as you soon leave the crowds behind. This is an interesting area of the Smokies to experience this spruce-fir ecosystem of highland Dixie. The A.T. traverses much of the spruce-fir ecosystem that covers 70,000 acres. Besides the Smokies, other noteworthy spruce-fir areas that the A.T. traverses are Roan Mountain in Tennessee and North Carolina and Mount Rogers in Virginia. Note the density of young red spruce growing on the forest floor. These evergreens are replacing full-grown red spruce that have fallen prey to the balsam woolly adelgid, a nonnative insect, feeding on these highland forests since the 1950s. Fraser firs' greatest concentrations are within the Smokies park, making the trees here critical to species survival. The park sprays a soapy insecticide in places to combat the adelgid.

Make the moderate climb to intersect the Appalachian Trail near Mount Buckley, elevation 6,500 feet, at 0.6 mile. Continue southbound on the A.T., dropping through an old burned-over section. The lack of tree cover opens vistas as far as the clarity of the sky allows. Drop into a saddle to briefly ascend again, topping out at a rock outcrop at 0.9 mile. This stone makes a wonderful bench from which to look far into North Carolina. Fontana Lake is way down there, to your south, and beyond that, the A.T. rises on ridges of the Nantahala National Forest on its way to Georgia. To your west stands now-wooded Silers Bald, where an A.T. shelter lies. To your right (north), Tennessee drops to the Tennessee Valley then back up to the Cumberland Plateau.

As you look out consider this: One-third of the Smoky Mountains National Park is cloaked in old-growth woodlands, the largest such tract in the East. More than 100 species of trees grow in the park. No fewer than 18 of these species are champion trees—that is, the largest individual trees in the entire United States of that particular type. When making the drive from Gatlinburg to Clingmans Dome, a park visitor can enjoy different forest types representative of the Appalachian Mountains from Maine to Georgia.

Backtrack from the west side of Mount Buckley, now northbound on the A.T. Meet the Clingmans Dome Bypass Trail then stay left on the A.T., still rising on the west flank of Clingmans Dome. The peak was named for Thomas Clingman, Confederate general and politician from North Carolina. Interestingly, after the Civil War, Clingman measured mountains in the Smokies region of North Carolina and Tennessee. He asserted that what was then called Smoky Dome was the highest point in the East. We know now ol' Clingman was off, Mount Mitchell being 6,684 feet high, 39 feet higher than the mountain bearing Clingman's name.

The A.T. leads to the base of Clingmans Dome tower at 1.5 miles. Climb the spiral stairway and hope the weather is sunny and clear, for you can get no higher on the A.T. If the weather is just so, many others will be with you. From here, it's all downhill to the parking area on the paved all-access trail.

Nearby Attractions

Newfound Gap Road, your access from Gatlinburg, Tennessee, or Cherokee, North Carolina, is great for auto touring.

Directions

From Great Smoky Mountains National Park Sugarlands Visitor Center, just outside of Gatlinburg, Tennessee, take US 441 South/Newfound Gap Road 13.1 miles to Newfound Gap. Veer right and drive 7 miles to the end of Clingmans Dome Access Road. Forney Ridge Trail starts at the tip end of the Clingmans Dome parking area. Clingmans Dome Access Road, the trail access and where this hike begins, is open April–November.

ALTERNATE DIRECTIONS: From Cherokee, North Carolina's Oconaluftee Visitor Center, drive 15.4 miles on US 441 North to Newfound Gap. Veer left and drive 7 miles to the end of Clingmans Dome Access Road. Forney Ridge Trail starts at the tip end of the Clingmans Dome parking area. Clingmans Dome Access Road, the trail access and where this hike begins, is open April–November.

Charlies Bunion

SCENERY: ★ ★ ★ ★ ★
TRAIL CONDITION: ★ ★ ★
CHILDREN: ★ ★
DIFFICULTY: ★ ★ ★
SOLITUDE: ★

THE VIEW INTO TENNESSEE FROM CRAGGY CHARLIES BUNION WAS ONCE
CAPTURED BY KODAKS, AND IS NOW CAPTURED BY SMARTPHONES.

GPS TRAILHEAD COORDINATES: N35° 36.660' W83° 25.518'

DISTANCE & CONFIGURATION: 8-mile out-and-back

HIKING TIME: 4.5 hours

HIGHLIGHTS: Views, spruce-fir forest, geology

ELEVATION: 5,015' at trailhead; 6,105' at high point

ACCESS: Fee and permit required if backpacking only

MAPS: Great Smoky Mountains National Park map; Trails Illustrated *#229 Great Smoky Mountains National Park*; USGS *Clingmans Dome* and USGS *Mount Le Conte*

FACILITIES: Restrooms, water at trailhead

CONTACT: Great Smoky Mountains National Park: 865-436-1200, **nps.gov/grsm**

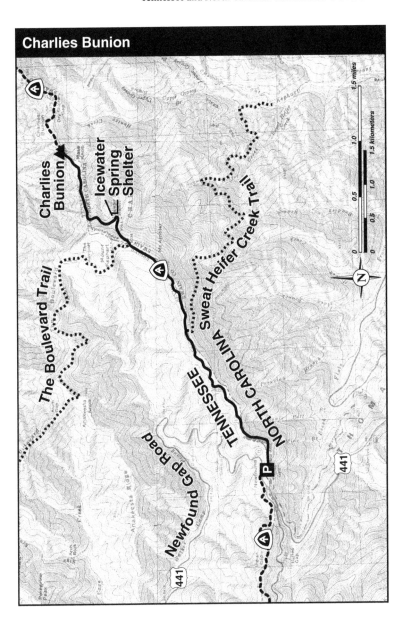

Charlies Bunion

Overview

Leave Newfound Gap and head northbound on the Appalachian Trail (A.T.). Rise amid rare spruce-fir forest with occasional clearings that present warm-up views. Pass Icewater Spring trail shelter before descending a knife-edge ridge. Come to the outcrop where astounding views into the Volunteer State and beyond open wide.

Route Details

The view from Charlies Bunion is arguably the park's finest. Unlike a view from a fire tower or a rounded peak, Charlies Bunion boasts a vista from a cliff face with an abrupt drop of more than 1,000 feet. There will also be fine views on your hike to the bunion, interspersed with sections of spruce-fir high-country forest. Since the park tries to keep Newfound Gap Road open year-round, this trek is a good way to jump into the maw of a high-country winter. Spring and fall are fine times when skies are clear. Summer will be busy—very busy.

Unusual for the timeworn Appalachian Range, the precipitous Charlies Bunion is the result of two events in the 1920s. A devastating fire raged over the area that is the bunion in 1925, denuding the vegetation clinging to the thin mountaintop soils. In 1929 heavy rains triggered a landslide of the burned-over area, leaving bare rock—and a great view—in its wake.

Head east from Newfound Gap on possibly the most-hiked 0.25 mile of the entire Appalachian Trail. In summer, Newfound

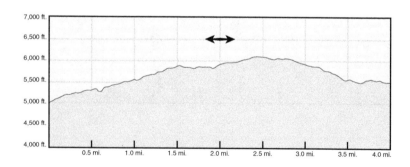

Gap can be a zoo and the A.T. packed with novices getting a taste of this special footpath, imagining themselves walking from Georgia to Maine. As you climb away from the gap, the throngs soon disappear, no matter the season. The trail is rocky, rooty, and often wet; use caution. Spruce-fir woodlands flank the track.

Continue to wind up the side of Mount Kephart, named for writer and early park proponent Horace Kephart. When the effort for a national park in the Smokies was underway, Kephart lived in Bryson City, North Carolina, just outside today's park boundary. Kephart often headed from town up nearby Deep Creek, where he would fish and camp and practice the woodcraft about which he wrote and which brought him fame. Many of his books are still in print. Two of the most famous are *Our Southern Highlanders,* about pre-park people and lifeways in the Smokies, and *Camping and Woodcraft*, a how-to manual for outdoorsmen of all stripes. This peak adds an additional lasting memorial to his legacy. While you are ascending the slope of Mount Kephart, the southern flank of Mount LeConte stands to your left.

At 1.7 miles, the Appalachian Trail levels out at the Sweat Heifer Creek Trail junction. The trail is often muddy here as it passes the 6,000-foot elevation mark only to descend to meet the Boulevard Trail at mile 2.7. The Boulevard Trail links the main crest of the Appalachians to Mount LeConte and is not nearly as easy as its name implies. Stay on the evergreen-flanked Appalachian Trail, opening up at the busy Icewater Spring trail shelter, at mile 2.9. The shelter is surrounded by a clearing and displays impressive views of the surrounding Southern highlands. Icewater Spring is just beyond the shelter. Its name is well deserved.

Beyond the spring, a 0.5-mile decline on a rocky, wet slope leads to a narrow stretch of the main state-line ridge. You can kick a rock off either side of the trail and it will drop a long way. At 3.6 miles, a good vista opens and you can see the rock point of Charlies Bunion below. Arrive at a trail junction at mile 4, just before Charlies Bunion. The Appalachian Trail leaves right. Carefully follow the slim trail 100 yards left to arrive at Charlies Bunion.

Below you lies the remote Greenbrier area of the park. To your left rises Mount LeConte. The green heath bald of Brushy Mountain is visible on LeConte. A sunny, clear day will allow an unparalleled view into the hills of East Tennessee, all the way to the Cumberland Plateau. At your feet, dark-eyed juncos and eastern chipmunks will be vying for some of your trail mix. This is a great place to really appreciate just how high the Smoky Mountains are and how cataclysmic events both recent and long ago can reveal the bedrock of the Smokies—and great views.

Nearby Attractions

Clingmans Dome, the highest point in the Smokies—and the entire Appalachian Trail—is just 7 miles away on seasonally open Clingmans Dome Road.

Directions

From Great Smoky Mountains National Park Sugarlands Visitor Center, just outside of Gatlinburg, Tennessee, drive 13.1 miles to Newfound Gap. The trailhead is at the parking area's left, near the large stone podium with the plaque on it.

ALTERNATE DIRECTIONS: From Cherokee, North Carolina's Oconaluftee Visitor Center, drive 15.4 miles on US 441 North to Newfound Gap. The trailhead is at the far end of the parking area as you come from the Tar Heel State.

SCENERY: ★ ★ ★ ★ ★
TRAIL CONDITION: ★ ★ ★ ★
CHILDREN: ★
DIFFICULTY: ★ ★ ★ ★ ★
SOLITUDE: ★ ★ ★

HISTORIC MOUNT CAMMERER TOWER LORDS OVER THE HILLS OF EAST TENNESSEE.

GPS TRAILHEAD COORDINATES: N35° 45.363' W83° 12.472'

DISTANCE & CONFIGURATION: 8-mile out-and-back

HIKING TIME: 4.5 hours

HIGHLIGHTS: Historic tower, views, wildflowers

ELEVATION: 2,240' at trailhead; 5,020' at high point

ACCESS: Fee and permit required if backpacking only

MAPS: Great Smoky Mountains National Park map; Trails Illustrated *#229 Great Smoky Mountains National Park*; USGS *Hartford* and USGS *Luftee Knob*

FACILITIES: Restroom, picnic area, campground at trailhead

CONTACT: Great Smoky Mountains National Park: 865-436-1200, **nps.gov/grsm**

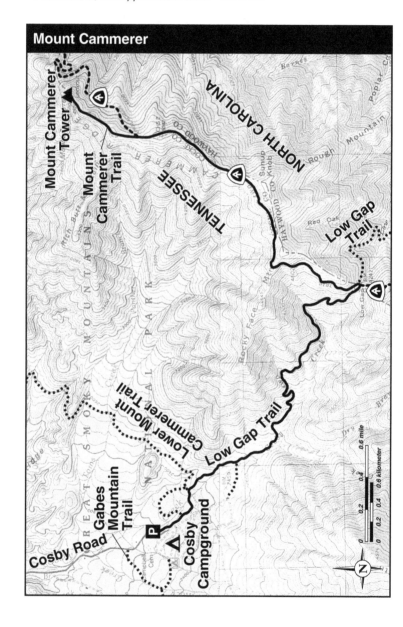

Mount Cammerer

Overview

Soak in boundless views from a historic, restored lookout tower. Leave Cosby Campground and head up Cosby Creek valley through gorgeous woodland to the state line. Meet the Appalachian Trail (A.T.) at Low Gap. Cruise the state line to emerge at an outcrop and tower where the world falls away.

Route Details

Called White Rock by Tennesseans and Sharp Top by Carolinians before the park's inception, this mountaintop rock outcrop was named in perpetuity for Arno B. Cammerer, former director of the National Park Service. No matter the name, this sentinel has incredible panoramas from its place on the Smokies' crest. A historic wood-and-stone fire tower, once long in disuse, has been restored by a group known as Friends of the Smokies. This restoration makes Mount Cammerer an even more desirable destination for Appalachian Trail hikers.

The trail's beginning, within the greater realm of Cosby Campground, can be a bit confusing, with numerous trail junctions in the first 0.5 mile. But a little persistence and soon you will be ascending the gorgeous valley of Cosby Creek, where tall trees shade mossy boulders and Cosby Creek forms a watery attraction alongside which proliferate wildflowers in spring. It is a steady climb to Low Gap, but

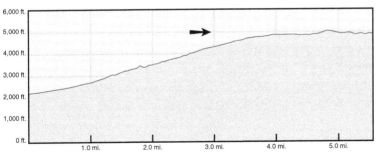

the trail is in good shape. From there, the A.T. has its ups, but the hardest part is over to Cammerer.

Leave the hiker parking area and drop to an old path of crumbling asphalt. Cosby Creek is downhill to your left. Soon pass the campground amphitheater. A cold-piped spring is on trail left just before the amphitheater. The now-lovely woodland around you was once farmland. The path soon splits as the Cosby Nature Trail meanders through the woods to the left. Stay with the signs indicating Low Gap, passing over two creeks via footbridges. The second creek is Cosby Creek. Reach the upper part of the Cosby Nature Trail. This time stay right. The Low Gap Trail soon reaches an open area and the Lower Mount Cammerer Trail at 0.4 mile.

Leave the trail junction and continue climbing toward Low Gap. This area was also once farmland but is now rich in wildflowers. Pass a water monitoring station on Cosby Creek just before reaching a trail junction at 0.8 mile. Here, a connector trail leads 0.4 mile back to Cosby Campground and 0.6 mile to Snake Den Ridge Trail. This connector allows hikers and equestrians to avoid the campground if going to Snake Den Ridge.

Stay with the Low Gap Trail, continuing the steady but not-too-steep uptick toward the Smokies' crest, now in tall woodland. You are walking the old maintenance road to the Mount Cammerer fire tower. The wide track allows you to look around more rather than watch your every step. Tulip trees, maple, preserved hemlock, and black birch form a green cathedral overhead. Moss and ferns grow on the bouldery ground, which becomes a wildflower garden in spring. Come back alongside Cosby Creek, where pretty cascades pour in white ribbons between mossy boulders. At mile 1.3, the trail makes the first of several switchbacks, leaving the dark creek-side world behind. The ascent steepens as the trail works the slopes of Rocky Face Mountain to your left. Cross a tributary at 1.8 miles. Keep rising. Step over now-tiny Cosby Creek again at mile 2.4.

The Low Gap Trail works around rock outcrops. The last stretch is a straight shot to make Low Gap and the Appalachian Trail at mile 2.9.

The elevation here is 4,242 feet. At Low Gap, turn left (northbound) on the A.T., and resume your ascent. A mile of steady climbing leads through northern hardwoods of cherry and yellow birch, along with scattered spruce. The Appalachian Trail levels out near Sunup Knob at mile 4. Winter views of the heath balds open along lower Mount Cammerer. Then the trail is as level as they come in the Smokies, rising slightly near the junction with the Mount Cammerer Trail at 5 miles.

Follow the Mount Cammerer Trail along the state-line ridge into mountain laurel. The A.T. drops toward Davenport Gap. After a slight dip, reach the outcrop and tower at mile 5.6. You do not need to get in the tower to enjoy the vistas from the jutting rocks, for you can see in every direction. The rock cut of I-40 is visible to your east, and the road follows the Pigeon River. Mount Sterling and its metal fire tower rise to your south. In the foreground to your north is the appropriately named Stone Mountain. Beyond Stone Mountain, Tennessee stretches until the horizon's end. Maybe a place this spectacular deserves three names.

Nearby Attractions

Located off the principal tourist circuit, cool, wooded Cosby Campground makes an ideal fall-camping base for exploring the virgin forests and high country of the northeastern Smokies.

Directions

From Gatlinburg, Tennessee, take US 321 North 18.1 miles, when it comes to a T intersection with TN 32. Follow TN 32 1.2 miles, turning right into the signed Cosby section of the park. After 1.9 miles up Cosby Road, watch for a road splitting left to the picnic area, the hiker parking area. Turn left here and immediately park. Low Gap Trail starts on the upper end of the parking area.

16

Max Patch

SCENERY: ★ ★ ★ ★ ★
TRAIL CONDITION: ★ ★ ★ ★
CHILDREN: ★ ★ ★ ★
DIFFICULTY: ★ ★
SOLITUDE: ★ ★

MAX PATCH IS OFTEN CALLED THE GRANDSTAND OF THE SMOKIES FOR VIEWS LIKE THIS.

GPS TRAILHEAD COORDINATES: N35° 47.789' W82° 57.750'

DISTANCE & CONFIGURATION: 2.7-mile loop

HIKING TIME: 1.5 hours

HIGHLIGHTS: Views from mountaintop bald

ELEVATION: 4,330' at trailhead; 4,629' at high point

ACCESS: No fees or permits required

MAPS: Trails Illustrated #782 *French Broad and Nolichucky Rivers;* Appalachian Trail Conservancy *TN–NC Maps 3 and 4;* USGS *Lemon Gap*

FACILITIES: None

CONTACT: Pisgah National Forest, Appalachian Ranger District: 828-689-9694, **www.fs.usda.gov/nfsnc**

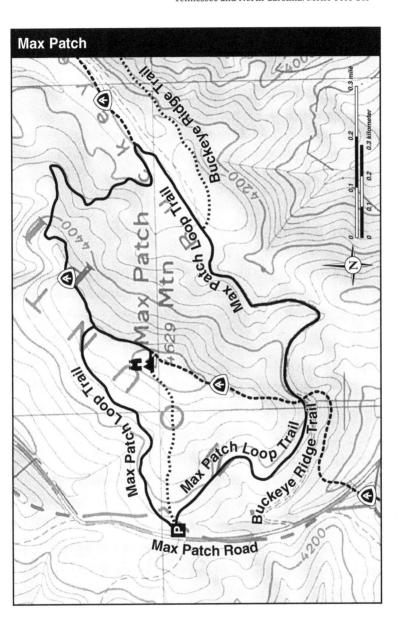

Max Patch

Overview

Make an easy circuit through and around this former mountaintop pasture, now a protected meadow with superlative views, known as being the Grandstand of the Smokies. First, the Max Patch Loop Trail traverses the western slopes opening into Tennessee. Take the short side trip to the 4,629-foot summit of Max Patch, soaking in 360-degree panoramas. Trace the Appalachian Trail (A.T.) northbound into highland forests. Return to the trailhead in a field-and-forest menagerie, soaking in more highland panoramas.

Route Details

There are those who argue for Max Patch as being the absolute best place to see the Southern Appalachians in all their glory. And it is hard to disagree. For not only can you see much of the Smokies' crest well enough to reel off specific peaks standing to your south, you can also see a whole lot of mountain country in the other three cardinal directions. And beauty can be had near as well: summer's colorful wildflowers; blackberry bushes heavily laden with dark fruit; fall's auburn grasses swaying in the breeze; a white carpet of snow in winter; and dizzyingly clear skies of spring, where the mountains seem close enough to touch. Of course, that is as long as the clouds and fogs are absent. Max Patch is an excellent starter high-country hike for kids, no matter their age. The loop has elevation changes under 500 feet and shortcuts if the 2.7 miles becomes too far.

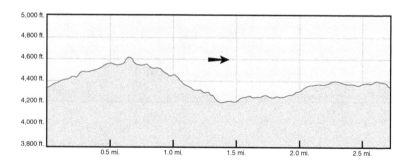

The most popular path is the one going directly up to the summit of Max Patch. It has no name. Our hike heads left on the Max Patch Loop Trail, following an old, grassy roadbed. Western panoramas open instantaneously, looking into Tennessee. Scattered trees and berry bushes begin to border the trail. Blackberries will ripen in early August. Both bears and people know this. Enter maple-dominated woodland at 0.2 mile. The main grasses of Max Patch rise to your right. At 0.3 mile, a short spur leads left to a spring box, a vestige from the days when cattle enjoyed the views—or at least the luxuriant grasses atop Max Patch—while grazing the summer away as farmers toiled below in the valleys, growing hay for the winter feeding season.

At 0.5 mile, the trail opens back to meadow. Ahead, you intersect the Appalachian Trail. Turn right (southbound) here, gunning for the high top of Max Patch, which you quickly reach. A U.S. Geological Survey marker denotes the peak. More likely, you will be looking out at the craggy panoramas in the expanse beyond the bald. The Great Smoky Mountains certainly stand out. Look first for Mount Cammerer, with its distinct curves and low tower. The A.T. goes right near it. Mount Sterling and its tall metal fire tower are easy to spot. And the mountains of that special national park go on. And to the east, lofty wooded knobs sway, roll, and dip until the land melds with the sky. Just below this point, you can see where this loop will lead. What a view!

Backtrack on the Appalachian Trail, heading northbound. Pass where you were earlier. The A.T. is marked with wooden trailside posts through the meadows, aiding wandering walkers in foggy or rainy weather. The A.T. descends north. At 1 mile, enter a hardwood forest. The trail curves on a rib ridge to meet a fenced-in spring and a small campsite at 1.4 miles. Ahead, squeeze your way through rhododendron thickets.

Reach a trail intersection at 1.5 miles. Turn right here, rejoining the Max Patch Loop Trail. Wander a mingling of meadow, brush, and trees. This is how former meadows regrow. Buckeye Ridge rises to your left and views of Max Patch open to your right, above the meadows to your right. At 1.7 miles, keep forward as the Buckeye

Ridge Trail, popular with equestrians, comes in on your left. Hop over a couple of spring branches in woods. At 2.3 miles, reach a four-way intersection. Here, the A.T. goes right uphill and left downhill while the Buckeye Ridge Trail follows an old roadbed. You take neither. Instead, stay straight on the loop trail, as the grassy path works on a side slope, the loop trail. Walk through a blend of small trees, grasses, and brush. More views open to your left. Return to the trailhead at 2.7 miles, completing the circuit.

Nearby Attractions

Round Mountain Campground, in Tennessee's Cherokee National Forest, is but a few miles away and makes a rustic warm-season overnighting area for exploring Max Patch and adjacent sections of the Appalachian Trail.

Directions

From Asheville, North Carolina, take I-40 West to Exit 7, Harmon Den. Turn right onto Forest Road 148/Cold Springs Creek Road, and continue 6.1 miles to reach a T intersection. Turn left here onto NC 1182/Max Patch Road. Follow NC 1182 1.8 miles to the Max Patch parking area on your right.

17

Lovers Leap

SCENERY: ★ ★ ★ ★
TRAIL CONDITION: ★ ★ ★
CHILDREN: ★ ★ ★
DIFFICULTY: ★ ★
SOLITUDE: ★ ★ ★

THIS OUTCROP OFFERS A PRECARIOUS VIEW FOR THE DARING OF THE FRENCH BROAD RIVER BELOW.

GPS TRAILHEAD COORDINATES: N35° 53.550' W82° 49.094'

DISTANCE & CONFIGURATION: 3.9-mile loop

HIKING TIME: 2 hours

HIGHLIGHTS: Views of French Broad River, trail town

ELEVATION: 1,375' at trailhead; 2,400' at high point

ACCESS: No fees or permits required

MAPS: Trails Illustrated *#782 French Broad and Nolichucky Rivers;* Appalachian Trail Conservancy *TN–NC Maps 3 and 4;* USGS *Hot Springs*

FACILITIES: None

CONTACT: Pisgah National Forest, Appalachian Ranger District: 828-689-9694, www.fs.usda.gov/nfsnc

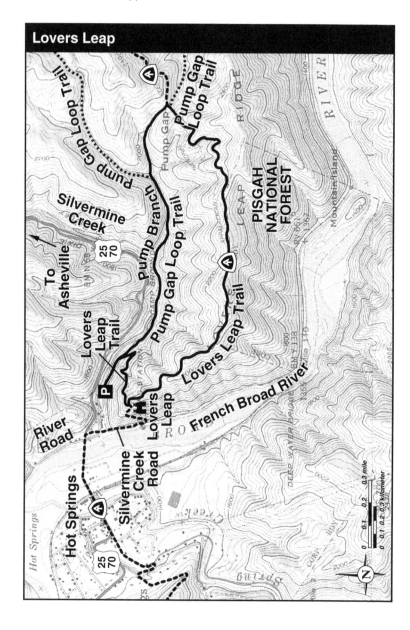

Overview

Enjoy a hike to a cliff top and a river view, starting at the trail town of Hot Springs, an officially designated Appalachian Trail Community. First, hike up a small mountain stream to a gap and the Appalachian Trail (A.T.). Trace the A.T. along Lovers Leap Ridge above the French Broad River. Find an outcrop jutting toward the river, where you can view Hot Springs and the mountains beyond. The hike culminates at Lovers Leap, with a fine vista. From there, descend back to the trailhead.

Route Details

The Appalachian Trail passes through several communities in the South. Some of these communities, such as Damascus, Virginia; Erwin, Tennessee; and Hot Springs, North Carolina, are known as trail towns, places where hikers are often seen and the outdoor life is popular with many residents. The A.T. literally goes through the heart of Hot Springs—a rising outdoor hub and one of three Appalachian Trail Communities in North Carolina—rimmed in mountains as it sits alongside the French Broad River. And yes, there are natural hot springs in Hot Springs, where you can soothe your body after a strenuous (or not-so-strenuous) hike. The hike to Lovers Leap is not strenuous and could be done in reverse, making an easier 1-mile round-trip. Additionally, the town of Hot Springs isn't just for hikers—it is also popular with rafters and kayakers, as well as campers.

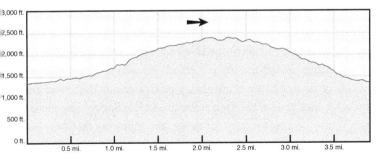

One advantage of this hike is the relatively low elevation. This makes it viable during colder times, when much of the A.T. high country is downright frigid or socked in with snow. Leave the Silvermine parking area and walk the gravel access road leading to Silvermine Group Campground. Silvermine Creek gurgles beside you. Soon rock-hop the stream. At 0.3 mile, make the group camp. Pass around a pole gate at the upper end of the camp. Pass by discarded national forest property. Look for a pair of concrete dynamite shacks, long in dereliction. The Pump Gap Loop Trail then morphs to a singletrack trail, entering the Silvermine Creek valley, cloaked in black birch, white pine, maple, and evergreens. The moist, mossy hollow, rife with wildflowers in spring, closes.

At 0.6 mile, the trail makes a short, abrupt climb. To your left, Silvermine Creek is not visible, since it is flowing under a culvert. Soon rejoin the creek, immediately crossing it, then climb away from the water. At 1 mile, an arm of the Pump Gap Loop Trail leaves left. You can lengthen this circuit hike by taking this spur. That trail circles back to Pump Gap, where you are headed. Our hike stays straight here, climbing. Trees tower above eye-level rhododendron. At 1.5 miles, reach Pump Gap and the Appalachian Trail.

Turn right (southbound) on the A.T. Climb a little as you wind in and out of shallow drainages. Make the crest of Lovers Leap Ridge at 2.1 miles. Pine, black gum, chestnut oak, and mountain laurel line the stony trail. Listen for the French Broad River below as it splashes over rocks and you roller coaster on the ridge crest. At 2.4 miles, reach a gap, then drop to the river side of the ridge. Ragged outcrops rise from the piney south-facing slope. At 2.8 miles, find a large campsite on your left. At 3.1 miles, look for a well-worn trail leading acutely left. Follow the side trail to an improbable rock rib ridge jutting toward the French Broad. Be careful scrambling out of this tapered outcrop. A forsaken pine tree guards the end of the rock. An open view of the French Broad and Hot Springs in a mountain frame are a just reward for those who tightrope their way out there. The French Broad River rises from the highlands of western

North Carolina near the town of Rosman, flowing approximately 100 miles, pouring past this outcrop into Hot Springs and beyond to Knoxville, Tennessee, where it meets the Holston River. Together they form the Tennessee River.

Resume the A.T. southbound, still descending. At 3.4 miles, come to a trail junction. Your return route, the Lovers Leap Trail, leaves right. First, follow the A.T. to two overlooks, the first very near the intersection, and second, follow the A.T. just a little farther to a switchback and a rock outcrop. This rock outcrop, with more open views, is Lovers Leap. Here, an American Indian princess leapt to her death after learning of the death of her one and only love at the hands of a rival suitor who wanted the princess for himself. This story is common in Cherokee lore.

Now backtrack a bit, then make a steady downgrade on the gravelly Lovers Leap Trail. At 3.7 miles, make a sharp switchback to the left, just above the Silvermine Group Campground. Work downhill to Silvermine Creek to reach the trailhead at 3.9 miles, ending the hike.

Nearby Attractions

The town of Hot Springs, North Carolina, offers not only nearby hiking and other outdoor sports but also dining and lodging. For more information, visit **hotspringsnc.org.**

Directions

From Asheville, North Carolina, take I-26 North 8.2 miles to Exit 19A. Merge onto US 25 North/US 70 West, and go 25.9 miles to Hot Springs. Just before crossing the bridge over the French Broad River, just east of Hot Springs, turn right onto River Road. Drive a very short distance to the river and turn left onto a paved road, Silvermine Creek Road, following it under the US 25/US 70 bridge. Stay left again as it curves up Silvermine Creek past houses. Reach the signed Silvermine parking area on your left, 0.3 mile from US 25/US 70.

SCENERY: ★ ★ ★ ★ ★
TRAIL CONDITION: ★ ★ ★
CHILDREN: ★
DIFFICULTY: ★ ★ ★ ★ ★
SOLITUDE: ★ ★ ★ ★

A BACKPACKER CROSSES BIG CREEK AT THE HIKE'S BEGINNING.

GPS TRAILHEAD COORDINATES: N36° 1.399' W82° 39.160'

DISTANCE & CONFIGURATION: 10.2-mile loop

HIKING TIME: 6.5-7.5 hours

HIGHLIGHTS: Cascade, 360-degree rocky views

ELEVATION: 2,400' at trailhead; 4,530' at high point

ACCESS: No fees or permits required

MAPS: Trails Illustrated *#782 French Broad and Nolichucky Rivers;* Appalachian Trail Conservancy *TN–NC Maps 3 and 4;* USGS *Greystone*

FACILITIES: None

CONTACT: Pisgah National Forest, Appalachian Ranger District: 828-689-9694, **www.fs.usda.gov/nfsnc**

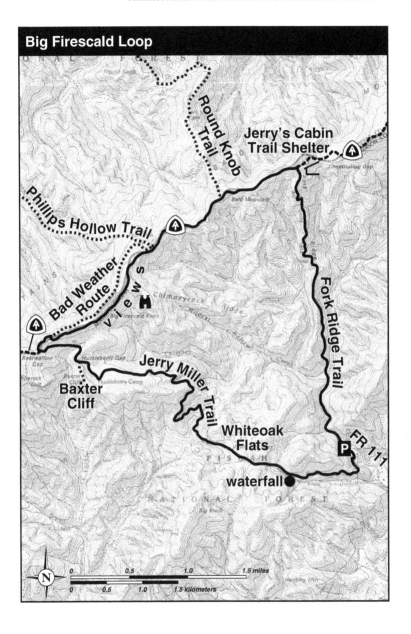

Big Firescald Loop

Overview

This loop is set in the Shelton Laurel Backcountry of the Pisgah National Forest. Jerry Miller Trail takes you to a 100-foot waterslide before opening onto Whiteoak Flats, a closing meadow. Ascend to the Appalachian Trail (A.T.). Walk the stony knife-edge delineating North Carolina and Tennessee. Incredible 360-degree views unveil atop Big Firescald Knob, a 0.5 mile of continuous outcrops opening into the Tar Heel State and the Volunteer State. A steep trip down Fork Ridge takes you back to the trailhead.

Route Details

Note the trailhead memorial to Jerry Miller, a Carolinian and national forest advocate. Bridge Big Creek on Jerry Miller Trail. This flat will fill with wildflowers in spring. Scale a ridge dividing Big Creek from Whiteoak Flats Branch, avoiding an old route that crossed private property. White trillium can be found here by the score. Turn into Whiteoak Flats Branch watershed at 0.3 mile. Head up the steep-sided valley among rhododendron, sourwood, pine, and magnolia.

The valley of Whiteoak Flats Branch closes in at 0.9 mile. Come near a noteworthy cascade to your left. Here, a long slide pours down the hollow and then drops in stages before slowing. Winter's barren trees reveal the full fall. The valley shuts and you take a short log bridge over now-gentle Whiteoak Flats Branch at 1.2 miles. Hop a tributary at 1.3 miles, then open onto what remains of Whiteoak Flats meadow.

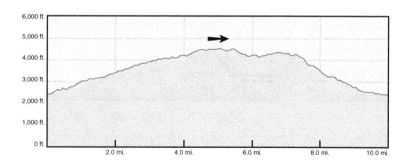

The former homestead is growing over with briers, pines, and tulip trees, yet you can still see surrounding ridges.

Whiteoak Flats meadow closes at 1.6 miles. Open onto a smaller clearing at 1.7 miles. Stay with the blazed trail, careful to avoid old roadbeds spurring from the primary trail. Take a sharp left at 2.1 miles. An old road goes straight here. The proper path is paint blazed; old roads fade and/or become overgrown. Rise to a dry ridge with black gum, pine, and mountain laurel. Jerry Miller Trail then turns into upper Chimney Creek valley, shaded by rhododendron arbors.

Tributaries of upper Chimney Creek sporadically spill over the trail. Rise to grassy Huckleberry Gap and a four-way intersection at 4 miles. To your right is a short path to a campsite. To your left, an unmarked trail leads atop a knob then sharply down to Baxter Cliff after 0.4 mile, with a view of Whiterock Cliff and Hickey Fork below.

Jerry Miller Trail leaves straight from Huckleberry Gap, curving around upper Hickey Fork to reach the Appalachian Trail at 4.5 miles. Turn right, northbound on the A.T., to quickly find another intersection. Here, the old A.T., now dubbed Bad Weather Route, stays left, while you stay right on Exposed Ridge Route, the newer A.T. section. Begin ascending among pale stone bluffs, boulders, and steps shaded by beech and yellow birch. Make a stony switchback at 4.7 miles. Head along the state-line crest among wind-stunted hardwoods.

At 5.1 miles, rise to Big Firescald Knob and begin a remarkable 0.5 mile of hiking. A jagged, irregular rock backbone rises above the trees. Looking into Tennessee, you see steep mountainsides give way to a patchwork quilt of farm and field. Looking into North Carolina, you see ridge after ridge extending easterly. During winter, look for the Jerry Miller Trail climbing toward Huckleberry Gap below, under the leafless trees. Stone steps, a result of backbreaking trail construction, lead through the craggy crest. Diminutive, windswept trees find a home in rock fissures, as do undersized rhododendron, blueberries, mountain laurel, and greenbrier. The going is slow, but maybe that is as it should be, given the incredible splendor. The A.T. enters more woods than rock at 5.6 miles.

Open to a rock slab and a north view of Big Butt and Green Ridge Knob, then find another overlook of Greene County, Tennessee, at 5.7 miles. Dip to meet Bad Weather Route at 6 miles. The rocky tread relents to tall woods and an undulating track. This area traverses the Bald Mountains, named for cattle-grazed meadows that once adorned their crests. Today, the forest has regenerated, and an amazing number of painted trillium and trout lilies carpet the forest floor in April.

At 6.7 miles, a roadlike trail leads left to Round Knob Picnic Area. Drift into a gap at 7.2 miles, then circle around the right side of Andrew Johnson Mountain. At 7.4 miles, reach Fork Ridge Trail (if you go 0.25 mile too far, you reach Jerry's Cabin trail shelter). Turn right on Fork Ridge Trail. Drop more than 1,000 feet in the next mile, flanked by rhododendron. Make a couple of upticks along the way, emerging in a trailhead parking area on FR 111 at 9.4 miles. From here, follow the forest road along trouty, sparkling Big Creek, crossing Chimney Creek by road ford at 9.5 miles, then Big Creek at 9.8 miles. Reach the Jerry Miller Trailhead at 10.2 miles, finishing the circuit.

Nearby Attractions

Shelton Laurel Backcountry has other trails that link to each other and to the Appalachian Trail for multiple loop possibilities.

Directions

From Asheville, North Carolina, take I-26 West to Exit 50, Flag Pond. Turn left onto Upper Higgins Creek Road, traveling 0.5 mile to TN 23. Turn right onto TN 23 North and follow it 2.1 miles to TN 352. Turn left onto TN 352 West. Enter North Carolina after 4.1 miles. The road becomes NC 212. Continue 3.2 miles beyond the state line; then turn right onto Big Creek Road, near Carmen Church of God. Follow Big Creek Road 1.2 miles. The road seems to end near a barn. Here, angle left onto Forest Road 111, taking the gravel road over a small creek. Enter Pisgah National Forest. At 0.4 mile beyond the barn, veer left onto a short spur road to dead-end at Jerry Miller Trailhead.

SCENERY: ★ ★ ★ ★
TRAIL CONDITION: ★ ★ ★ ★
CHILDREN: ★ ★ ★
DIFFICULTY: ★ ★
SOLITUDE: ★ ★ ★ ★

VIEWS ALONG THE A.T., SUCH AS THIS ONE AT THE HIGH ROCKS, INSPIRE HIKERS
TO NEW HEIGHTS.

GPS TRAILHEAD COORDINATES: N36° 1.922' W82° 25.219'

DISTANCE & CONFIGURATION: 3.4-mile out-and-back

HIKING TIME: 2.5 hours

HIGHLIGHTS: View from outcrop, solitude

ELEVATION: 3,200' at trailhead; 4,270' at high point

ACCESS: No fees or permits required

MAPS: Trails Illustrated *#782 French Broad and Nolichucky Rivers;* Appalachian Trail
Conservancy *TN–NC Maps 3 and 4;* USGS *Chestoa*

FACILITIES: None

CONTACT: Pisgah National Forest, Appalachian Ranger District: 828-689-9694,
www.fs.usda.gov/nfsnc

High Rocks Vista

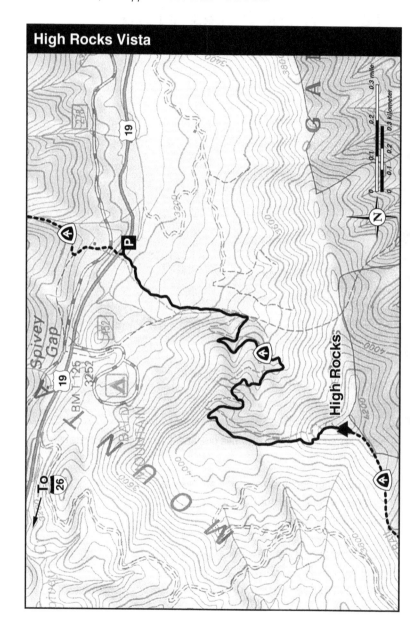

Overview

Join the Appalachian Trail (A.T.) in a secluded locale near Spivey Gap, at the North Carolina–Tennessee state line. Your southbound track takes you over the headwaters of Big Creek. Hike through an upland cove, passing a wildlife clearing. Rise to the stone outcrop of High Rocks, where an open slab avails extensive views of the surrounding mountains.

Route Details

The Appalachian Trail's first thousand miles cover only four states—Georgia, North Carolina, Tennessee, and Virginia. We might want to include West Virginia too, as a part of the A.T. runs along the Virginia–West Virginia border near the New River Valley and up by the Potomac River. For hikers trekking the Appalachian Trail in the South, that adds up to a lot of mileage, numerous access points, and many highlights, such as the High Rocks, to visit.

This section of the A.T., winding through the Bald Mountains, straddles the Tennessee–North Carolina state line. The A.T. crosses US 19W here, creating a convenient access, and avails hikers a nice walk to a big gray outcrop complete with a vista that offers solitude unseen at many other A.T. overlooks. From the parking area on US 19W, pick up a blue-blazed trail leading down from the parking area. Meet the white-blazed Appalachian Trail in just a few feet, amid dense cover of rhododendron. Join the A.T. and immediately step

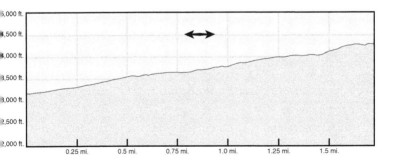

over Big Branch on some conveniently placed, very large stepping-stones. Keep south, passing a trail sign indicating various mileages for southbound hikers.

The A.T. wanders uphill in an upland cove, passing a few camp-sites situated among white pines, black birch, and oaks. At 0.2 mile, the A.T. comes alongside a grassy opening. These wildlife clearings provide additional habitat amongst the great forests of the Southern Appalachians. Where the woods and grass meet is called an edge, and it is in these edges where plants from both habitats overlap and create an ecotone. Ecotones can be rich with food, a place where berries grow, for example. In addition, deer and even bear browse on the grass of the wildlife clearings. Sometimes, land managers plant grasses and/or crops in wildlife clearings to supplement natural offerings.

The A.T. continues climbing into steeper wooded terrain. At 0.4 mile, join stone steps ascending a draw. Reach a ferny, mossy boulder garden, then turn sharply right. At 0.5 mile, a wooden span leads across a tinkling spring, as much pebbles as moving water. As you climb, the wide expanse of Flattop Mountain, rising from the north side of Spivey Gap, reveals itself. Turn into a tulip tree–filled hollow at 0.6 mile. Here, the Appalachian Trail is simply laboring up the side of a slope, easing the climb with switchbacks.

A discerning eye can still detect the old path of the A.T., which ran directly up the mountainside. When trails are laid out in that manner, not only are they difficult to hike but they are also erosive, as storm water runs directly down the path, gullying the course.

The trail switchbacks again at 0.8 mile, curving through a boulder garden. You are gaining elevation all the while. Yellow birch and cherry—representatives of northern hardwoods—begin to appear. At 1.2 miles, the A.T. turns sharply left on an outcrop. Flattop Mountain looms across Spivey Gap. Head south, then reach a gap on the shoulder of High Rocks at 1.4 miles. This is your first level ground since the trailhead.

Resume climbing, up the north slope of High Rocks. Wind among boulders in the forest. Stone steps aid your passage among these rock giants. Views open to the east, into North Carolina. The A.T. works over to the west side of the ridge, then dips along the base of a towering gray outcrop. You are just below the actual High Rocks but would need ropes to access it from this point. Instead, let the A.T. take you past the outcrop, descending to reach a signed trail intersection at 1.7 miles.

Head left on the blue-blazed spur. The spur rises to a narrowing crown, where stunted evergreens and hardwoods anchor to thin soils in rock crevices. The main path leads through crowded boulders then instantaneously opens onto a veritable dance floor of open flat rock. Here, views open in the distance. To the left (southwest), the knob of now-wooded Little Bald stands forth. The South Indian Creek valley and its tributaries, each forming its own valley, lie below. The crest of the Tennessee–North Carolina state line curves in an arc. Flint Mountain and Big Butt form distinctive peaks. To the right, you can gaze northeast into waves of mountains. Yes, High Rocks is a worthy destination, and a place to linger, before backtracking to the trailhead.

Nearby Attractions

The Appalachian Trail northbound from this trailhead travels 11 miles to the Nolichucky River, passing one trail shelter along the way. The Nolichucky River is a popular kayaking and rafting destination should you desire to complement your hike with a whitewater thrill ride. Outfitters are located on the river near the officially designated Appalachian Trail Community of Erwin, Tennessee.

Directions

From Exit 43 on I-26 near Erwin, Tennessee, take US 19W South 1.1 miles, then veer left, staying with US 19W South. Enter North Carolina, and after a total of 8.8 miles from I-26, you will come to the Appalachian Trail crossing and a parking area on your right.

20

Highlands of Roan

EXTENSIVE VIEWS OPEN AS THE A.T. DROPS OFF ROUND BALD.

SCENERY: ★ ★ ★ ★ ★
TRAIL CONDITION: ★ ★ ★ ★
CHILDREN: ★ ★ ★ ★
DIFFICULTY: ★ ★
SOLITUDE: ★

GPS TRAILHEAD COORDINATES: N36° 6.386' W82° 6.629'

DISTANCE & CONFIGURATION: 4.8-mile out-and-back

HIKING TIME: 3 hours

HIGHLIGHTS: Mile-high meadows, open balds, spruce-fir forests

ELEVATION: 5,500' at trailhead; 6,170' at high point

ACCESS: No fees or permits required

MAPS: Trails Illustrated *#783 South Holston and Watauga Lakes;* Appalachian Trail Conservancy *TN–NC Maps 1 and 2;* USGS *Carvers Gap*

FACILITIES: Restroom at trailhead

CONTACT: Cherokee National Forest, Watauga Ranger District: 423-735-1500, **www.fs.usda.gov/cherokee**

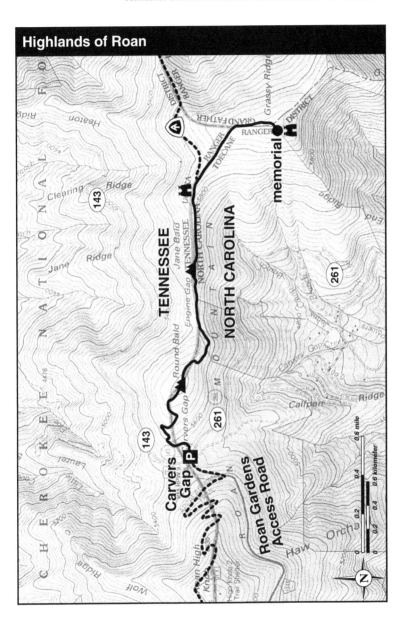

Highlands of Roan

Overview

Leave mile-high Carvers Gap on the Appalachian Trail (A.T.), strad-dling the Tennessee–North Carolina state line. Quickly surmount two grassy balds presenting views galore. Leave the A.T. at Grassy Ridge, where more views await above 6,000 feet. End your hike at a view and a plaque memorializing a highlander native to our area. This walk can easily be shortened for kids and less-able A.T. enthusiasts.

Route Details

Roan Mountain is a special place on the A.T. When recalling the most spectacular sections of the Appalachian Trail, thru-hikers regularly mention Roan Mountain. Under clear skies, trail trekkers atop The Roan will capture far-reaching, 360-degree panoramas between patches of dense spruce-fir forests, rhododendron gardens, and brush thickets.

Do not look for solitude here, as others will be enjoying the superlative scenery, save for during the week or when temperatures are low. Take the Appalachian Trail northbound from Carvers Gap by cutting through a fence on a gravel track. Curve up the west slope of Round Bald, entering a dark thicket of red spruce and Fraser fir. On the forest floor, moss-capped boulders contrast with fallen bronze needles. Leave the forest after switchbacking uphill. Open onto a grassy slope punctuated by evergreen tree stands and rhododendron thickets. Peer back across Carvers Gap and the looming mass of Roan Mountain.

At 0.6 mile, reach the crest of Round Bald. The grassy moun-taintop avails 360-degree vistas and is a great place for a picnic or short kid-friendly hike. The state of Tennessee stretches north and the Tar Heel State extends south. Lucky hikers will encounter blue skies. Even at that, clouds and fog often pour over this mile-high ridge, obfuscating the landscape beyond. At 1.1 miles, the A.T. bot-toms out at Engine Gap. Rise from the gap, passing over and around emergent rock outcrops, and beside wind-stunted bushes and trees. At 1.3 miles, a hard-to-resist outcrop draws hikers to its boulders.

Here, nature's stone seats open down to the hills of East Tennessee. Somewhere down there is my home in Johnson City.

The top of Jane Bald crests out just ahead. Jane Bald is a mix of grasses, shrubs, and small trees, trying to morph to forest. Balds, or open meadows such as Jane Bald, are one of the great mysteries of the Southern Appalachians. The origin of these mountaintop fields is not clear, although natural fires, clearing by Indians, and grazing animals have historically kept the trees at bay. Goats have been experimentally used atop The Roan, though mowing is the primary bald-maintaining technique here.

Descend from Jane Bald and rise to a prominent vista at 1.7 miles. Look back on Jane Bald and Round Bald, with forested Roan Mountain forming a dusky frame. At 1.8 miles, the Appalachian Trail splits near an outcrop. At this junction, the white-blazed A.T. leaves left for more balds, whereas the trail to Grassy Ridge heads right. Aim for Grassy Ridge, taking the lesser-trod right fork. Ascend southeasterly on a narrow, sometimes rutted path, still straddling the Tennessee–North Carolina line. Push past low brush, wind-sculpted trees, and tightly grown thickets of rhododendron.

You are soon above 6,000 feet. Open onto the grassy part of Grassy Ridge at 2.1 miles. Spruce and fir trees, rising in dense groves, break up the flat green continuum. Astonishing landscapes distract you from your footsteps. You have about leveled off. At 2.4 miles, the trail divides. Stay right here and soon reach a notable gray outcrop with a vista allowing looks back to the trailhead and just about every

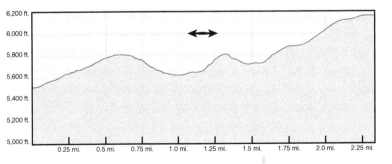

direction your eyes can go. On this rock, you will find a prominently displayed plaque erected by the U.S. Forest Service. It honors Cornelius Rex Peake. The inscription states: "A special man who loved God, his country, his fellow men and this land; a legacy from his forefather. Born in the valley below, April 3, 1887, buried near his birthplace March 23, 1964. Because of his love of nature, his long and close association with this mountain, no one was better versed on the Roan and its people."

If we could all be so close to the land. . . . Beyond this outcrop and the hike's turnaround point, trails extend farther out Grassy Ridge, through fields and into spruce forests. Nevertheless, there is more than ample beauty along this hike to sate even a man such as Cornelius Rex Peake . . . and us.

Nearby Attractions

During late June, the world-famous rhododendron gardens of Roan Mountain will be blooming. A nature trail exploring the gardens is accessible from the other side of Carvers Gap. From Carvers Gap, you take the auto road up to the trailhead.

Directions

From Johnson City, Tennessee, take US 321 North/TN 67 East, following signs to Elizabethton. Travel 9.9 miles to reach US 19E and a traffic light (from Bristol take US 11E South 12 miles to this same intersection on US 19E South, except you will keep straight through the traffic light). Turn right here, now joining US 19E South/Veterans Memorial Parkway toward Roan Mountain and Mountain City, Tennessee, and Boone, North Carolina. Follow US 19E 16.5 miles to TN 143 in the town of Roan Mountain. Turn right onto TN 143 and follow it 12.6 miles to Carvers Gap, at the Tennessee–North Carolina state line. A small parking area is on the right.

21

Big Hump Mountain

FALL WILDFLOWERS BLOOM ON THE GRASSY FIELDS BELOW BIG HUMP MOUNTAIN.

SCENERY: ★ ★ ★ ★ ★
TRAIL CONDITION: ★ ★ ★ ★
CHILDREN: ★ ★
DIFFICULTY: ★ ★ ★ ★
SOLITUDE: ★ ★

GPS TRAILHEAD COORDINATES: N36° 7.018' W82° 2.930'

DISTANCE & CONFIGURATION: 8.8-mile out-and-back

HIKING TIME: 5 hours

HIGHLIGHTS: Historic connector path, superlative views from open balds

ELEVATION: 4,220' at trailhead; 5,587' at high point

ACCESS: No fees or permits required

MAPS: Trails Illustrated #783 *South Holston and Watauga Lakes;* Appalachian Trail Conservancy *TN–NC Maps 1 and 2;* USGS *Carvers Gap* and USGS *White Rocks Mountain*

FACILITIES: None

CONTACT: Cherokee National Forest, Watauga Ranger District: 423-735-1500, www.fs.usda.gov/cherokee

Big Hump Mountain

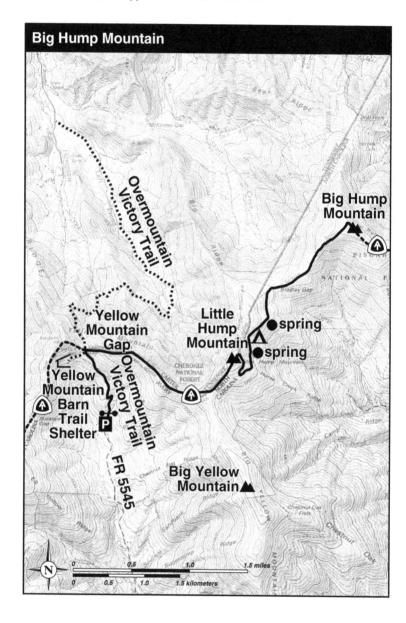

Overview

Start on the Revolutionary War–era Overmountain Victory Trail and rise to the Appalachian Trail (A.T.). From there, straddle the Tennessee–North Carolina state line in a mix of forests, meadows, and fields presenting first-rate vistas. Cross over Little Hump Mountain, then make a grassy ramble down to Bradley Gap. A final push leads to Big Hump Mountain and 360-degree mountain panoramas that cap off this top-notch trek.

Route Details

This hike's beginning roughly follows the route of the Overmountain Men—pioneers of North Carolina, Virginia, and what became Tennessee—who mustered at Sycamore Shoals before embarking eastward over the mountains to take on the British, providing an important victory that helped turn the tide of the Revolutionary War in the South.

Leave the trailhead on Overmountain Victory Trail. Pass around the pole gate into a small clearing to the right of the parking area, not up gated FR 5545. Soon enter a forest of maple, yellow birch, haw, and buckeye on a doubletrack path. A stream gurgles to your right. At 0.2 mile, come to a field. Here, turn acutely left and bisect the meadow. This turn, signed with a brown post, is easily missed. If you keep straight on the doubletrack, you will immediately cross the stream you've been paralleling by culvert. This is the wrong way, though you can eventually

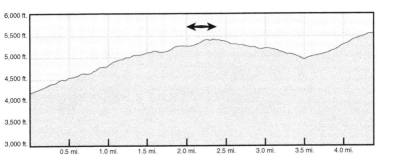

reach the A.T. Instead, bisect the aforementioned meadow, then join a doubletrack path climbing parallel and to the left of the meadow. Continue ascending in woods, though you can see the clearing to your right. Pass through full-blown forest. At 0.7 mile, you are again running alongside another meadow to your right. Reach the well-used blue-blazed spur to the Yellow Mountain Barn trail shelter just before coming to Yellow Mountain Gap and the Appalachian Trail at 0.8 mile.

Harken back to 1780, late September it was, when the Overmountain Men marched through Yellow Mountain Gap in the snow, fighting for American independence. The 640 patriots, who knew this route as Bright's Trace, took roll here, then spent a subfreezing night before descending toward Roaring Fork and on to Kings Mountain, where they slew the dreaded Patrick Ferguson and his band of Tories. Our hike is much less hazardous, as we turn right (northbound) on the A.T. Quickly climb from woods onto a meadow with fine views of the Roaring Fork valley below, the valley through which you came. Note the fields down there. As you climb, look back at the Yellow Mountain Barn trail shelter, backed by the Appalachian crest. The A.T. enjoys some level stretches with a foot-friendly trail bed. The trail is canopied in places. At 1.9 miles, open onto the grasses of Little Hump Mountain. Tennessee views open wide. White Rocks Mountain and the town of Roan Mountain stand below. The jagged crest of Carolina's Grandfather Mountain climbs the sky.

Pass a beckoning outcrop just before topping out on Little Hump Mountain at 2.3 miles. Soak in the nearly 360-degree views. Big Hump Mountain stands to the east. This is a fine turnaround point for those seeking a less-strenuous hike. Otherwise, leave Little Hump and drift through dense stands of stunted birch alternating with open slopes on the east side of Little Hump. Step over a trailside rocky spring at 2.8 miles. Pass a campsite on your right at 2.9 miles. The A.T. descends, passing a spur trail to another spring at 3.1 miles. Open onto continuous meadow just beyond the spring. Here, the massif of Big Hump rises, centered by grasses and bordered by wind-sculpted trees and brush, mixed with gray rock outcrops.

The A.T. takes you farther down, however, to reach Bradley Gap at 3.5 miles. There is nary a tree around. Begin working upward along the spine of the Appalachians. Stellar views into the two states provide a distraction to your heavy breathing while making the 600-foot ascent from Bradley Gap. Pass over a fence at 4.1 miles. This fence encloses grazing cattle, without which these balds would completely reforest themselves. The U.S. Forest Service also uses mowing to keep the trees at bay.

Pass an outcrop with views into Tennessee before making a sharp right turn. Make the final few feet to the tiptop of Big Hump Mountain, elevation 5,587 feet, at 4.4 miles. A sheer, utter magnificence of mountains stretches into the yon. When I think of the best destinations on the A.T. in the South, Big Hump Mountain comes to mind. My favorite vista from here is back toward Roan Mountain, with the meadows of Bradley Gap in the fore. Your backtrack will reveal more views you missed on the way out.

Nearby Attractions

The historic Overmountain Victory Trail continues from Yellow Mountain Gap for 3.6 miles into Tennessee.

Directions

From downtown Elk Park, North Carolina, just east of the Tennessee state line, take US 19E South 1 mile, and then stay right on US 19E toward Spruce Pine, North Carolina. Follow US 19E South a total of 9.2 miles from Elk Park; then turn right onto Roaring Creek Road, just before reaching McCoury's Rock Freewill Baptist Church. Follow Roaring Creek Road 2.2 miles to a Y intersection, and stay right as Jerry's Creek Road turns left. At 3.5 miles, the paved road becomes gravel Forest Road 5545. Continue up the gravel track to end at a parking area at 4.6 miles from US 19E. Overmountain Victory Trail is to your right as you reach the trailhead.

22

Laurel Falls

SCENERY:	★ ★ ★ ★ ★
TRAIL CONDITION:	★ ★ ★
CHILDREN:	★ ★
DIFFICULTY:	★ ★ ★
SOLITUDE:	★

LAUREL FALLS IS AN AQUATIC ALTERNATIVE TO THE RIDGE-RUNNING SEGMENTS OF THE APPALACHIAN TRAIL.

GPS TRAILHEAD COORDINATES: N36° 17.123' W82° 9.132'

DISTANCE & CONFIGURATION: 4.8-mile out-and-back

HIKING TIME: 3.5 hours

HIGHLIGHTS: Laurel Falls, rock bluffs, other geological features

ELEVATION: 1,860' at trailhead; 2,180' at high point

ACCESS: No fees or permits required

MAPS: Trails Illustrated #783 *South Holston and Watauga Lakes;* Appalachian Trail Conservancy *TN–NC Maps 1 and 2;* USGS *Elizabethton*

FACILITIES: None

CONTACT: Cherokee National Forest, Watauga Ranger District: 423-735-1500, **www.fs.usda.gov/cherokee**

Laurel Falls

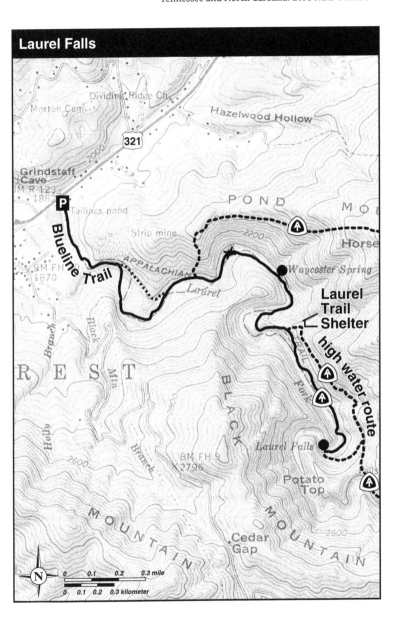

Overview

This hike travels to an aquatic feature along the Appalachian Trail (A.T.)—Laurel Falls. First, follow an old railroad grade into the heart of the Laurel Fork Gorge on the Blueline Trail. Pass a sheer rock bluff, the first of many geological features, before meeting the Appalachian Trail. Continue deeper up the Laurel Fork valley, climbing a rock spine before descending to Laurel Fork again. Squeeze past another bluff before reaching Laurel Falls. This brawling cataract drops some 60 feet into a deep churning pool and is popular with summertime swimmers.

Route Details

Laurel Fork Gorge is hemmed in by Black Mountain on one side and Pond Mountain on the other. Over time, Laurel Fork has cut through the layers of stone—leaving behind boulder fields, rock piles, and steep cliffs. The watershed was logged around a century back. This logging railroad grade forms the basic trail bed. Considering the inhospitable terrain, it is hard to believe anyone would attempt cutting through this gorge with a railroad. The forest has recovered nicely, and in 1986, most of the lower gorge became part of the Cherokee National Forest's Pond Mountain Wilderness. The Appalachian Trail traverses the heart of the gorge and the wilderness.

Leave the Hampton parking area on the Blueline Trail. It follows the old railroad grade, then leaves acutely left away after 0.25 mile, avoiding an old creek crossing. Pass under a power line clearing, then reenter woods. At 0.4 mile, enter the Pond Mountain Wilderness.

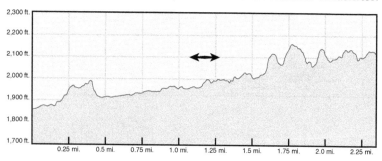

Just ahead, the Blueline Trail splits. Stay right, descending to flats along Laurel Fork. The tea-colored stream flows in shoals and pools, bordered by sand and gravel bars. At 0.5 mile, a huge stone bluff rises across the stream. Continue upstream in rich forest of beech, sugar maple, black birch, and tulip trees with tangles of rhododendron and mountain laurel. Dog hobble and ferns thicken the ground cover. White pines tower above all.

At 0.7 mile, the Blueline Trail split comes in on your left. Blueline Trail squeezes past a streamside outcrop. At 0.9 mile, walk around a conspicuous boulder in the middle of the trail. Continue up streamside flats, meeting the Appalachian Trail at 1 mile. It has descended from Pond Mountain. Keep straight (southbound) on the Appalachian Trail. Talus slopes fall off Pond Mountain to your left. At 1.2 miles reach a footbridge that crosses over to the right bank of Laurel Fork. Tunnel through rhododendron on a sandy track.

Rock outcrops remain visible throughout the foreboding gorge. Bridge the stream yet again at 1.4 miles. Just ahead, meet Waycoster Spring, used by passersby from Cherokee Indians to yesteryear's loggers to today's Appalachian Trail thru-hikers. Occasional campsites are scattered in the flats.

At 1.6 miles, the path leaves Laurel Fork and ascends a stony, rooty track up to a rocky, pine-clad ridge, fringed with galax. Chestnut oaks and hickories reflect the dry ridge. Laurel Fork is curving around this outcrop that you have climbed. Soak in views of the stream and the imposing canyon. At 1.8 miles, the trail splits. The blue-blazed A.T. high water route leaves left toward Laurel Trail Shelter. Stay right with the white-blazed Appalachian Trail, quickly descending back to Laurel Fork. Streamside slabs make for fine water accesses and relaxation spots. At 2.2 miles, the Appalachian Trail is forced to the edge of Laurel Fork by a jutting outcrop. The A.T. squeezes by here directly along the stream. If Laurel Fork is flooded, this route is impassable, hence the high water route.

Watch for an impressive bluff just past this trail squeeze. Continue up the rugged gorge on an exceedingly rocky track. Laurel

Falls becomes visible through the trees, and you reach it at 2.4 miles. The watercourse is tumbling over a stone rampart in a froth of whitewater, framed in thick woods under an open sky. A huge pool, rife with tricky undercurrents, stretches between you and the falls. If you want to swim, stay back from the falls itself. On nice weekend days, hikers will be gathered here, soaking in the scenery. Scores of boulders make for ample seating to observe the falls.

On your return trip, you can simply backtrack or continue the Appalachian Trail southbound up a series of steep steps to reach an old railroad grade. Here, the A.T. leaves right but the A.T. high water route leaves left, passing through a railroad cut then cruising mid-slope along the gorge. It offers views of Black Mountain across Laurel Fork and then meets the Laurel Trail Shelter, a small, three-sided stone structure. From there the route descends back to the A.T. This alternate adds about 0.2 mile to your hike and a 300-foot climb from Laurel Falls to the high water route.

Nearby Attractions

Cherokee National Forest's Dennis Cove Campground, upstream of Laurel Falls, presents more hiking and fishing opportunities.

Directions

From Johnson City, Tennessee, take US 321 North/TN 67 East, following signs to Elizabethton. Travel 9.9 miles to reach US 19E and a traffic light (from Bristol take US 11E South 12 miles to this same intersection on US 19E South, except you will keep straight through the traffic light). Turn right here, now joining US 19E South/Veterans Memorial Parkway toward Roan Mountain and Mountain City, Tennessee, and Boone, North Carolina. Follow US 19E 5.2 miles to the left turn for Hampton and Watauga Lake, US 321 East/TN 67 East. Turn left onto TN 67 and follow it 1.2 miles to the Laurel Falls Trailhead on your right.

SCENERY: ★ ★ ★ ★
TRAIL CONDITION: ★ ★ ★ ★
CHILDREN: ★ ★ ★
DIFFICULTY: ★ ★
SOLITUDE: ★ ★

THE A.T. WINDS ATOP POND MOUNTAIN IN THE BACKGROUND AND ALONG WATAUGA LAKE IN THE FOREGROUND.

GPS TRAILHEAD COORDINATES: N36° 18.130' W82° 7.701'

DISTANCE & CONFIGURATION: 5.4-mile out-and-back

HIKING TIME: 3.5 hours

HIGHLIGHTS: Watauga Lake, Watauga Dam

ELEVATION: 1,970' at trailhead; 2,240' at high point

ACCESS: No fees or permits required

MAPS: Trails Illustrated *#783 South Holston and Watauga Lakes;* Appalachian Trail Conservancy *TN–NC Maps 1 and 2;* USGS *Elizabethton* and USGS *Watauga Dam*

FACILITIES: Picnic area, restrooms, swim beach in season

CONTACT: Cherokee National Forest, Watauga Ranger District: 423-735-1500, **www.fs.usda.gov/cherokee**

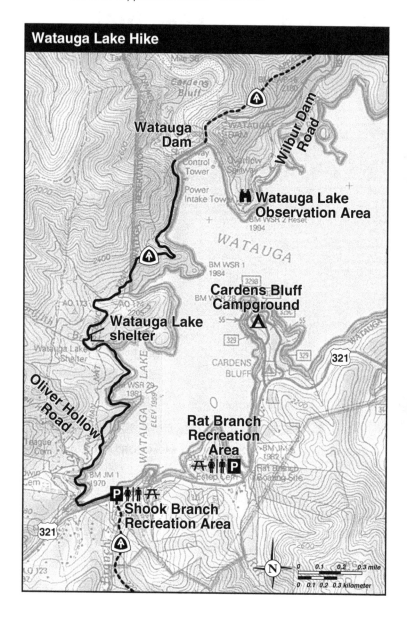

Watauga Lake Hike

Overview

Soak in this highlight-filled lakeside ramble. Join the Appalachian Trail (A.T.) as it curves along the shore of Watauga Lake, bordered by mountain vistas aplenty and swimming opportunities too. Cruise away from the lake, passing a pair of pre-lake homesites. Next, stop by a trail shelter before visiting Watauga Dam. The dam offers wide-ranging panoramas of the surrounding land and waterscape.

Route Details

Interestingly, from your starting point at the Shook Branch Recreation Area, you can look across Watauga Lake to your destination, Watauga Dam. While you walk to the dam, mountain views will be present most of the hike. Leave the auto turnaround, northbound on the Appalachian Trail (even though you are traveling south at the hike's origin) and immediately bridge Shook Branch. Just ahead, a set of wooden steps comes in from US 321–TN 67. Continue straight on the A.T., circling around the first of two small tributaries feeding Watauga Lake.

Bridge the first tributary at 0.2 mile. When the lake is drawn down in winter, scan for old roads and such that were inundated after the lake was flooded. Come very near houses and Oliver Hollow Road, in earshot of US 321–TN 67's rumbling traffic. At 0.5 mile, the A.T. works around an iron gate. Cruise the lakeshore, passing campsites and swimming spots. Pond Mountain Wilderness rises across

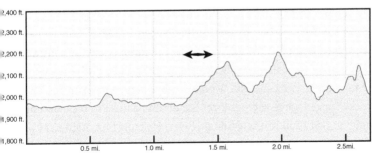

141

the water. The trail wanders away from Watauga Lake, climbing over a richly forested hill, still roughly paralleling the shoreline. At 0.8 mile, the singletrack A.T. turns sharply left, working into a lake cove.

Now the shore stays close enough to allow nearly continuous lake views, if not occasional lake accesses. At 1.2 miles, the A.T. joins a roadbed left over from pre-lake days. Turn into a hollow, passing an old homesite on the left. Note the planted yuccas and escaped periwinkle, both common indicators of former dwelling sites. The trail gently ascends the roadbed, and comes to a second homesite at 1.3 miles. This area has rock piles, old metal washtubs, cans, and other relics—even a rocked-in basement. Ironically, the pine-shaded flat is now used as a campsite by A.T. hikers.

At 1.4 miles, step over the branch that created the homesite hollow, rising along a south-facing ridge full of oaks and pines. Top out at 1.5 miles, then descend into the rhododendron-heavy valley of Griffith Branch, a perennial stream. Reach the bottom of the hollow, then find the spur trail leading left to the Watauga Lake trail shelter at 1.6 miles. The spur crosses Griffith Branch and finds a clearing, whereupon a three-sided, tin-roofed, wooden shelter stands. A picnic table, fire ring, and bear-proof food-hanging pole complement the shelter.

Beyond the shelter, the A.T. crosses Griffith Branch, then climbs 200 feet to a peninsula jutting into Watauga Lake. At this point, you are nearly 300 feet above the impoundment, which at full pool is 1,959 feet in elevation. The A.T. quickly drops to the shore again, reaching an extremely rocky area. Return to the shoreline at 2.3 miles. The slope here is steep, however.

The A.T. reaches an asphalt road and the greater dam area at 2.5 miles. Open onto Watauga Dam at 2.7 miles. View the contrast between sides of the dam. Upstream stretches a smooth impoundment bordered by majestic wooded mountains. Downstream, the rocky rugged gorge through Iron Mountain testifies to rock-eroding aquatic pulsation of the Watauga River. Holston Mountain rises in the distance.

The dam, centered at the upper end of the Watauga River Gorge, stands 318 feet. Construction of Watauga Dam began in 1942, but World War II put it on hold; it was completed in 1948. The impoundment has 105 miles of shoreline and covers nearly 6,500 acres at full pool. Its deepest spot is a whopping 281 feet! This dam inundated many a homestead. The most famous community was Butler. These lands were commandeered by the United States government by eminent domain. Much of the surrounding land was already in the hands of the Cherokee National Forest. A significant portion of the shore and surrounding mountains create what many believe to be one of the South's most scenic lakes. Watauga Dam is a good place to turn around. However, the A.T. travels another mile north to reach Iron Mountain Gap and Wilbur Dam Road.

Nearby Attractions

Cherokee National Forest's Cardens Bluff Campground is just down the road from the Shook Branch Recreation Area trailhead. It offers waterfront camping on Watauga Lake during the warm season.

Directions

From Johnson City, Tennessee, take US 321 North/TN 67 East, following signs to Elizabethton. Travel 9.9 miles to reach US 19E and a traffic light (from Bristol take US 11E South 12 miles to this same intersection on US 19E South, except you will keep straight through the traffic light). Turn right here, now joining US 19E South/Veterans Memorial Parkway toward Roan Mountain and Mountain City, Tennessee, and Boone, North Carolina. Follow US 19E 5.2 miles to the left turn for Hampton and Watauga Lake, US 321 East/TN 67 East. Turn left onto TN 67 and follow it 3.2 miles to the Shook Branch Recreation Area on your left. Follow the entrance road to its end at an auto turnaround and the A.T. In winter, the recreation area is gated, but there is a small parking area 0.2 mile west of the Shook Branch entrance road. Steps lead to the A.T. from this parking area.

Views from Vandeventer

> SCENERY: ★ ★ ★ ★ ★
> TRAIL CONDITION: ★ ★ ★
> CHILDREN: ★
> DIFFICULTY: ★ ★ ★ ★
> SOLITUDE: ★ ★ ★

GAZING UPON WATAUGA LAKE FROM THE VANDEVENTER SHELTER

GPS TRAILHEAD COORDINATES: N36° 19.710' W82° 6.700'

DISTANCE & CONFIGURATION: 9.2-mile out-and-back

HIKING TIME: 5.5 hours

HIGHLIGHTS: Laurel Branch Wilderness, lake views, trail shelter

ELEVATION: 2,380' at trailhead; 3,610' at high point

ACCESS: No fees or permits required

MAPS: Trails Illustrated #783 South Holston and Watauga Lakes; Appalachian Trail Conservancy TN–NC Maps 1 and 2; USGS Watauga Dam

FACILITIES: Picnic area, boat launch near trailhead

CONTACT: Cherokee National Forest, Watauga Ranger District: 423-735-1500, www.fs.usda.gov/cherokee

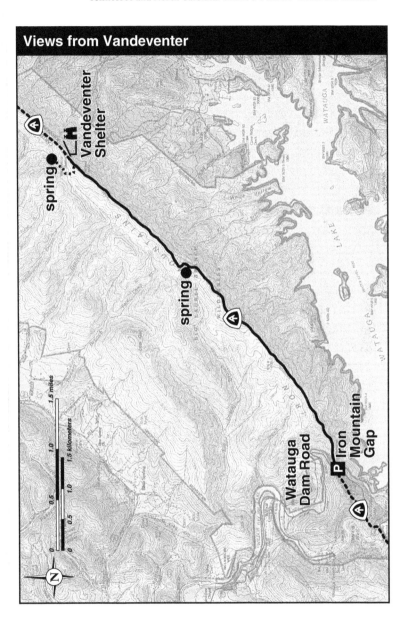

Views from Vandeventer

Vandeventer Shelter

spring

spring

Watauga Dam Road

Iron Mountain Gap

Overview

This hike travels the spine of Iron Mountain, using the Appalachian Trail (A.T.) to reach a trail shelter and a fine view. Enter Laurel Branch Wilderness at the trailhead, climbing by switchbacks to the ridge crest. Occasional outcrops provide warm-up views. The richly forested mountain eventually leads to Vandeventer trail shelter, directly behind which is a rock crag presenting panoramas of Watauga Lake and a host of mountains beyond.

Route Details

This hike is best enjoyed when the skies are clear. I recommend doing it from early fall through late spring, especially after fronts have passed through. The trek can be a hot one during summer with the lack of water and potentially hazy skies being pitfalls then. The Appalachian Trail crosses Watauga Dam Road at Iron Mountain Gap. This is where you start this hike. Parking spots are stretched along the road here, but if you cannot find one, just drive on down toward the observation and picnic area overlooking Watauga Lake. Leave Iron Mountain Gap, northbound on the Appalachian Trail. Immediately reach a sign indicating the Laurel Branch Wilderness, a federally designated wild area encompassing the crest of Iron Mountain and its tributaries running down both sides of the ridge, including all the way down to Watauga Lake on the southeast side of Iron Mountain. Designated by Congress in 1986, the wilderness area encompasses

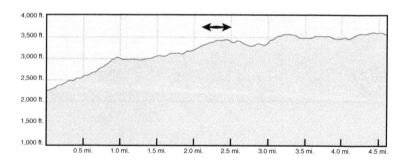

more than 6,360 acres. This hike stays within the wilderness for its entire length. Shortly pass a trailside signboard. Make your way uphill in prototype pine-oak-hickory woods, found on south-facing and dry slopes of the Cherokee National Forest. Black gum, sassafras, and sourwood add floral variation. The trail soon slips to the Watauga Lake side of the ridge. Make the first of several switchbacks that ease what was formerly a steep ascent up the nose of Iron Mountain. The practiced eye can see the route of the old A.T. while navigating these switchbacks. Please stay with the rerouted trail—not only does it make the hiking easier, it also prevents erosion.

The switchbacks and climbs continue. Note the stone steps in spots. Hats off to the Tennessee Eastman Hiking and Canoe Club for their work maintaining this section of the Appalachian Trail. Most of the entire A.T. is maintained by volunteer clubs. Consider joining them to help the A.T. stay in good shape. At times you will look southeast over the lake and at other times northwest toward Holston Mountain. In winter, your views will be nearly continuous.

Around 1 mile, the climbing eases and you enter a copse of Carolina hemlock. This is an often compact, conical evergreen with needles spreading in all directions versus the needles of an Eastern hemlock, which spread in two rows on either side of the branch. Carolina hemlock occurs—not surprisingly—in western North Carolina, as well as East Tennessee, southwest Virginia, and even bits of Georgia and South Carolina. It grows on dry slopes like this, unlike moisture-loving Eastern hemlock. The evergreen also seems to be less susceptible to the hemlock woolly adelgid, which is decimating hemlocks throughout the East. Pockets of rhododendron keep the trailside green too.

The main climb is over, but there are more undulations ahead, and a general upward trend. The ridge crest is often rocky. At 1.2 miles, come to a grassy flat with the sitting rocks that beckon a stop. The ridgeline is narrow, with the southeast slope being amazingly precipitous. At 1.5 miles, a short spur trail leads right to an outcrop and a tree-framed view of Watauga Lake and the mountains beyond.

Remain on the ridge, gently undulating. Pass another outcrop and view at 1.8 miles. This view is somewhat limited by the vegetation. At 2 miles, come to another outcrop and panorama. Here, you can clearly see the TN 67 bridge spanning Watauga Lake, with the balance of mountains stretching easterly to the horizon. At 2.6 miles, a spur trail leads right to a wooded knob and little campsite.

The white-blazed Appalachian Trail continues tracing Iron Mountain in a nearly arrow-straight northeast direction. Black birch, red maple, and goosefoot maple increase in number with the increasing elevation. You are now above 3,000 feet. Drop left off the ridge and descend into a hollow. Reach a small spring at 3 miles. This upwelling can nearly run dry by late summer and may need to be dug out. Climb from the hollow to rejoin the top of Iron Mountain at 3.3 miles. The ridge narrows and a rocky spine rises, forcing you to walk just below the stony hogback.

The trail continues to play tag with the crest, going atop the ridge where it can, sometimes retreating to a side slope when the rocks are impassable. At 4.5 miles, look left for a blue-blazed spur trail heading to a chilly spring. Stay straight with the Appalachian Trail. Descend a bit, then reach the Vandeventer trail shelter at 4.6 miles. The worn-down, three-sided, cinder-block structure is no match for the splendor of Iron Mountain. Vandeventer Shelter was built in 1961 and shows its age. Nevertheless, a rock outcrop rises beyond the shelter, and needs no human augmentation. Climb atop the gray stone and look out. Below, Watauga Lake forms a flat shimmer pocked with islands, peninsulas, and coves. Pond Mountain and White Rocks Mountain frame the lake. In the distance, Roan Mountain, Grandfather Mountain, and myriad peaks of North Carolina's Pisgah National Forest extend to horizon's end. Make sure to sign the trail register in the shelter before backtracking.

Nearby Attractions

The Tennessee Valley Authority's Wilbur Dam and Watauga Dam area have picnic areas, boat launches, and even a campground. For more information, visit **tva.com.**

Directions

From Johnson City, Tennessee, take US 321 North/TN 67 East, following signs to Elizabethton. Travel 9.9 miles to reach US 19E and a traffic light (from Bristol take US 11E South 12 miles to this same intersection on US 19E South, except you will keep straight through the traffic light). Turn right here, now joining US 19E South/Veterans Memorial Parkway toward Roan Mountain and Mountain City, Tennessee, and Boone, North Carolina. Follow US 19E 0.3 mile, and then turn left onto Siam Road at a traffic light. Follow Siam Road 3.5 miles to meet Wilbur Dam Road at a T intersection. The Watauga River is dead ahead in 0.6 mile. Turn right to stay on Wilbur Dam Road. At 2.6 miles, make sure to stay left toward OVERLOOK and LAKE RECREATION. At 4.2 miles, come to Iron Mountain Gap and the Appalachian Trail. Parking will be on your left.

Cross Mountain

SCENERY: ★ ★ ★ ★ ★
TRAIL CONDITION: ★ ★ ★ ★
CHILDREN: ★ ★ ★
DIFFICULTY: ★ ★
SOLITUDE: ★ ★ ★

BACKPACKER CROSSES THE OPEN MEADOWS OF CROSS MOUNTAIN ON A
WHEELCHAIR-ACCESSIBLE PORTION OF THE A.T.

GPS TRAILHEAD COORDINATES: N36° 28.882' W81° 57.629'

DISTANCE & CONFIGURATION: 1-mile out-and-back; 5.8-mile out-and-back option

HIKING TIME: 1 hour; 3.5 hours for 5.8-mile option

HIGHLIGHTS: Panoramas from Osborne Farm, Appalachian Trail shelter

ELEVATION: 3,510' at trailhead; 4,130' at high point

ACCESS: No fees or permits required

MAPS: Trails Illustrated #783 South Holston and Watauga Lakes; Appalachian Trail
Conservancy TN–NC Maps 1 and 2; USGS Doe and USGS Shady Valley

FACILITIES: None

CONTACT: Cherokee National Forest, Watauga Ranger District: 423-735-1500,
www.fs.usda.gov/cherokee

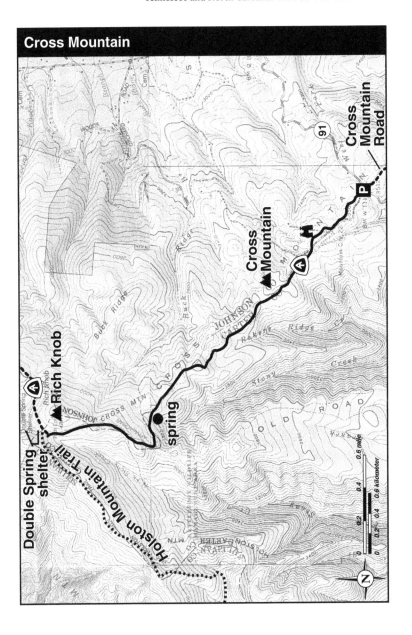

Cross Mountain

Cross Mountain Road

91

Cross Mountain

Rich Knob

Double Spring shelter

spring

JOHNSON

Holston Mountain Trail

Overview

The first 0.5 mile of this Appalachian Trail (A.T.) hike is for everybody (including those in wheelchairs), a universal access pathway over a view-laden meadow. The highlights come early as you trace the A.T. across the open fields of the old Osborne Farm. Here, far-reaching panoramas stretch north into Shady Valley and beyond into the Virginia highlands. The gently rising track enters woods after a mile of open meadows. From there you can make your way to Double Spring Shelter, an A.T. accommodation set in a hollow on Holston Mountain, and then backtrack.

Route Details

Several decades past, when the Appalachian Trail was originally laid out, certain sections went through private property. Such was the case atop Cross Mountain, a ridge linking Holston and Iron Mountains where Mr. and Mrs. Lester Osborne had a farm. Straddling the Johnson County–Carter County line, the open meadows of their place provided stunning views, but it *was* private property. Eventually, the A.T. was rerouted around their farm. Fast-forward to September 25, 2001, when the Osbornes sold their farm to the Nature Conservancy, which in turn sold it to the U.S. Forest Service, and it became part of Tennessee's Cherokee National Forest.

The Tennessee Eastman Hiking and Canoe Club, which maintains the Appalachian Trail in these parts, sprang into action, rerouting

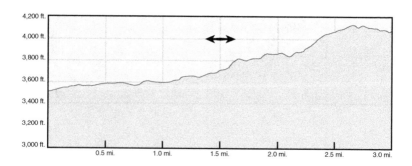

the Appalachian Trail over the mountaintop meadows, restoring the views that we can enjoy today. As an added benefit, the first 0.5 mile of the trail was made wheelchair accessible, an unusual thing for the Appalachian Trail. This first 0.5 mile is 3 feet wide and covered with hard-packed gravel. It makes for an easy start to the hike and lures in not only wheelchair hikers but also casual strollers who happen upon the path then enjoy those panoramas. This 0.5-mile part of the trail did not come cheaply either—more than $18,000. Today, the Osborne farmhouse has been removed, but some outbuildings remain, reflecting its agricultural heritage. Fences crisscross the 250-acre tract. You will traverse some of them on this hike.

Leave the parking area, crossing to the west side of TN 91. A gravel road extends west, but the hike works through a gate, following the white-blazed Appalachian Trail into open grassy pasture. Do not be surprised if cattle are grazing in the meadow—they help keep it from growing over in trees and obscuring the gorgeous views. Continue following the gravel all-access trail as it rolls over grassy hills. Ahead, weathered outbuildings come into view, and you will pass near them. Views open. To your west, the direction you are hiking, Holston Mountain forms a rampart and is the ridge the A.T. follows beyond Cross Mountain. To your right the patchwork fields of Shady Valley spread out below. Iron Mountain forms the eastern flank of Shady Valley. When the skies are clear, you will see the dark mass of Mount Rogers—Virginia's highest point—and Whitetop Mountain, the signature peaks of the Mount Rogers high country.

Locust posts, blazed in white, keep you on the correct path over the open meadows. When the skies are foggy, rainy, or otherwise inclement, these posts help hikers find their way. At 0.5 mile, the gravel, all-access portion of the Appalachian Trail ends at a contemplation bench. The splendor of Johnson County, Tennessee, opens before you. The ecologically significant cranberry bogs of the Osborne property are just below. Shady Valley is the most southerly location of cranberry bogs in the United States. This is a good place for less able hikers to turn around.

Continue following the posts to reach the end of pasturage and a stile at 1 mile. Enter woods and continue westerly under hardwoods and pines, as well as evergreen swaths of rhododendron and mountain laurel. The A.T. gently moves uphill, northwesterly along Cross Mountain. At 2 miles, pass a rocked-in spring and campsite just to the right of the trail. This flow forms Stony Creek's headwaters. Work uphill, rising to a gap at 2.7 miles. Rich Knob stands just to your right. Descend on a south-facing slope from the gap, drifting to a white pine–laden hollow and the Double Spring Shelter at 2.9 miles. Here, the concrete-block, three-sided refuge lies in the flat. A spur trail to a spring leads left and the Appalachian Trail turns uphill to the right, joining Holston Mountain and heading northeast to Damascus, Virginia, and points beyond. This is a good place to turn around; however, make sure to sign in at the trail register in the shelter.

Nearby Attractions

The community of Shady Valley presents an annual Cranberry Festival the second weekend in October.

Directions

From Bristol, Tennessee, take US 421 South 18.9 miles to Shady Valley and a four-way stop. Turn right here onto TN 91 South and follow it 3.6 miles to the Cross Mountain trailhead, on your left.

ALTERNATE DIRECTIONS: From Johnson City, Tennessee, take US 321 North/TN 67 East, following signs to Elizabethton. Travel 9.9 miles to reach US 19E and a traffic light (from Bristol take US 11E South 12 miles to this same intersection on US 19E South, except you will keep straight through the traffic light). Turn left here, now joining US 19E North just 0.2 mile to cross the Watauga River. Turn right onto TN 91/Stony Creek Road. Follow TN 91 18.4 miles to reach a gap with Cross Mountain Road to your right. The parking area is on the right just past Cross Mountain Road.

A CONEFLOWER BRIGHTENS A FALL DAY. *(See page 144.)*

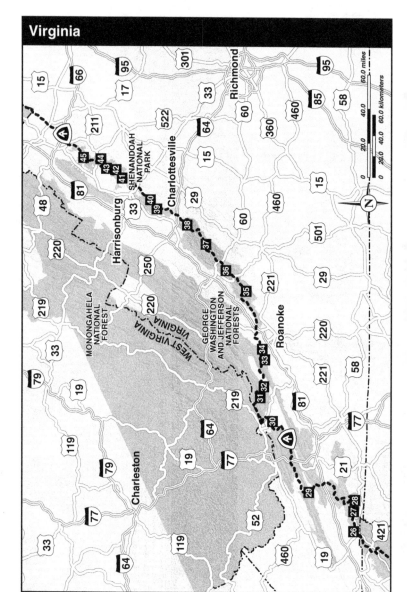

Virginia

THE FIELDS AND FORESTS OF WILBURN VALLEY, AS SEEN FROM AN OUTCROP ON PEARIS MOUNTAIN *(See page 179.)*

SCENERY: ★ ★ ★ ★
TRAIL CONDITION: ★ ★ ★ ★ ★
CHILDREN: ★ ★
DIFFICULTY: ★ ★ ★
SOLITUDE: ★ ★

THE FAMED VIRGINIA CREEPER TRAIL AND THE EVEN MORE FAMOUS A.T. RUN IN CONJUNCTION NEAR DAMASCUS, "THE FRIENDLIEST TOWN ON THE TRAIL."

GPS TRAILHEAD COORDINATES: N36° 38.124' W81° 47.537'

DISTANCE & CONFIGURATION: 5.9-mile loop

HIKING TIME: 3.5 hours

HIGHLIGHTS: Trail town, streams, Appalachian Trail, views

ELEVATION: 1,910' at trailhead; 2,950' at high point

ACCESS: No fees or permits required

MAPS: Trails Illustrated #786 Mount Rogers National Recreation Area; Appalachian Trail Conservancy SW VA Maps 3 and 4; USGS Damascus

FACILITIES: Restroom, water, picnic area at Town Park

CONTACT: Mount Rogers National Recreation Area: 276-783-5196, tinyurl.com/mtrogersnra

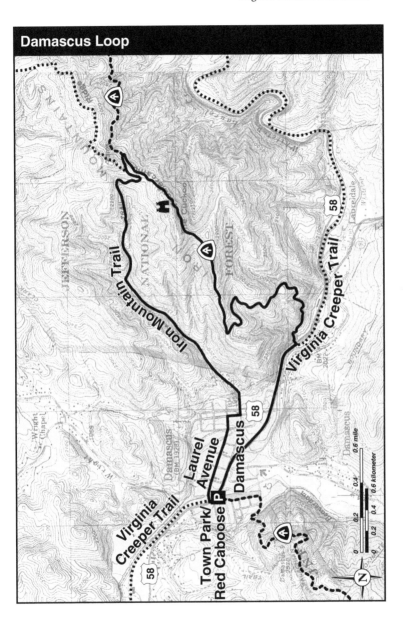

Damascus Loop

Overview

This fun and unusual hike incorporates the trail town of Damascus, an official Appalachian Trail Community, with national forest trails in its shadow. Leave Damascus Town Park on the Virginia Creeper Trail, which is wheelchair accessible. Along the way, you will see Damascus and the streams that flow through it. Leave the Creeper Trail for the Appalachian Trail (A.T.). Take America's most famous footpath up through wooded ridges. Pass a rewarding view of adjacent mountains. Meet the Iron Mountain Trail. Dip into a hollow and return to Damascus, rejoining the A.T. as it parades directly through downtown.

Route Details

The Appalachian Trail passes through several communities in the South. Some of these communities, such as Damascus, Virginia; Erwin, Tennessee; and Hot Springs, North Carolina, are known as trail towns, places where hikers are often seen and the outdoor life is popular with many residents. Damascus, Virginia, is the consummate trail town—at the confluence of the Appalachian Trail, the Virginia Creeper Trail, and a few hundred other miles of paths within the Mount Rogers National Recreation Area, as well as the adjacent Cherokee National Forest in Tennessee.

Part of the lure of this hike is walking through the town of Damascus. Here you can get a little exercise, see the trail community, and even grab a meal while you are in town. But the hike also has a wild side when it climbs away from town and onto nearby Iron Mountain.

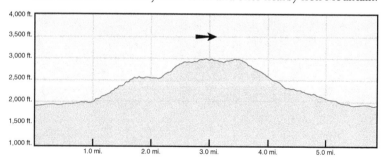

Leave the Damascus Town Park on the Virginia Creeper Trail. It immediately bridges Beaverdam Creek and passes through a residential area of town. Shortly span Whitetop Laurel Creek as you follow an old railroad line that once headed deep into the mountains. Come back alongside US 58 near what used to be the infamous Dot's Inn diner. Here, the A.T. and Virginia Creeper Trail run in conjunction. Leave the heart of Damascus and walk next to US 58.

At 1 mile, your level hiking ends for a while and you gain 1,000 feet in the next 2 miles. Follow the Appalachian Trail as it turns left, crosses US 58, and ascends a stairway, the Steps of Damascus, into the woods. A roadside spring flows left of the steps. Start up Feather Camp Ridge in gum-oak-maple woods. Holly and white pines add an evergreen touch. Angle uphill in and out of intermittent stream drainages. Imagine Appalachian Trail thru-hikers climbing this hill, fully loaded with supplies just purchased in Damascus. Rise into xeric woods of white oak, sourwood, and hickory on a sandy track. Briefly level off at 1.5 miles. Ahead, sporadic views open west of the South Fork Holston Valley. Achieve the ridge crest, then make a sharp switchback to the right at 2.2 miles. Keep climbing the nose of a ridge amid white pines and chestnut oaks. Level off at 2.5 miles. The singletrack path works around a couple of knobs. At 3 miles, a clear view opens across the Whitetop Laurel valley into the Cherokee National Forest to the south and also to the east of Whitetop Mountain. Elevation-wise, this is the high point of the hike, a little shy of 3,000 feet.

The A.T. continues easterly, descending past a shaded outcrop and popular stopping point. At 3.4 miles, intersect the Iron Mountain Connector Trail. Turn left here and wind uphill, meeting the Iron Mountain Trail at 3.5 miles. Turn left again. Begin your journey back to Damascus on the Iron Mountain Trail, the former route of the A.T. a half century back. It's downhill almost all the way to downtown. Make a hard right at 3.6 miles. The wider track, open to bikes, enters a hollow. A stream builds to your left. Evergreens of rhododendron and white pine keep the hollow colorful even in winter. Step over the unnamed stream at 4.3 miles. Begin a pattern of continually crisscrossing the creek. Ferns, wildflowers, and beech trees increase in number. The descent is continuous. Emerge from the national forest at 5 miles. Stay with a paved road heading downhill through Mock Hollow, lined with houses. Meet US 58 at 5.3 miles and return to level walking. Cross US 58 and turn right. Even though you are walking through town, you are officially back on the Appalachian Trail. Ahead, turn left, staying with US 58 West where it diverges from VA 91. Bridge Whitetop Laurel Creek. You are in the heart of Damascus.

On your way through town, make sure to stop at Mount Rogers Outfitters, the iconic hiking and backpacking store. They are not only well stocked with the latest gear but are also friendly locals who truly appreciate the Appalachian Trail. Other offerings as you pass through town range from ice cream to pizza to bicycle rentals, even hostels. Make sure to take advantage of these trailside treats. It isn't often that bona fide hikes take us through trail towns with all their amenities. Finally, bridge Beaverdam Creek and return to the red caboose and Damascus Town Park, completing your hike at 5.9 miles.

Nearby Attractions

The Virginia Creeper Trail, a multiuse path that was once a railroad line, leaves from Damascus 16 miles west to Abingdon (an officially designated Appalachian Trail Community) and 17 miles east into the heart of Mount Rogers National Recreation Area. Shuttles and bike rentals are available throughout Damascus.

Directions

From Bristol, Virginia, take I-81 North to Exit 19 for US 11/US 58 toward Abingdon/Damascus. Turn right onto US 58 East and go 9.9 miles to Damascus, Virginia. Park in the lot near the red caboose at Town Park, just before US 58 bridges Beaverdam Creek.

27

Mount Rogers
via Elk Garden

SCENERY: ★ ★ ★ ★ ★
TRAIL CONDITION: ★ ★ ★ ★
CHILDREN: ★ ★
DIFFICULTY: ★ ★ ★
SOLITUDE: ★ ★

VIEW OF WHITETOP MOUNTAIN AND ELK GARDEN

GPS TRAILHEAD COORDINATES: N36° 38.767' W81° 34.984'

DISTANCE & CONFIGURATION: 8.8-mile out-and-back

HIKING TIME: 4.5 hours

HIGHLIGHTS: Highest point in Virginia, views, meadows

ELEVATION: 4,460' at trailhead; 5,729' at high point

ACCESS: No fees or permits required

MAPS: Trails Illustrated *#786 Mount Rogers National Recreation Area*; Appalachian Trail Conservancy *SW VA Maps 3 and 4*; USGS *Whitetop Mountain*

FACILITIES: None

CONTACT: Mount Rogers National Recreation Area: 276-783-5196, **tinyurl.com/mtrogersnra**

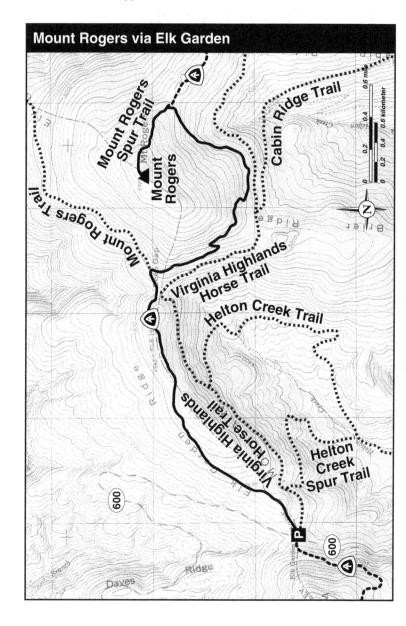

Mount Rogers via Elk Garden

Overview

This heavily used section of the Appalachian Trail (A.T.) offers a series of views from the moment it leaves Elk Garden. Along the way, it passes through a rare and lofty spruce-fir forest. Numerous rock outcrops jut above meadows where wild ponies graze and blueberries ripen late in summer. To reach Mount Rogers, Virginia's highest point, the hike leaves the A.T. on the Mount Rogers Spur Trail through open slopes before entering a dense spruce-fir forest where the actual high point stands.

Route Details

There are no views from Mount Rogers, Virginia's high point. However, you will be treated to an abundance of panoramas along the way, making the hike more than worth it, even if you are not a peak bagger. Leave VA 600 and Elk Garden to pass through a wide metal gate. The Virginia Highlands Horse Trail heads forward on a dirt path toward Deep Gap. The A.T. veers left through open country, uphill. Wood posts topped with white blazes mark the trail. Brier Ridge stands off to the right. Evergreen-topped Mount Rogers rises in the background. Views are numerous. Cows and horses may be grazing the fields and are the sole reason for the fields not returning to woods. Wind-sculpted hawthorn trees break up the landscape. The ridge of Iron Mountain, former route of the A.T., stands to your left. Look back toward Whitetop Mountain too.

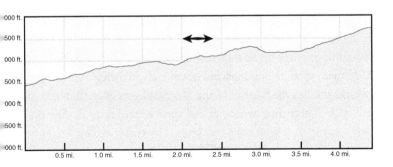

Transition into full woods, clearing a walk-through fence stile and enter Lewis Fork Wilderness at 0.5 mile. Moderately ascend through a rocky, northern hardwood forest, primarily red maple, along with beech and yellow birch. Level off at 1.1 miles. Mainly stay atop the ridge on an easy walk. At 1.8 miles, pass a blue-blazed trail leading right to a campsite before reaching the actual Deep Gap at 1.9 miles. Deep Gap is closed to camping. Across the gap, the Virginia Highlands Horse Trail has come 1.7 miles from Elk Garden. A blue-blazed spur trail leads right across the horse trail to a spring.

Keep forward on the A.T., shortly passing another spring. At 2.1 miles, intersect the Mount Rogers Trail. It leaves left 5.5 miles down to Fairwood Valley and Grindstone Campground. The A.T. turns sharply right here, and begins a long curve around the south slope of Mount Rogers. Pass some impressive outcrops. By 2.3 miles, red spruce and Fraser fir trees appear among the northern hardwoods. A clear section of trail allows views back to Elk Garden. At 3 miles, come to a meadow and old fence line. Brier Ridge stands across the grassy gap below. If you walk out in the open, a vista of Whitetop Mountain awaits, along with the Elk Garden parking area. An old blue-blazed spur trail crosses open slopes to the Virginia Highlands Horse Trail below.

The A.T. continues curving around the side of Mount Rogers. Numerous streams flow from the mountaintop across the path. Open into a field, broken with spruce, fir, cherry, and hawthorn trees at 3.6 miles. Wide vistas stretch east toward Wilburn Ridge. Intersect the Mount Rogers Spur Trail at 3.9 miles.

Leave the Appalachian Trail and walk northwest through a field broken by cherry, spruce, Fraser fir, and mountain ash trees. Note that no fires or camping are allowed beyond this point. Pine Mountain, with its outcrops and open fields, is visible to the right. Behind you lies the balance of the Mount Rogers High Country. At 4.2 miles, enter thick woods of red spruce and Fraser fir. The primary way to distinguish the two trees is by their needles. Fraser fir trees are flat, fragrant, and friendly, meaning they are wider on one side than the other, smell strongly of evergreen, and are pliable to the touch. Fraser fir is the only native Southern fir, growing in the mountains of Virginia, North Carolina, and Tennessee (they don't grow in Georgia). The needles of red spruce are squared off, don't smell as strong, and are stiff to the touch. They grow mostly in New England and Canada but range southward down the spine of the Appalachians into Tennessee.

Keep ascending on a sometimes-muddy path through sunlight-blocking woods, where moss grows on fallen trees and anything else not moving. Climb sharply just before reaching the rocky summit of the mountain. At 4.4 miles, look on the rock outcrop for a survey marker, indicating the actual high point of Mount Rogers, elevation 5,729 feet.

Nearby Attractions

Forest Road 89, located a short way past the Elk Garden trailhead, offers a scenic drive along the slopes of Whitetop Mountain.

Directions

From the red caboose at Town Park in Damascus, Virginia, where US 58 meets South Beaver Dam Avenue, drive 11 miles east on US 58. Here, US 58 curves right; keep straight, now on VA 603/Konnarock Road. Stay on VA 603 for 2.6 miles to VA 600/Whitetop Road. Turn right onto VA 600 and follow it 5.1 miles to the Elk Garden trailhead, where the A.T. crosses VA 600.

28

Mount Rogers High Country

SCENERY: ★ ★ ★ ★ ★
TRAIL CONDITION: ★ ★ ★ ★
CHILDREN: ★ ★
DIFFICULTY: ★ ★ ★ ★
SOLITUDE: ★

THE APPALACHIAN TRAIL WANDERS THROUGH THE WINDSWEPT TERRAIN OF VIRGINIA'S ROOFTOP.

GPS TRAILHEAD COORDINATES: N36° 38.007' W81° 30.505'

DISTANCE & CONFIGURATION: 11.4-mile loop

HIKING TIME: 7 hours

HIGHLIGHTS: Wild ponies, designated wilderness, rock outcrops

ELEVATION: 4,670' at trailhead; 5,480' at high point

ACCESS: Entrance fee required

MAPS: Trails Illustrated #786 Mount Rogers National Recreation Area; Appalachian Trail Conservancy SW VA Maps 3 and 4; USGS Whitetop Mountain and USGS Trout Dale

FACILITIES: Campground, picnic area, restrooms, water at state park

CONTACT: Mount Rogers National Recreation Area: 276-783-5196, tinyurl.com/mtrogersnra

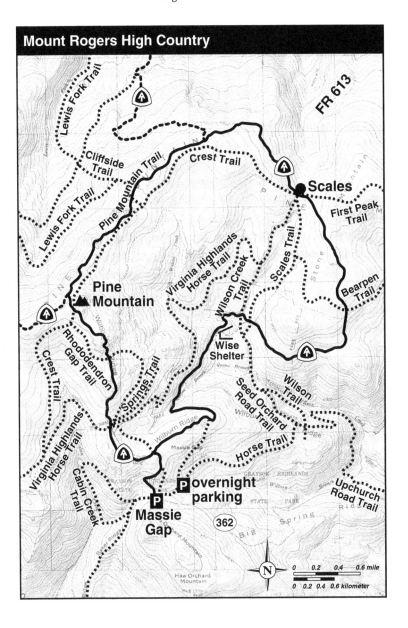

Mount Rogers High Country

Lewis Fork Trail

Cliffside Trail

Crest Trail

FR 613

Pine Mountain Trail

Scales

Lewis Fork Trail

First Peak Trail

Virginia Highlands Horse Trail

Wilson Creek Trail

Scales Trail

Pine Mountain

Bearpen Trail

Rhododendron Gap Trail

Crest Trail

Springs Trail

Wise Shelter

Wilson Trail

Seed Orchard Road Trail

Virginia Highlands Horse Trail

Cabin Creek Trail

Horse Trail

overnight parking

Upchurch Road Trail

Massie Gap

362

N

0   0.2   0.4   0.6 mile

0   0.2   0.4   0.6 kilometer

Overview

From Grayson Highlands State Park, you will join the Appalachian Trail (A.T.) as it rambles over Virginia's rooftop, where open fields provide extensive panoramas of surrounding stone monoliths, evergreen forest, and wild ponies. Pass through Little Wilson Creek Wilderness. Explore a mosaic of environments en route to Pine Mountain. Ramble atop a mile-high ridge. Rejoin the A.T. as it traverses rocky and open Wilburn Ridge.

Route Details

The Mount Rogers High Country is arguably the most scenic swath of land in the Old Dominion through which the A.T. travels. This loop picks up the A.T. near Massie Gap at Grayson Highlands State Park, where you then circle the lofty Wilson Creek drainage. Here wild ponies graze on windswept open ridges formerly cloaked in rare spruce-fir forest, first cut in the 1880s. Virginia's crest was stripped bare; farmers and cattle grazers followed. Now, despite grazing by cattle and the wild ponies, the Mount Rogers High Country is slowly growing in with trees and brush—the entire ecosystem is a study in forest succession. Be apprised that the weather can be cloudy, windy, foggy, rainy, and sometimes all the above any time of year. Be prepared. In winter, conditions can be downright harsh.

From Massie Gap, you will take Rhododendron Trail within Grayson Highlands State Park, established in 1965, around the same time the U.S. Forest Service acquired the adjacent high country and rerouted the Appalachian Trail from nearby Iron Mountain through the newly purchased lands. Trace Rhododendron Trail north toward a fence line. Pass through a gate and then curve into open terrain. At 0.3 mile, merge with the Virginia Highlands Connector Trail, which has also come from Massie Gap. The two paths share the same wide, rocky treadway to meet the Appalachian Trail at 0.5 mile.

Turn right (northbound) on the A.T. Work through open terrain and big vistas of Pine Mountain and Stone Mountain, where you will be. At 1.2 miles, meet the Appalachian Spur Trail, which leads to the state park's overnight parking lot. Drop off the view-laden lands and curve into wooded Quebec Branch watershed. Bridge the highland stream and cross a fence stile at 1.8 miles. These fences keep wild ponies and cattle grazing where they are supposed to be. You will be passing around, over, and through many more stiles ahead.

The A.T. joins an old roadbed. The walking is easy. By 2.6 miles, you are again passing through a mix of small meadows and woods; then reach the Wise trail shelter. This three-sided wooden affair is set in a flat above Big Wilson Creek. Continuing, the A.T. crosses a stile and bridges Big Wilson Creek, cloaked in rhododendron. The trail then turns down Big Wilson Creek and goes through a swampy area, where nimble-footed hikers boulder-hop and keep their toes dry. Cross the Wilson Creek Trail, then bridge a tributary of Big Wilson Creek and reach the low point of the hike at 2.9 miles. At 3 miles, reach the wide and rocky Scales Trail. The A.T. leads left briefly in conjunction with the Scales Trail then curves right to reach a stile and the Little Wilson Creek Wilderness. Ascend through ferny woods, mixed with spruce. At 4.3 miles, reach yet another trail intersection, crossing Bearpen Trail. Just ahead, leave the wilderness for open slopes, dotted with bushes. You are working atop ferny Stone Mountain. Drift into the gap known as Scales, a trailhead and major trail intersection, at 5.5 miles. In days of yore at summer's end, cattle grazing the high country would be taken off the mountain. Farmers got better prices for their livestock when weighed and sold up here,

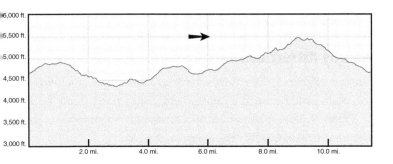

rather than walking cattle down the mountain back to their farms, lending the name Scales to this locale.

The A.T. bisects Scales corral and passes trail intersections. Veer right away from the corral to enter a field broken by trees. Mostly climb away from Scales in a mix of spruce with beech and yellow birch. Streamlets flow off the slopes of Pine Mountain. At 6.8 miles, you have reached 5,000 feet and a trail intersection. Leave the Appalachian Trail and head left on the lesser used Pine Mountain Trail. The walking is easy and more level than not. Cross a couple of fences, wending through a mosaic of spruce, meadow, northern hardwoods, rhododendron thickets, and rocks.

Open to a large meadow at 7.4 miles. Wilburn Ridge and Mount Rogers stand tall. Cross a tiny stream before intersecting the Lewis Fork Trail at 7.7 miles. Stay straight with the Pine Mountain Trail, ascending through trees, then rocks and dense rhododendron thickets, to meet the A.T. at 8.8 miles, in Rhododendron Gap. Here, you will turn left (northbound) again. Ahead, cross famed Wilburn Ridge, a massif of open rock and grasses, with mixed vegetation copses. The panoramas of the Virginia Highlands will stun.

Ahead, cross the Crest Trail, then the Wilburn Ridge Trail at 9.4 miles and the Rhododendron Gap Trail at 9.6 miles. You are above a mile high here. At 10.3 miles, come to a stile and Grayson Highlands State Park. Trails branch off like spokes of a wheel. You stay straight on the A.T., at this point a level, grassy roadlike path. Soak in vistas of Little Wilson Creek watershed before leaving right on the A.T. at 10.9 miles. From here, backtrack to Massie Gap, recalling the views and landscapes of Virginia's rooftop.

Nearby Attractions

Grayson Highlands State Park, where this hikes begins, is a full-service state park, featuring a campground, hiking trails, picnic areas, and more. A pioneer homestead area offers a glimpse into life in the Grayson Highlands before there were state parks.

THE WILD PONIES ARE A MAJOR ATTRACTION IN THE MOUNT ROGERS HIGH COUNTRY.

Directions

From Exit 14 on I-77 near Hillsville, Virginia, take US 58 West 49 miles (turning left just before Wilson Creek to remain on US 58) to Grayson Highlands State Park. Enter the park on VA 362 and follow it 3.5 miles to reach Massie Gap on your right. Parking is along the road on the right.

ALTERNATE DIRECTIONS: From Damascus, Virginia, take US 58 East 26 miles to Grayson Highlands State Park. Enter the park on VA 362 and follow it 3.5 miles to reach Massie Gap on your right. Parking is along the road on the right.

29

Chestnut Knob

SCENERY: ★ ★ ★ ★ ★
TRAIL CONDITION: ★ ★ ★ ★
CHILDREN: ★
DIFFICULTY: ★ ★ ★ ★
SOLITUDE: ★ ★ ★ ★

THE CHESTNUT KNOB TRAIL SHELTER WAS ONCE A FIRE WARDEN'S CABIN.

GPS TRAILHEAD COORDINATES: N37° 1.362' W81° 25.498'

DISTANCE & CONFIGURATION: 9.2-mile out-and-back

HIKING TIME: 5 hours

HIGHLIGHTS: Historic stone fire warden cabin, views of Burkes Garden, wide open meadows

ELEVATION: 2,320' at trailhead; 4,390' at high point

ACCESS: No fees or permits required

MAPS: U.S. Forest Service *Jefferson National Forest;* Appalachian Trail Conservancy *SW VA Maps 1 and 2;* Trails Illustrated *Map #787 Blacksburg New River Valley;* USGS *Hutchinson Rock*

FACILITIES: None

CONTACT: George Washington and Jefferson National Forests, Eastern Divide Ranger District: 540-552-4641, **www.fs.usda.gov/gwj**

Chestnut Knob

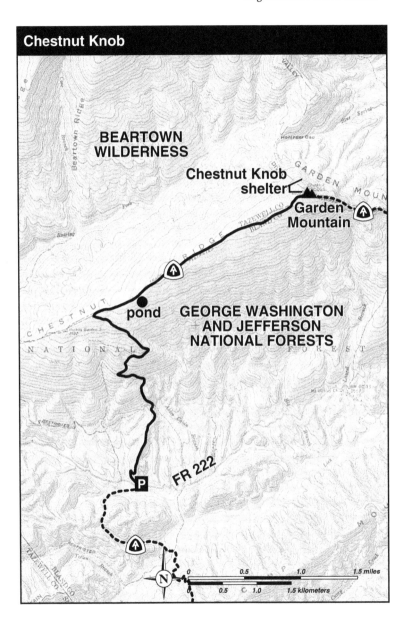

Overview

Take this lesser trod part of the Appalachian Trail (A.T.) past open meadows with breathtaking vistas to reach an old stone fire warden's cabin atop Chestnut Knob. From this point, you can gaze upon Burkes Garden, one of Virginia's most lovely rural farmlands.

Route Details

Hikers can use the Appalachian Trail to peer down on Burkes Garden, the largest historic rural district in Virginia, and the state's highest valley, standing over 3,000 feet above sea level. You climb from Lick Creek valley to the crest of Chestnut Ridge. Once atop this ridge crest, pass through a series of highland meadows, kept open by the U.S. Forest Service. Break 4,000 feet to reach Chestnut Knob and a cleared view of Burkes Garden. Here, you can also visit the enclosed stone cabin of a former fire warden who maintained a now-dismantled tower. Today, the stone cabin is an Appalachian Trail shelter, used by backpackers traversing the highlands of the Old Dominion.

Start the hike by leaving Forest Road 222, northbound on the Appalachian Trail. Ascend the south slope of lower Chestnut Ridge. Switchback uphill to join a rib ridge and then level off. At 0.9 mile, the A.T. climbs in earnest in rocky oak woods. Cross a small stream at 1.2 and 1.5 miles. At 2.4 miles, reach the crest of Chestnut Ridge. Turn right, heading northeast into a meadow and southward vistas. Pass through more meadows, some dotted with apple trees. At 2.7

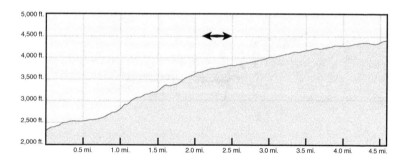

miles, come near a pond. Look back for more views. Bisect meadows broken by woods. At 3.9 miles, the A.T. leaves the upper end of a huge meadow, reentering woods on a doubletrack path, bordered by extremely rocky terrain. Hike atop open rock slabs. Drop to a gap at 4.4 miles. A path leads right to a spring. A small pond is nearby. Stay straight on the A.T. to enter a final meadow. At 4.6 miles, come to the Chestnut Ridge trail shelter. The stone structure was once a fire warden's cabin. The concrete pillars of the former fire tower stand nearby. Seize views down into Burkes Garden.

Here is how the valley got its name: Back in the mid-1700s, a survey party was in these parts. The surveying party camped in the valley below. James Burke had cook duties and peeled some potatoes while preparing supper. When the survey crew returned next year, a potato patch had sprung up from his peelings. His fellow surveyors jokingly named the spot Burkes Garden. Burke later came back with his family and settled here and had the last laugh.

Back in the 1970s, the U.S. Forest Service stopped using fire towers as such, with stationary wardens manning them. Most towers were dismantled, including this one on Chestnut Knob. However, the value of the stone warden's cabin was apparent to them and will be to you. In 1994 the cabin was rehabilitated and then altered to become an Appalachian Trail shelter. Unlike most A.T. trail shelters, it is completely enclosed with a wooden door and windows. Inside stand several bunks and a table.

As lonely as it was for the fire warden, the Chestnut Knob Shelter is a welcome sight for Appalachian Trail thru-hikers seeking refuge from high-country chills. An overlook of Burkes Garden opens from the northeast side of the knob. Burkes Garden is the most notable and most scenic agricultural valley in Virginia. There is only one natural entrance to the level vale enfolded by high ridges. Burkes Garden Creek flows from the ridge-rimmed valley, creating the access portal. Burkes Garden is dotted with dairy farms and other operations that recall a way of life left behind in our digital world.

There are only two ways in or out of the valley—one the afore-mentioned natural portal of Burkes Garden Creek and the other a torturous mountain road that the A.T. crosses—which creates iso-lation. However, the residents of Burkes Garden (numbering under 500) like it that way. The A.T. continues along the east side of Burkes Garden atop Garden Mountain for 6 miles before dropping to Hunt-ing Camp Creek.

Note: It is a 2,100-foot climb from the trailhead to the Chest-nut Knob Shelter at the hike's end. This hike is best under clear skies. The views are truly breathtaking from multiple points along the way, including a view of Virginia's high point of Mount Rogers. Be apprised the open highland meadows are subject to wind and rain. I would not want to be there during a thunderstorm. Furthermore, allow ample time for the hike in order to soak in the views along the way.

Nearby Attractions

The community of Burkes Garden holds a fall festival focusing on farm life and agricultural heritage on the last Saturday in September.

Directions

From Exit 52 on I-77 near Bland, Virginia (an official Appalachian Trail Community), take VA 42 West/US 52 West 4.2 miles; then stay right with VA 42 West as it diverges from US 52. Follow VA 42 10.2 more miles to reach the hamlet of Ceres. Here, turn right onto VA 625/Poor Valley Road. At 0.4 mile, it turns to gravel. At 6.7 miles, Poor Valley Road becomes Forest Road 222. It is a total of 8 miles from Ceres to the Appalachian Trail parking area on your left, where the A.T. crosses FR 222.

SCENERY: ★ ★ ★ ★
TRAIL CONDITION: ★ ★ ★ ★
CHILDREN: ★ ★
DIFFICULTY: ★ ★ ★
SOLITUDE: ★ ★ ★

THE A.T. BREAKS THROUGH THESE STONE GATES ATOP PEARIS MOUNTAIN.

GPS TRAILHEAD COORDINATES: N37° 19.757' W80° 45.063'

DISTANCE & CONFIGURATION: 5-mile out-and-back

HIKING TIME: 3 hours

HIGHLIGHTS: Multiple vistas, challenging climb

ELEVATION: 2,005' at trailhead; 3,680' at high point

ACCESS: No fees or permits required

MAPS: Trails Illustrated *#787 Blacksburg/New River Valley*; Appalachian Trail Conservancy *SW VA Maps 1 and 2*; USGS *Narrows*

FACILITIES: None

CONTACT: George Washington and Jefferson National Forests: 540-552-4641, www.fs.usda.gov/gwj

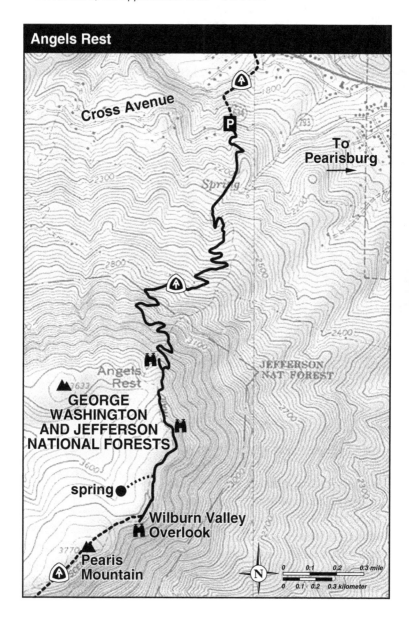

Angels Rest

Cross Avenue

To Pearisburg

Spring

JEFFERSON NAT FOREST

Angels Rest

GEORGE WASHINGTON AND JEFFERSON NATIONAL FORESTS

spring●

Wilburn Valley Overlook

Pearis Mountain

N

| 0 | 0.1 | 0.2 | 0.3 mile |

| 0 | 0.1 | 0.2 | 0.3 kilometer |

Overview

This Appalachian Trail (A.T.) trek climbs the northeast shoulder of Pearis Mountain to three vistas. Start near the town of Pearisburg, an officially designated Appalachian Trail Community, then trace a series of switchbacks up a thickly wooded ridge. Once on the crest, enter a boulder garden to emerge at Angels Rest and its view of the New River Valley. From there, head south along Pearis Mountain, passing a lesser view before reaching Wilburn Valley Overlook, presenting bucolic Virginia countryside set between long ridges.

Route Details

This is a classic mountain climb to a view—or three views in this case. You will earn your reward as the hike ascends nearly 1,700 feet from the trailhead. However, bear in mind that the trail is well maintained and well graded, and does not have any insanely steep segments, making it doable by average hikers who take their time.

From Cross Avenue, join the Appalachian Trail southbound as it quests for the crest of Pearis Mountain. Switchback on a steep slope, cloaked in hardwoods. The trail curves in and out of drainages cutting down the north slope of Pearis Mountain. Mossy boulders are scattered in the woods. Cross a trickling branch at 0.5 mile, still ascending. Briefly join an old logging road at 0.7 mile. Stay with the white blazes as thoughtless hikers are creating erosive paths while shortcutting the switchbacks.

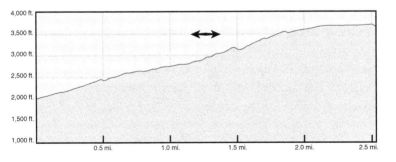

At 1.1 miles, the path crosses a rocky wet-weather drainage then passes by an impressive oak on trail right at 1.2 miles. Break the 3,000-foot barrier by 1.4 miles. You have climbed 1,000 feet with less than 700 to go. At 1.5 miles, the trail leads you across a rock garden, but at least it is on a level stretch. At 1.7 miles, tunnel into a rhododendron thicket.

Upon reaching a cluster of truck-sized boulders at 1.8 miles, you have made the crest of Pearis Mountain. While amid the gray giants, watch for the spur trail leading right to Angels Rest. It leads to an outcrop and a view. The scene is a mix of land and water, civilization and backcountry. Here, you can look down on the New River, as well as the towns of Narrows and Pearisburg (both are designated as official Appalachian Trail Communities). Sturdy Peters Mountain guards the rear. It is amazing how the New River—a truly big waterway at this point—looks so small from Angels Rest.

Funny thing about the New River, purportedly the second-oldest river on the planet. How did it get that name? While Virginia was still an English colony, a man named Abraham Wood sent two men west to what was then terra incognita. The two explorers—Thomas Batts and Robert Fallam—came upon this large, previously unmapped waterway. When drawing a map of the newly explored territory, they wrote *new river* on it and then promptly forgot about it. Later, Batts and Fallam turned in their map to a cartographer, and *new river* became the New River, an accident of history. That is fodder for an Appalachian Trail hiker looking out from such a perch.

After soaking in the vista from Angels Rest, even resting perhaps, backtrack to the A.T., then resume your southbound course. The trail slices betwixt more boulders then levels off. Enjoy your well-earned walk, from here a nearly level course winding through oaks and mountain laurel. Parallel the southeast edge of the ridge, getting glimpses of lands below. At 2.2 miles, a short path leads left to an outcrop and a warm-up view of the Wilburn Valley. Beyond here, the walking remains glorious. At 2.4 miles, a blue-blazed spur trail leads right to a spring. However, this spring is known to dry up in late summer and early fall. A little more walking brings you to the rocky brow of Pearis Mountain. At 2.5 miles, a short spur leads left to a flat rock and an easterly panorama of Wilburn Valley, part of the great Walker Creek watershed that you look down upon below. This scene is decidedly more agricultural than the view from Angels Rest. Patterns of farm fields dot the lowlands. Wooded Walker Mountain rises as a backdrop to the scene. Relax and enjoy the panorama that was well worth the climb.

Nearby Attractions

The New River offers paddling and angling opportunities galore. Multiple launch points and outfitters make a float trip on the river a breeze. Also, historic downtown Pearisburg, very near the trailhead, is worth exploring.

Directions

From Exit 118 on I-81 near Christiansburg, Virginia, take US 460 West 32.4 miles to the second exit for Pearisburg, Virginia, VA 100 South/US 460 Business East. Follow this exit as it heads into Pearisburg. After traveling 0.2 mile, turn right onto Johnston Avenue, just past the right turn to VA 100 North. Johnston Avenue is a residential street. Follow Johnston Avenue just 0.1 mile, and then veer right onto Morris Avenue. Morris Avenue turns into Cross Avenue. Drive for a total of 0.7 mile to the A.T. crossing from US 460 Business East. Do not park at the exact trail crossing as it is on a curve. Rather, park on the left about 150 feet after the A.T. crossing. Space is limited, so be courteous.

31

Mountain Lake Wilderness

SCENERY: ★ ★ ★ ★ ★
TRAIL CONDITION: ★ ★ ★ ★
CHILDREN: ★ ★
DIFFICULTY: ★ ★ ★ ★
SOLITUDE: ★ ★

SALT POND MOUNTAIN LOOMS ACROSS WAR SPUR BRANCH FROM WAR SPUR LOOKOUT.

GPS TRAILHEAD COORDINATES: N37° 24.725' W80° 31.367'

DISTANCE & CONFIGURATION: 10.5-mile out-and-back; 0.5-mile out-and-back; or 9-mile loop using forest road

HIKING TIME: 6 hours; 0.5 hour; or 5 hours

HIGHLIGHTS: Two views, backcountry, spruce highland plateau, varied hike possibilities

ELEVATION: 3,970' at trailhead; 3,420' at low point

ACCESS: No fees or permits required

MAPS: Trails Illustrated *#787 Blacksburg/New River Valley;* Appalachian Trail Conservancy *Central VA Maps 3 and 4;* USGS *Interior* and USGS *Waiteville*

FACILITIES: None

CONTACT: George Washington and Jefferson National Forests: 540-552-4641, **www.fs.usda.gov/gwj**

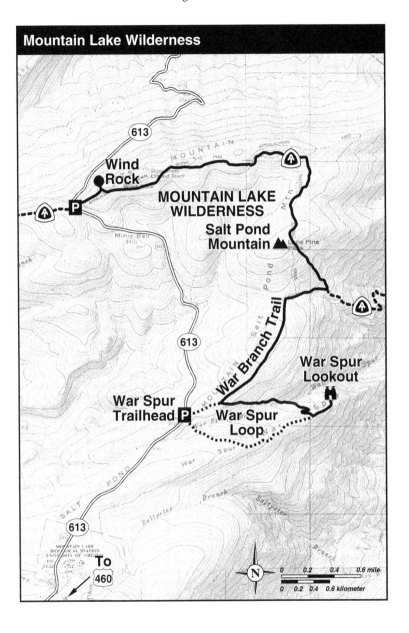

Mountain Lake Wilderness

613

Wind
Rock

P

MOUNTAIN LAKE
WILDERNESS

Salt Pond
Mountain ▲

613

War Branch Trail

War Spur
Lookout

War Spur
Trailhead P

War Spur
Loop

613

To
460

N 0   0.2   0.4   0.6 mile
   0 0.2 0.4 0.6 kilometer

Overview

This hike enters Mountain Lake Wilderness and quickly reaches Wind Rock and extensive views. Then the Appalachian Trail (A.T.) traverses a high plateau in a forest recalling New England. The hike splits off and heads for War Spur Lookout and more vistas. From there, you can backtrack or make a loop using the forest road upon which you drove to the trailhead. A third possibility is a short walk to Wind Rock and back.

Route Details

This hike starts in the unnamed gap between Big Mountain to the west and Potts Mountain to the east. Join the A.T., northbound, and head east toward Wind Rock. Enter the Mountain Lake Wilderness. The trail is well trammeled here. A slight uptick through northern hardwoods leads to Wind Rock after 0.25 mile. Split left from the A.T. and reach the crag of Wind Rock. Rocky Mountain and Fork Mountain stand in the fore, while Peters Mountain forms a long ridge and the boundary of West Virginia and Virginia. To the south, Big Mountain runs south. From Wind Rock, lesser hikers can turn back to the trailhead, and judging by the A.T. as you continue, most hikers do turn back.

The Appalachian Trail continues easterly along Potts Mountain. Begin to look for occasional spruce trees that survive on this cold, elevated plateau that also harbors short, squat hardwoods

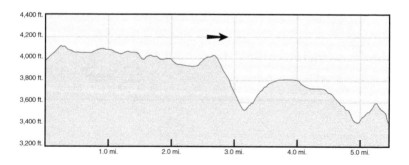

carpeted with ferns. At 1.6 miles, come near an intermittent stream and campsite. Keep easterly in this highland wilderness. At 2 miles, the Appalachian Trail abruptly turns right (south) and now begins rolling on the elevated plateau of Salt Pond Mountain. The walking is glorious. Enjoy the backcountry while scoping for spruce trees, not to be confused with hemlocks that can also be found among the hardwoods here.

At 2.7 miles, the A.T. drops off the slope of Salt Pond Mountain. At 3.2 miles, reach a trail intersection, ending your descent. Turn right onto War Branch Trail. This path proceeds to regain the lost elevation. You are back on the nearly level shoulder of Salt Pond Mountain by 3.5 miles. At 3.6 miles, look for a silted-in pond on trail right. Turn southwesterly and relish in more easy highland wilderness walking, a rare combination. Pass a second filled-in pond at 4.3 miles. At 4.4 miles, meet the War Spur Loop. Head left here, then descend into the War Spur Branch valley. The path finagles through rocks and rhododendron thickets while crossing War Spur Branch at 4.9 miles. This little valley stays cold to cool year-round, judging by the preponderance of spruces. This is the low point of the hike, at a little over 3,400 feet. Note the tea-colored water here. Ascend from War Spur Branch and reach an intersection at 5.3 miles. Head left to the War Spur Lookout, descending in woods. At 5.5 miles, the trail emerges onto a cliff, the War Spur Lookout. Here, Salt Pond Mountain looms across War Spur Branch. Potts Mountain extends to the horizon. Glimpse down to the Johns Creek valley in the distance.

The view is a fitting reward for a hike through the 10,753-acre wilderness that the Old Dominion shares with West Virginia. What is wilderness anyway? After 18,600 pages of testimony and the consolidation of 65 bills, the Wilderness Act of 1964 was passed by Congress. The legal definition of wilderness, spelled out in the bill, is as follows: "A wilderness, in contrast with those areas where man and his works dominate the landscape, is hereby recognized as an area where the earth and its community of life are untrammeled by man, where man . . . is a visitor and does not remain." Ranging from 6 to over 9 million acres in size, wilderness areas have multiple uses, such as hiking, hunting, canoeing, climbing, fishing, and camping. Virginia has 24 wildernesses, mostly located in the mountains. Mountain Lake Wilderness was established in 1984.

At this point, you have two choices. The first choice is a simple backtrack, and that will get you back to the trailhead after 5.5 more miles. The other alternative is to take the War Spur Loop out to Mountain Lake Road, then follow the gravel road into the Little Stony Creek drainage then up to the parking area near Wind Rock. If you do this, you will reach the road at 6.7 miles, bridge Little Stony Creek at 7.4 miles, then return to the trailhead at 9 miles.

Nearby Attractions

You will pass Mountain Lake Lodge on the way to the trailhead. Situated on a natural highland tarn—only one of two natural lakes in Virginia—it has been the site of hotels and summer visitors since the early 1800s. The resort is surrounded by a large nature preserve that offers more trails of its own. For more information, please visit **mtnlakelodge.com.**

Directions

From Exit 118 on I-81 near Christiansburg, Virginia, take US 460 West for 19 miles to VA 700/Mountain Lake Road. Turn right onto VA 700 East toward Mountain Lake. Follow VA 700 East for 6.6 miles to Mountain Lake. Here, Mountain Lake Road becomes VA 613. Stay with it another 5.4 miles for a total of 12 miles from US 460 to the Appalachian Trail crossing. The parking area is on the left just before the crossing.

32

Kelly Knob

SCENERY: ★ ★ ★
TRAIL CONDITION: ★ ★ ★
CHILDREN: ★ ★
DIFFICULTY: ★ ★
SOLITUDE: ★ ★ ★ ★

THIS VISTA-LADEN STONE PERCH AWAITS YOU ATOP KELLY KNOB.

GPS TRAILHEAD COORDINATES: N37° 22.359' W80° 26.770'

DISTANCE & CONFIGURATION: 4-mile out-and-back

HIKING TIME: 2.5 hours

HIGHLIGHTS: Solitude, high country, view

ELEVATION: 3,260' at trailhead; 3,800' at high point

ACCESS: No fees or permits required

MAPS: Trails Illustrated #787 Blacksburg/New River Valley; Appalachian Trail Conservancy Central VA Maps 3 and 4; USGS Newport

FACILITIES: None

CONTACT: George Washington and Jefferson National Forests, Eastern Divide Ranger District: 540-552-4641, **www.fs.usda.gov/gwj**

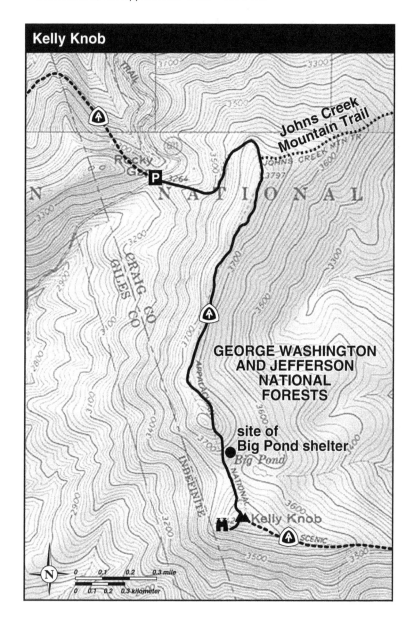

Kelly Knob

Overview

This fairly easy hike to a view offers solitude aplenty, sometimes hard to find on the Appalachian Trail (A.T.). Start your hike at remote Rocky Gap, north of Blacksburg, then make a quick but short climb to the crest of Johns Creek Mountain. From there, it is an easy walk to Kelly Knob, where a spur leads to an outcrop and views of the New River Valley and adjoining mountains.

Route Details

Rocky Gap is little used as a trailhead, judging by the limited parking spaces. However, it is not difficult to reach, yet seems to be off the radar for most Appalachian Trail hikers. From the direction you drove, the Appalachian Trail goes either right or left. Head right (northbound) on the Appalachian Trail. Here, the A.T. follows an old jeep road easterly and uphill. You are already at 3,200 feet in elevation, so the weather should be cooler than the lowlands below. Oaks, mountain laurel, and maple flank the uphill path. A practiced eye will be able to spot bush-sized regenerating chestnut trees. Look for the chestnut's long, serrated leaves.

The American chestnut tree was once the dominant giant of the Southern Appalachians. This tree formerly ranged from Maine to Mississippi. In Virginia, chestnuts grew to massive proportions. The fruit of this tree was very important. Chestnut acorns fed everything from bears to birds. Humans ate them too. Remember the words

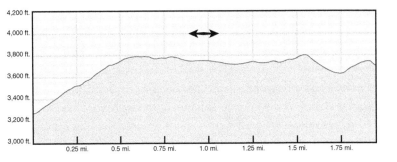

from the Christmas carol, "chestnuts roasting on an open fire." The tree also provided excellent wood for everyday use by pioneers. It was also coveted by the timber companies, which harvested the titans.

The day of the mighty chestnut is gone—for now. In the early 1900s, Asian chestnut trees were imported to the United States, bringing a fungus with them. The Asian trees had developed immunity to the fungus, but the American chestnut was helpless. Before long, chestnuts were dying in the Northeast, and the blight worked its way south, reaching Virginia in the 1920s. Two decades later, all the giant chestnuts were slain. But there is hope. To this day, chestnut trees such as you see beside the trail sprout from the roots of the ancients, growing up but always succumbing to the blight. Hopefully, these chestnuts are building a resistance to the blight and will one day tower over the mountains again, long after we are gone. Scientists are expediting this process, and experiments are underway to graft American chestnut trees with the Asian chestnuts in an effort to develop a blight-resistant American chestnut.

At 0.3 mile, walk next to a trailside boulder that has become a resting bench. Pass an outcrop to your left at 0.4 mile with partial views. The trail levels off at 0.5 mile. Congratulations, you just climbed 500 feet. Just ahead, intersect the Johns Creek Mountain Trail. It leaves left for VA 658. The walking is easy now as you head south along a level crest. Drop off a little bouldery spot at 0.9 mile, then resume easy walking over small flat stones resembling tile. Descend a little to reach a gap at 1.7 miles. Here, a faint trail leaves left a short distance to the site of the Big Pond trail shelter, now dismantled. There is still a seldom-used campsite at this small flat.

It is but a small climb to Kelly Knob, which you reach at 1.9 miles. A sign indicates a blue-blazed path leaving right. Follow the spur southwest and downhill to reach a narrow stone brow. Turn right here and soon emerge at an open outcrop, elevation 3,700 feet. The stone base of the outcrop is fissured, so you have to hop over cracks to explore. Stepping out to the main overlook, the Sinking Creek Valley, flanked by Johns Creek Mountain and Clover Hollow

Mountain, stretches to the west. The New River, into which Sinking Creek flows, is down there too. To the north, the high plateau of Salt Pond Mountain rises wide. And you will likely share this view with nothing but the wind! Solitude is yours—and one of the primary lures of this hike.

Nearby Attractions

Along the way to the trailhead, you will pass the Sinking Creek Covered Bridge. There is a small park and wayside near the bridge on your right. The bridge was built in 1916 and is owned and maintained by Giles County. The 70-foot-long span was left in place after a nearby new bridge was built in 1949.

Directions

From Exit 118 on I-81 near Christiansburg, Virginia, take US 460 West for 17.3 miles; then turn right onto VA 42 East toward Newport. Follow VA 42 East as it winds through Newport for a total of 1 mile, and then turn left onto VA 601/Clover Hollow Road. Stay with VA 601 for 5 miles. Here, paved Clover Hollow Road leaves left and turns into VA 602, but you stay straight, joining gravel Laurel Springs Road. Stay with Laurel Springs Road for 1.6 miles to reach Rocky Gap. There are just a few parking spots, so be courteous with your spacing.

SCENERY: ★ ★ ★ ★ ★
TRAIL CONDITION: ★ ★ ★
CHILDREN: ★ ★
DIFFICULTY: ★ ★ ★
SOLITUDE: ★

VIEW FROM DRAGONS TOOTH

GPS TRAILHEAD COORDINATES: N37° 22.716' W80° 9.370'

DISTANCE & CONFIGURATION: 4.9-mile loop

HIKING TIME: 3 hours

HIGHLIGHTS: Panoramas from Dragons Tooth, Devils Seat, rock scrambling

ELEVATION: 1,800' at trailhead; 3,020' at high point

ACCESS: No fees or permits required

MAPS: Trails Illustrated #787 Blacksburg/New River Valley; Appalachian Trail Conservancy Central VA Maps 3 and 4; USGS Glenvar

FACILITIES: Restroom at trailhead

CONTACT: George Washington and Jefferson National Forests, Eastern Divide Ranger District: 540-552-4641, **www.fs.usda.gov/gwj**

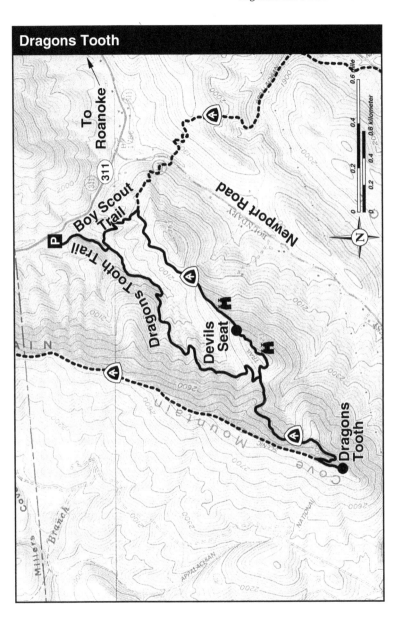

Overview

This deservedly popular circuit hike travels up Cove Mountain to a vertical stone slab providing 360-degree panoramas. Along the way, you will ascend a small stream valley then meet the Appalachian Trail (A.T.). From there, the A.T. traverses boulder fields and upturned rock slabs that require some scrambling. Climb the Dragons Tooth, then return via the A.T., passing more views, including the Devils Seat.

Route Details

This is a fun, popular, yet challenging hike to a geological formation that is fascinating to see, while providing a vista from its tiptop. Be apprised that part of the hike, a part that is on the Appalachian Trail, does require a modicum of rock scrambling using hands and feet. That being said, the hike is done by thousands every year. And the hike certainly shows off the Appalachian Trail in a spectacular setting.

Start out on Dragons Tooth Trail. The singletrack path quickly leads away from the large parking area into the valley of a tributary of McAfee Run. Small bridges pass smaller tributaries. After 0.25 mile, you reach a trail intersection and the loop portion of the hike. Stay right with Dragons Tooth Trail. Begin crisscrossing the stream of the valley you are ascending. The small watercourse can nearly go dry in summer, but stepping-stones will aid your passages when the stream is higher. Rise into classic pine, oak, and hickory woods with a smattering of sassafras. Occasional switchbacks ease the ascent. Wander

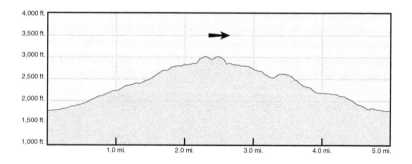

through quiet coves of tulip trees, and then reach Lost Spectacles Gap and the Appalachian Trail at 1.4 miles. Turn right (southbound) here on the Appalachian Trail. Begin a benign climb toward the crest of Cove Mountain.

Then things change. A sign accurately warns you of extremely rocky trail ahead. However, it is not simply rocks in the trail, but big boulders, naked rock slabs, and upturned formations that challenge the hiker. Stone steps help in places. Pines and black gum trees find their place in the thin soils and lichen-covered boulders. At 2 miles, the trail becomes normal again, for a minute, and then you renew your close relationship with the geology of Cove Mountain. The pathway begins angling up a sloped rocky slab and opens onto your first great view of the Catawba Creek valley below and Fort Lewis Mountain to the southeast. Beyond the view, you will be using all fours. Two spots have iron rungs placed into the rock for improved hand and foot placement. Exciting!

At 2.2 miles, leave the Appalachian Trail left, joining the ridgetop spur to the Dragons Tooth. The blue-blazed spur curves right around some upturned rocks, a preview of what you are about to reach. Break the 3,000-foot barrier. At 2.4 miles, come to the Dragons Tooth, an upturned rock that does have a canine appearance. There are other, lesser "teeth" as well. Views can be had from its base, but far better ones await atop the tooth. Walk around the far side of the pillar then scramble to its narrow apex. It is a little scary up there but worth the 360-degree visions of the ridges and valleys near and far. Sinking Creek Mountain stands to the northwest and marks the Virginia–West Virginia boundary. Craig Creek Valley stretches into the distance. A menagerie of southwest-to-northeast-running parallel ridges and valley proffer a panorama of the first order.

Be careful descending the narrow Dragons Tooth, especially when it is wet or other hikers are on it. Once on terra firma, backtrack on the spur, and then backtrack on the A.T., now northbound. Descending the rock slabs and stone steps is harder than climbing them in a way. Return to Lost Spectacles Gap at 3.2 miles. Continue northbound on the A.T., now covering new terrain. Switchback uphill through laurel, galax, and oak. Regain the ridge crest among squat pines, blueberry, and mountain laurel. Pass an outcrop and a southerly view at 3.4 miles. Ahead, keep an eye peeled for a short spur trail leaving left to a squarish rock with a north-facing perch. This is the Devils Seat. Beyond McAfee Run below, the ridge of North Mountain stands tall and proud. Resume the A.T. as it makes a rocky downgrade over a slender ridgeline. At 3.7 miles, reach another southerly view. You have descended quite a bit, and Catawba Creek valley is much closer.

A continual downgrade leads you to the Boy Scout Trail at 4.3 miles. Leave the A.T. for the foot-friendly, pine needle–carpeted path. The Boy Scout Trail switchbacks downhill in thickening woods. Come along a little drainage, then, at 4.6 miles, return to the Dragons Tooth Trail. From here, it is a simple backtrack to the trailhead, completing the hike.

Nearby Attractions

The hike to the famed McAfee Knob, another Appalachian Trail icon, is just 4.6 miles away on VA 311 toward Roanoke. See the next page.

Directions

From Roanoke, Virginia, take I-81 South to Exit 141. Turn left onto VA 419 North and go 0.3 mile; then turn right onto VA 311 North and follow it 9.6 miles. Turn left into the signed parking area for Dragons Tooth.

34

McAfee Knob

SCENERY: ★ ★ ★ ★ ★
TRAIL CONDITION: ★ ★ ★ ★
CHILDREN: ★ ★
DIFFICULTY: ★ ★ ★
SOLITUDE: ★

THE PROTRUSION OF MCAFEE KNOB IS PERHAPS THE MOST PHOTOGRAPHED SPOT ON THE ENTIRE APPALACHIAN TRAIL.

GPS TRAILHEAD COORDINATES: N37° 22.812' W80° 5.360'

DISTANCE & CONFIGURATION: 7.8-mile out-and-back

HIKING TIME: 4.5 hours

HIGHLIGHTS: Views from most-photographed trailside vista in Virginia

ELEVATION: 1,950' at trailhead; 3,150' at high point

ACCESS: No fees or permits required

MAPS: Trails Illustrated *#788 Covington/Allegheny Highlands*; Appalachian Trail Conservancy *Central VA Maps 3 and 4*; USGS *Catawba*

FACILITIES: None

CONTACT: George Washington and Jefferson National Forests, Eastern Divide Ranger District: 540-552-4641, **www.fs.usda.gov/gwj**

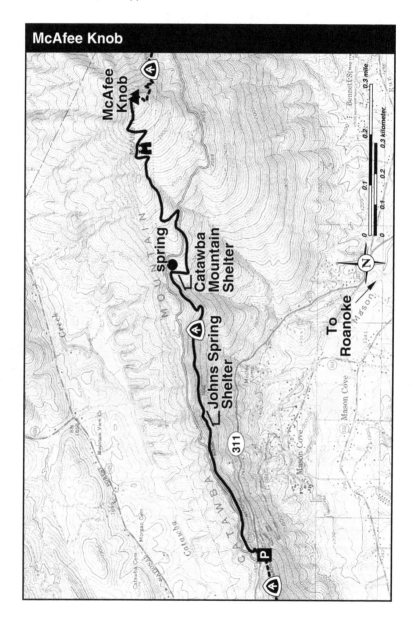

Overview

Take a hike to the outcrop of McAfee Knob, arguably the icon of the Appalachian Trail (A.T.) in Virginia. Start at busy VA 311 and trace the A.T. northbound along Catawba Mountain. The moderate hike skirts past two trail shelters then works up the slope of McAfee Knob. Open onto a long brow of overhanging rock where a mass of mountain lands extend to the horizon. An alternate return route is possible via a fire road.

Route Details

This busy hike deserves its popularity. McAfee Knob is great not only for snapping pictures of hikers standing atop its overhang but also for enjoying the far-reaching views from the outcrop. At the same time, expect no solitude. The first part of the adventure is crossing VA 311 from the trailhead parking lot. It is a semi-blind curve, and you just have to listen for approaching cars, then go. Join the Appalachian Trail northbound. Quickly pass under a brushy power line crossing. By 0.1 mile, you have gained the crest of Catawba Mountain. Ascend via wood and earth steps. Catawba Creek valley falls away to your left, backed by North Mountain. Views also open right (east) toward the Roanoke Valley.

At 0.3 mile, reach a trail intersection and informational kiosk. Here, the Appalachian Trail leaves right and a short path splits left then reaches the fire road running the length of Catawba Mountain.

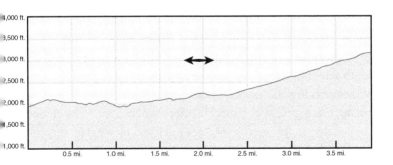

Stay with the Appalachian Trail, briefly stopping at the southerly overlook near the kiosk. Now the A.T. resumes its easterly tack, running beneath the mountain crest. Pass over and near open rock slabs and stony segments. Bridges rise above some of the slabs, and they are especially appreciated when the slabs are wet or icy. At 1 mile, pass just above the Johns Spring trail shelter. The wooden structure is set in a small cove. Not only do Appalachian Trail thru-hikers use this shelter, but it is also popular with local backpackers. Campers are asked to stay only at shelters and designated camping areas along Catawba Mountain to concentrate the heavy use at them.

Climb from the shelter to enter oaks, pine, gum, and sassafras. Pass by more rock slabs and bridges traversing them. At 2.1 miles, the A.T. curves just below a box spring that can run dry by late summer or early fall. Just ahead, pass the spur to the Catawba Mountain Shelter. This three-sided wooden refuge is set in a small cove as well. The A.T. passes some designated campsites then turns uphill; then begins the first real climb of the day. You have gained only 250 feet in elevation thus far. By 2.6 miles, you have gained another 200 feet and reach the fire road. This fire road can be used as a return route starting to the trailhead from this point. You cut off 0.5 mile of distance on a more foot-friendly track, but the fire road isn't the A.T.

Onward to McAfee Knob, staying with the Appalachian Trail and still climbing. At 3.1 miles, bisect a power line clearing. The uptick continues as the A.T. runs parallel to the clearing. This is a good area to see wildlife around dusk or dawn. By 3.4 miles, you have gained the crest of Catawba Mountain. Views once again open to the north. Walk along the rock brow and keep climbing to reach what seems a trail intersection at 3.6 miles. Nevertheless, the only way to go is left, as the trail leading right is closed. Begin curving around the south side of McAfee Knob. Pass an agglomeration of giant squared-off boulders in silent repose. Hikers have created side trails, passing among these geological giants. The Appalachian Trail turns around the boulders in its quest for McAfee Knob and then passes through brushy, wind-stunted woodland. At 3.9 miles, the A.T. takes you to the western edge of McAfee Knob. Take the short spur left to the stony edge of the mountain. Here you see the overhanging rock outcrop so often seen in photos. The area is truly picturesque—a large upthrust outcrop overlooking the Catawba Creek valley and a host of ridges and valleys to the north and west. If you continue along the outcrop rim, it curves around to the right enough to allow northeasterly views of the Roanoke Valley. This is a popular spot, and you will likely share it with others. No camping is allowed directly on the knob, but nearby camping areas on both sides of McAfee Knob allow backpackers to view the sunset from the outcrop, then return to their campsites. Sunrise, sunset, midday—it doesn't matter. What matters is getting to McAfee Knob. It is one of the jewels in the crown of the Appalachian Trail in the South.

Nearby Attractions

The hike to the Dragons Tooth—with its 360-degree views—is just 4.6 miles farther down VA 311. See page 194.

Directions

From Roanoke, Virginia, take I-81 South to Exit 141. Turn left onto VA 419 North and go 0.3 mile; then turn right onto VA 311 North and follow it 5.6 miles. As you approach the gap in Catawba Mountain, look for the yellow hiker road-crossing sign, and turn left into the large parking area for McAfee Knob.

35

Apple Orchard Falls Loop

SCENERY: ★ ★ ★ ★
TRAIL CONDITION: ★ ★ ★ ★
CHILDREN: ★ ★ ★
DIFFICULTY: ★ ★
SOLITUDE: ★ ★

THE UPPER PART OF APPLE ORCHARD FALLS AS IT SPILLS OVER A LEDGE

GPS TRAILHEAD COORDINATES: N37° 30.466' W79° 31.448'

DISTANCE & CONFIGURATION: 5.1-mile loop

HIKING TIME: 3 hours

HIGHLIGHTS: Apple Orchard Falls, view

ELEVATION: 3,450' at trailhead; 2,420' at low point

ACCESS: No fees or permits required

MAPS: Trails Illustrated *#789 Lexington/Blue Ridge Mountains;* Appalachian Trail Conservancy *Central VA Maps 1 and 2;* USGS *Arnold Valley*

FACILITIES: None

CONTACT: George Washington and Jefferson National Forests, Glenwood–Pedlar Ranger District: 540-291-2188, **www.fs.usda.gov/gwj**

Overview

Leave the Blue Ridge Parkway at Sunset Fields and descend Apple Orchard Mountain to tall and varied Apple Orchard Falls. From there, loop via the Cornelius Creek Trail to meet the Appalachian Trail (A.T.). A high-country ramble on the slope of Apple Orchard Mountain leads you back to the parkway.

Route Details

You may not want to leave your starting point on the Blue Ridge Parkway. Sunset Fields Overlook provides a western vista from atop lofty Apple Orchard Mountain, so named for the rounded-off, weathered oaks that grow atop it, resembling ranks of apple trees. Nevertheless, the Appalachian Trail is calling, and so is high Apple Orchard Falls, tumbling in its wide-ranging fashions, a menagerie of cascades in one location.

The first part of the Apple Orchard Falls Trail is asphalt, all access (including wheelchairs for the first 200 feet), leading across the small roadside meadow. From there, join a singletrack natural surface path descending into rich hardwoods. Circle around an upland cove. At 0.2 mile, intersect the Appalachian Trail. This will be your return route. For now, stay straight with the Apple Orchard Falls Trail as it begins a headlong descent along a fast-gathering,

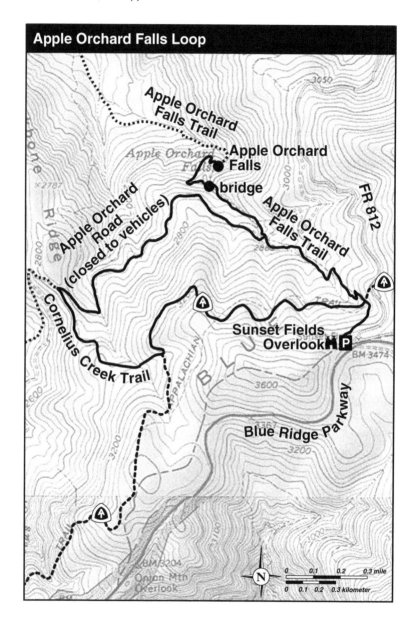

Apple Orchard Falls Loop

Apple Orchard Falls Trail

Apple Orchard Falls

bridge

Apple Orchard Falls Trail

FR 812

Apple Orchard Road (closed to vehicles)

Cornelius Creek Trail

Sunset Fields Overlook

BM 3474

Blue Ridge Parkway

BM 3204
Onion Mtn
Overlook

0   0.1   0.2   0.3 mile
0   0.1   0.2   0.3 kilometer

N

unnamed tributary of North Creek, making small cascades as it follows the rules of gravity. At 0.6 mile, spot some old rock walls from a hardscrabble farm. Life must have been tough up here, with cold winters; thin, sloped soils chock-full of rocks; and extreme isolation. At 0.8 mile, come to Apple Orchard Falls Road, closed to vehicles. Keep straight, still descending on the Apple Orchard Falls Trail. Step over a trickling branch contributing its waters to Apple Orchard Falls, then rejoin the main creek, which has now picked up steam and volume as it dashes betwixt boulders. At 1 mile, squeeze through a boulder garden, a stone portal of sorts, then cross the main creek on a hiker bridge, near a campsite and a small ledge waterfall.

The valley opens beyond the bridge, and you make a wide switchback. Work down an amazing number of wooden stairs, daring for Apple Orchard Falls. Pass a big boulder and cleared overlook at 1.2 miles. Here, you can gaze westerly into ridges and hills toward the James River valley. Look for the bolts of a bench once connected to the boulder. Continue negotiating wooden steps through rhododendron and mountain laurel. At 1.3 miles, reach a bridge crossing the base of Apple Orchard Falls. The span makes for an ideal viewing platform. Look up—from here you can see the cataract spill over an open ledge then slide down an angled chute. From there the foam encounters a huge mid-cataract boulder, where water disperses into multiple spills and then filters into a rock jumble as it passes underneath the bridge. There is a little bit of everything in this waterfall.

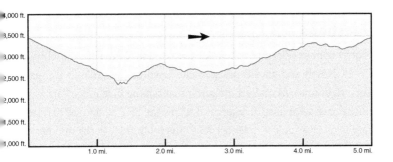

Beyond here, the Apple Orchard Falls Trail continues down to North Creek, but we backtrack away from the falls, returning to Apple Orchard Road at 2 miles. Turn right (west) on the former forest road turned trail. The roadbed is still grassy, but trees are closing in these days. The walking is easy on the north slope of Apple Orchard Mountain. At 2.7 miles, turn into a stream valley. Ahead, step over this unnamed branch, then rise to meet the Cornelius Creek Trail at 3.1 miles. Head left here, joining a ridgeline clad in galax, laurel, and oaks. Climb, then dip to a gap at 3.4 miles and a small campsite. Ahead, recross the aforementioned branch, then rise to meet the Appalachian Trail at 3.6 miles. From here, head left (northbound) on the A.T. The master path of the East wanders in and out of rich coves of Apple Orchard Mountain, where sturdy, gray-trunked tulip trees fashion a regal mantle. Stinging nettle will border the path in late summer. The trail undulates but little, making for easy walking. Bisect a mossy boulder garden at 4.3 miles. At 4.9 miles, the A.T. returns you to the Apple Orchard Falls Trail. From here, it is a simple backtrack to the trailhead. If it's late afternoon, consider lingering at the Sunset Fields Overlook to watch Sol sink below the mantle of Old Dominion ridges fading into the distance.

Nearby Attractions

This part of the Blue Ridge Parkway makes for an alluring drive as it travels from the lowest part of the parkway in Virginia at the James River to the highest stretch of atop Apple Orchard Mountain.

Directions

From Roanoke, Virginia, take I-81 North to Exit 162. Turn right onto US 11 North and go 4.6 miles to the town of Buchanan, Virginia. Turn right onto VA 43 East. Follow it to reach the Blue Ridge Parkway (BRP) after 4.7 miles. Turn left and follow the BRP 12.4 miles to Sunset Fields Overlook at milepost 78.4. The trailhead is in the middle of the parking area.

36

Ottie Powell Memorial

SCENERY: ★ ★ ★ ★
TRAIL CONDITION: ★ ★ ★ ★
CHILDREN: ★ ★ ★
DIFFICULTY: ★ ★
SOLITUDE: ★ ★ ★ ★

IT IS EASY TO SEE WHY A FIRE TOWER WAS ERECTED HERE, WITH THESE VIEWS NORTH ALONG THE BLUE RIDGE.

GPS TRAILHEAD COORDINATES: N37° 40.446' W79° 20.065'

DISTANCE & CONFIGURATION: 3.8-mile out-and-back

HIKING TIME: 2.5 hours

HIGHLIGHTS: Trail ghosts, views, trail shelter, memorial

ELEVATION: 2,140' at trailhead; 3,320' at high point

ACCESS: No fees or permits required

MAPS: Trails Illustrated *#789 Lexington/Blue Ridge Mountains;* Appalachian Trail Conservancy *Central VA Maps 1 and 2;* USGS *Buena Vista*

FACILITIES: None

CONTACT: George Washington and Jefferson National Forests, Glenwood–Pedlar Ranger District: 540-291-2188, **www.fs.usda.gov/gwj**

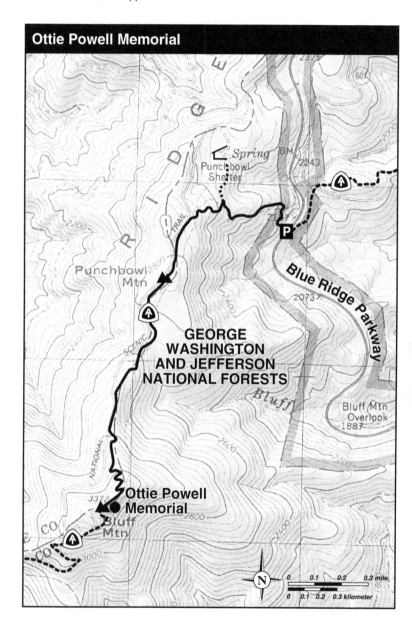

Ottie Powell Memorial

Overview

Trace the Appalachian Trail (A.T.) up to Bluff Mountain, the site of a fire tower that still presents wide vistas. There lies the memorial to little Ottie Powell, lost a century back. His body was found atop Bluff Mountain, and his story became legend. Even now, Ottie's ghost is said to haunt nearby Punchbowl Mountain trail shelter—which you will visit en route to Bluff Mountain.

Route Details

It was late fall 1891, and 4-year-old Ottie Powell walked to one-room Dancing Creek School in the shadows of the Blue Ridge. A cold spell had used up the school's wood supply, so Ottie and other students headed into the nearby forest to fill the school's iron stove. It wasn't long before the students were back in their desks—except Ottie. Soon, the whole community was searching for little Ottie. The cloudy November day quickly faded to dusk. Rain fell. Still the search continued. At one point, more than 1,000 people were searching for Ottie. Hopes shrank as the spring of 1892 arrived with nary a sign of Ottie Powell. Later that spring, bear hunters were tracking the Blue Ridge. One of their dogs stopped tracking and started howling from atop Bluff Mountain, more than 2,400 feet above Dancing Creek School.

There lay the remains of little blue-eyed and sandy-haired Ottie Cline Powell. From the contents of his stomach, detectives concluded Ottie perished of hypothermia his first night lost. Yet how did he get

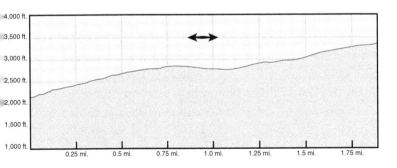

7 miles distant and 0.5 mile higher than the schoolhouse? This question remains unanswered to this day.

Ottie Cline Powell was buried near his home. Ottie's tale became the stuff of legend when a local Virginia resident wrote a book about him, even building a cross atop Bluff Mountain. By then, Bluff Mountain was part of the Washington National Forest. Officials erected a steel fire tower atop Bluff Mountain. The Appalachian Trail ran beneath it.

Hikers visiting the mountain grew curious about the cross, perpetuating the legend of Ottie Powell. Later, the bronze memorial we see today was laid. The fire tower, in existence since 1917, was dismantled. Today's hikers see four concrete tower supports and stairs going nowhere, except a few feet higher atop Bluff Mountain.

Even without the tower, a cleared view reveals the Maury River valley to the west, still farther to Lexington, Mill Mountain, and West Virginia. To the east, the James River valley courses through knobby hills, Richmond bound. The Blue Ridge rolls north to Shenandoah National Park and is what the A.T. follows from here.

Some say Ottie Powell's spirit can be sensed atop Bluff Mountain. Visitors regularly adorn Ottie's memorial with flowers and toys. Campers at Punchbowl Mountain shelter swear they can hear Ottie's voice pealing through the wind-whipped leafless trees of November.

You will reach the shelter after leaving the Blue Ridge Parkway and the trailhead, southbound on the Appalachian Trail. Ascend a hardwood hollow. At 0.4 mile, come to a trail intersection. I recommend you take the spur trail right. It leads 0.25 mile to the Punchbowl Mountain trail shelter, a typical three-sided, wooden A.T. overnighting place—except for the Ottie Powell part. Nearby a pond stands silent. A small stone-encased spring gurgles close by. If you camp here, bring your best flashlight for the long, potentially scary night ahead and maybe an electronic device for recording your ghost sighting.

Return to the A.T. and continue the hike to Bluff Mountain. Ascend beneath chestnut oaks growing amid mountain laurel and gray boulders covered in lichens. At 0.6 mile, catch your breath as the A.T. levels off after rising 600 feet. Surmount gentle Punchbowl Mountain at 0.8 mile. Descend amid rhododendron and laurel to reach a gap at 1.1 miles. From here, begin your conquest of Bluff Mountain. At 1.5 miles, the Appalachian Trail makes a series of switchbacks among diminutive pines. By 1.8 miles, views are opening through the trees to the east. Hold on, because you arrive at the grassy apex of Bluff Mountain at 1.9 miles. You will find the memorial to Ottie Powell, the fire tower foundations, those inspiring panoramas of the lands beyond . . . and maybe a ghost.

Nearby Attractions

Otter Creek Campground is situated about 10 miles south of the trailhead on the Blue Ridge Parkway. It offers 45 tent and 24 trailer campsites. The campground also has restrooms with flush toilets and water. Many of the campsites are along Otter Creek. It is generally open early May–October. Check ahead for exact dates at **nps.gov/blri.**

Directions

From Exit 188 on I-81, take US 60 East to and through Buena Vista for a total of 8 miles to reach the Blue Ridge Parkway. Take the Blue Ridge Parkway southbound for 6.1 miles to the Punchbowl Mountain Overlook, milepost 51.5, on your left. The "overlook" is actually a parking area for the Appalachian Trail and offers no views. From there, take the A.T. southbound, joining it across the parkway from the overlook. Do *not* follow the A.T. northbound, directly from the overlook.

37

The Priest

SCENERY: ★ ★ ★ ★
TRAIL CONDITION: ★ ★ ★
CHILDREN: ★ ★ ★
DIFFICULTY: ★ ★
SOLITUDE: ★ ★

VIEWS FROM THE PRIEST STRETCH OUT ACROSS THE TYE RIVER VALLEY.

GPS TRAILHEAD COORDINATES: N37° 49.834' W79° 5.026'

DISTANCE & CONFIGURATION: 3.6-mile out-and-back

HIKING TIME: 3 hours

HIGHLIGHTS: Views from The Priest, federally designated wilderness

ELEVATION: 3,035' at trailhead; 4,063' at high point

ACCESS: No fees or permits required

MAPS: Trails Illustrated *#789 Lexington/Blue Ridge Mountains;* Appalachian Trail Conservancy *Central VA Maps 1 and 2;* USGS *Massies Mill*

FACILITIES: Restroom at trailhead

CONTACT: George Washington and Jefferson National Forests, Glenwood–Pedlar Ranger District: 540-291-2188, **www.fs.usda.gov/gwj**

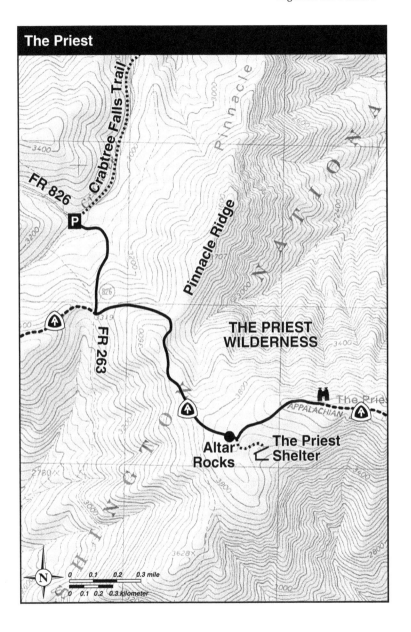

The Priest

Crabtree Falls Trail

Pinnacle

Pinnacle Ridge

FR 826

P

FR 263

NATIONA

THE PRIEST
WILDERNESS

The Prie

APPALACHIAN

Altar
Rocks

The Priest
Shelter

WASHINGTON

N

0   0.1   0.2   0.3 mile

0   0.1 0.2 0.3 kilometer

Overview

This Appalachian Trail (A.T.) hike leads through the Priest Wilderness to a 4,000-foot-high outcrop and a stellar view of the Tye River Valley and mountains beyond. From this same trailhead, you can also hike to Crabtree Falls, Virginia's highest fall and arguably the highest cataract in the East.

Route Details

Even if you don't bag two hikes from this trailhead and only hike to The Priest, then you will be well rewarded. The hike to The Priest travels through the Priest Wilderness, a 5,963-acre reserve set aside in the year 2000. The wilderness encompasses the highest part of The Priest mountain, as well as springs and streams spilling off it. The reason for the peak's name has been lost to time, although a pair of massive boulders near the top looks suspiciously like an altar. The Appalachian Trail will take you aside this altarlike boulder stack. Speculate for yourself if that is where the name came from. The hike also leads near a shelter set beside a spring on a shoulder of the mountain. Just like everything else around here, the shelter goes by the name The Priest.

The parking area for this hike is primarily used to access the upper end of Crabtree Falls. This area is known as Crabtree Meadows. As late as the 1930s, Crabtree Meadows was occupied by several mountain families. Crabtree Meadows is also the best place to access

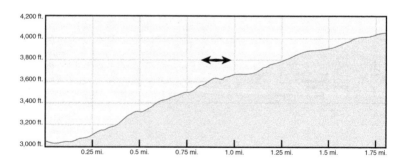

The Priest, even though it requires a 0.5-mile hike on an abused gravel road suitable only for four-wheel-drive enthusiasts. You cannot get a passenger car up the last part of the gravel road under any circumstances, so don't even think about it. Instead, follow the rough forest road beyond the Crabtree Meadows parking area, crossing upper Crabtree Creek. Ascend on the gravel track past a few campsites and what's left of Crabtree Meadows on your right. The track steepens among oaks, maples, and ferns. It quickly becomes evident that no passenger vehicle could make it up this road.

At 0.5 mile, level off in an unnamed gap, elevation 3,319 feet. Turn left (northbound) on the Appalachian Trail, leaving the erstwhile forest road. Walk under short, stunted maples and oaks on a pebbly path. A sign welcomes you to the Priest Wilderness. Continue ascending on a steady grade. At 0.8 mile, the A.T. passes a gap to the left from which Pinnacle Ridge stretches. Turn south and shortly level off in rocky woods. Dip to a gap at 1.1 miles. At 1.4 miles, pass the Altar Rocks, a pair of linked boulders that recalls a priest's altar. Perhaps this is from which the name derived.

The spur trail to The Priest trail shelter leaves right just beyond the Altar Rocks. The Priest shelter, just a short piece down the spur, is a three-sided wooden affair in a grassy flat next to a spring.

Stay northbound on the Appalachian Trail. Begin the final ascent to the peak of The Priest, breaking the 4,000-foot mark. At 1.8 miles, a well-used spur trail leads left to an outcrop running along the brow of the mountain. Before you opens a panorama of mountains, a wilderness landscape devoid of civilization's signs. Below, the Tye River gathers its tributaries, including Crabtree Creek. From the left, the outcrops of Pinnacle Ridge stand out. Beyond, the Big Levels on the Blue Ridge Parkway, then Torry Ridge, then the Devils Knob and Three Ridges Wilderness form a left-to-right frame. On a clear day, Massanutten Mountain can be seen in the most distant distance.

After backtracking to the trailhead, and if you have extra time and energy, visit Crabtree Falls. Crabtree Falls is Virginia's claim to having the highest waterfall east of the Mississippi. Of course, that depends on how you define a waterfall. Any way you slice it, Crabtree Falls is the highest waterfall in Virginia. Crabtree Falls is divided into five major waterfalls along Crabtree Creek. The creek drops 1,200 feet over 0.5 mile, with one tumble of 500 feet. Remember the old TV show *The Waltons*? They portrayed a Virginia mountain family. The show is linked to Crabtree Falls. The falls were not shown on television, but the name was mentioned several times during the life of the program, usually in reference to a Sunday outing.

Nearby Attractions

From this very trailhead, you can hike the Crabtree Falls Trail 1 mile to the upper part of the falls.

Directions

From Lexington, Virginia, take I-81 North to Exit 205 for VA 606. Turn right onto VA 606 1.5 miles to Steeles Tavern and US 11. Turn left onto US 11 North and proceed 0.1 mile; then turn right onto VA 56 East and follow it 9.1 miles to the right turn onto Forest Road 826. Drive 3.8 miles to reach the trailhead on the left. This is also the upper trailhead for Crabtree Falls. The four-wheel-drive road continuing past the trailhead is FR 263 and is not recommended. Walk 0.5 mile from the trailhead.

38 **Humpback Rocks Loop**

SCENERY: ★ ★ ★ ★ ★
TRAIL CONDITION: ★ ★ ★
CHILDREN: ★ ★ ★
DIFFICULTY: ★ ★
SOLITUDE: ★ ★

HIKERS RELAX ATOP THE PANORAMA-RICH HUMPBACK ROCKS.

GPS TRAILHEAD COORDINATES: N37° 58.363' W78° 53.950'

DISTANCE & CONFIGURATION: 4.8-mile loop

HIKING TIME: 2.5 hours

HIGHLIGHTS: Historic homestead, extensive panoramas

ELEVATION: 2,320' at trailhead; 3,260' at high point

ACCESS: No fees or permits required; check **nps.gov/blri** for real-time information regarding road closures in winter.

MAPS: Trails Illustrated *#789 Lexington/Blue Ridge Mountains;* Appalachian Trail Conservancy *Central VA Maps 1 and 2;* USGS *Sherando*

FACILITIES: Restrooms, water fountain, gift shop, picnic tables

CONTACT: Blue Ridge Parkway: 828-298-0398, **nps.gov/blri**

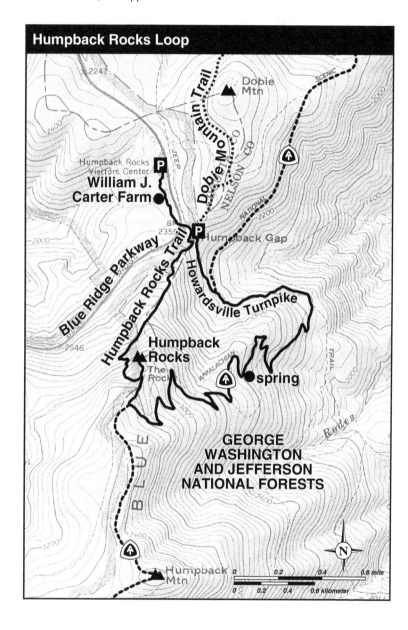

Humpback Rocks Loop

Overview

This Blue Ridge Parkway hike begins at a fine visitor center and then leads to the Carter Place, a highland pioneer farmstead, replete with historic structures. After exploring the homestead, make the rocky ascent to the Humpback Rocks, where you soak in wide prospects of the Shenandoah Valley and mountains beyond. Descend on the Appalachian Trail (A.T.) in a series of switchbacks. Finally, the circuit traces old Howardsville Turnpike back to the trailhead.

Route Details

This hike starts at the northern end of the Blue Ridge Parkway, at the Humpback Rocks Visitor Center, your entryway to the 469-mile mountain road linking Shenandoah National Park to Great Smoky Mountains National Park. The Mountain Farm Trail (which is wheelchair accessible for the first 0.25 mile) leaves the visitor center, housing a small museum, to where William J. Carter homesteaded. The park service has re-created this farmstead to the 1890s era, using authentic local structures, though none from Carter himself.

Carter settled here after receiving a land grant from the state of Virginia. The state wanted settlers in the mountains west of the Piedmont to provide a defensive bulwark against Indian attacks from the west. William J. Carter picked a good spot, mostly level, despite being atop the mountainous Blue Ridge. Stroll through the split-log-fence-bordered grounds to view a log cabin—the symbol of the early

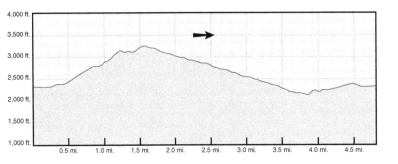

Appalachian frontier. Find the curious storage shed, a mix of rock and wood. And then there's the barn. Note the wood shingle roof atop it. Ahead, find a pigpen and springhouse. Springs were of paramount consideration when settlers sought locations for their homesteads. The homestead is a fun place to explore for kids of all ages.

At 0.3 mile, the trail leaves the farm, passes through a gate, and heads toward Humpback Gap. Make sure to look up at the Humpback Rocks while crossing the Blue Ridge Parkway. In Carter's day, they were simply known as The Rocks and were a point of reference for passersby on the Howardsville Turnpike. At 0.4 mile, reach a trailhead kiosk and alternate parking area in Humpback Gap. Join the Humpback Rocks Trail, formerly the route of the A.T. Now you earn your view from the Humpback Rocks. The wide and sometimes busy trail is shaded by hardwoods, but a little tree cover does not make the path less steep.

At 0.8 mile, a user-created shortcut leads left to the Humpback Rocks. Avoid this erosive closed trail. Stay with the blue-blazed Humpback Rocks Trail. At 1 mile, the path winds upward into a massive boulder garden. It took a lot of muscle power to create the stair-like path through the wonderment of geology. At 1.3 miles, the Humpback Rocks Trail meets the spur trail to Humpback Rocks. Follow the gentle spur to emerge at the enormous crag at 1.4 mile. The prospects are wide and distant. Below, the William J. Carter Farm looks little, and, in a way, it is hard to believe you just climbed that. To your north, the spine of Shenandoah National Park stretches to the horizon. Looking west, the Shenandoah Valley forms a patchwork of field and forest. Behind it rise the Alleghenies, which delineate the Virginia–West Virginia border. Turn around and look east to the Piedmont as it stretches toward the sea. Make sure to visit the multiple overlooks atop Humpback Rocks.

Rejoin the Humpback Rocks Trail to meet the Appalachian Trail at 1.6 miles. This is the hike's high point. The A.T. is descending off the crest of Humpback Mountain. Head left (northbound) on the A.T. as it descends a series of switchbacks, tempering the steepness of this east-facing hillside. The downhill makes for easy travel. At 2.9 miles, you pass a marked spring. At 3.1 miles, the trail bisects a campsite in a flat. After a while, the Appalachian Trail joins the Howardsville Turnpike, a former wagon road linking the Shenandoah Valley to the west with the Piedmont to the East.

Though most rocks were removed, the turnpike is no modern highway, but it was for its time. A few streams flowing off Humpback Mountain flow across the turnpike. At 4.2 miles, the A.T. splits right (north), aiming for Shenandoah National Park a few miles distant. Keep straight on the Howardsville Turnpike, drifting into Humpback Gap at 4.5 miles. From there, backtrack through the William J. Carter Farm to complete the hike.

Nearby Attractions

During summer weekends, farm demonstrations, gardening, and period reenactments are engaged at the William J. Carter Farm. Also, Sherando Lake is a fun George Washington National Forest campground destination.

Directions

From Exit 99 on I-64 near Waynesboro, Virginia, an officially designated Appalachian Trail Community, take the Blue Ridge Parkway south 5.9 miles to the Humpback Rocks Visitor Center on your right. The Mountain Farm Trail leading through the farm and to the loop part of the hike leaves south from the visitor center. Check **nps.gov/blri** for real-time information regarding road closures in winter.

39

Blackrock Summit

SCENERY: ★ ★ ★ ★

TRAIL CONDITION: ★ ★ ★ ★ ★

CHILDREN: ★ ★ ★ ★ ★

DIFFICULTY: ★

SOLITUDE: ★ ★

THIS TALUS SLOPE ON BLACKROCK MOUNTAIN OFFERS DISTANT VIEWS OF SHENANDOAH NATIONAL PARK.

GPS TRAILHEAD COORDINATES: N38° 13.371' W78° 44.010'

DISTANCE & CONFIGURATION: 1.1-mile loop

HIKING TIME: 1 hour

HIGHLIGHTS: Wide-ranging panoramas from boulder jumble peak

ELEVATION: 2,940' at trailhead; 3,140' at high point

ACCESS: National park entrance fee required; Skyline Drive may close in winter; call 540-999-3500 for the latest road conditions.

MAPS: Potomac Appalachian Trail Club *Map 11 AT and other trails in Shenandoah National Park South District;* Trails Illustrated *Map #228 Shenandoah National Park;* USGS *Browns Cove*

FACILITIES: None

CONTACT: Shenandoah National Park: 540-999-3500, **nps.gov/shen**

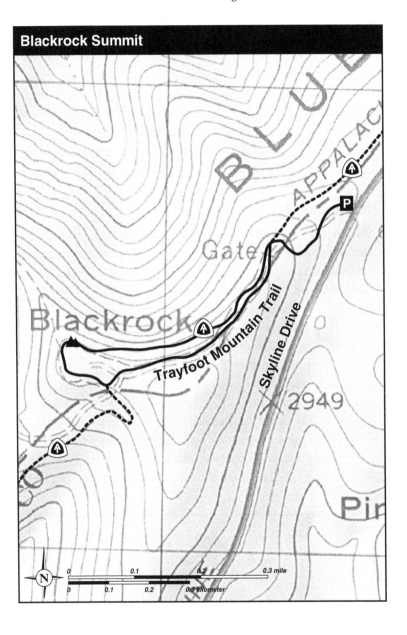

Blackrock Summit

Overview

This child-friendly, geologically fascinating loop has fun written all over it. Make an easy walk from Shenandoah's Skyline Drive to an incredible rock jumble on the Appalachian Trail (A.T.). Views extend for miles in multiple directions from the summit of boulder-strewn Blackrock. After gaining views from several spots, reenter woods, cruising back to the trailhead. Elevation changes are minimal, relaxation spots are ample, and boulder scrambling is an amusing option.

Route Details

Shenandoah National Park is known for its overlooks and vistas accessible from Skyline Drive. However, as hikers know, the best views are those earned on foot. But not everyone can tramp for miles to an overlook. However, this short loop around the summit of Blackrock is doable by just about everyone from 4 to 84. Start at nearly 3,000 feet, then make your way up the Trayfoot Mountain Trail on a wide track, topping a hill. Meet the Appalachian Trail, then follow that famous footpath northbound. Open onto an incredible rock jumble. Views extend for miles in multiple directions. Kids can have a ball scrambling over massive boulders to reach the summit of Blackrock. Adults can stay on the Appalachian Trail, which has been cleared of stones. After gaining views from several spots, reenter woods, working your way back to the trailhead. This highland walk is best whenever the skies are clear, whether it is winter, spring, or fall. Summer

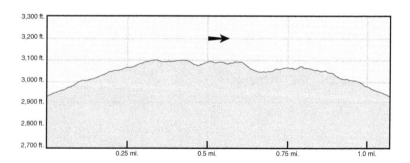

will often be hazy yet has its share of clear days. Also, the optional rock scrambling atop Blackrock is safest when the terrain is dry.

A large sign at the hike's beginning details the tightly woven trail network lacing the crest of Blackrock. You walk under a mixed canopy of locust and other hardwoods. The large flowering black cohosh exhibits its fragrant white cylindrical flowers in midsummer. To the left of the trail, brushy woods proliferate. Curve uphill, then come to the Appalachian Trail at 0.1 mile. A few short steps connect the A.T. to the Trayfoot Mountain Trail here. For now, stay straight on the wide Trayfoot Mountain Trail, resuming an uptick, topping out at 0.3 mile. A hill rises yet higher to your left. Observe how the trail was used as a fire line. To the left, you will see old blackened trunks amid the regrowth, whereas to the right of the trail, the woods exhibit no signs of burn within the past decade.

The slope opens to your left. Blackberries attract man and beast alike. At 0.5 mile, come to a four-way intersection. Here, you meet the Appalachian Trail yet again. Another map displays the trail system here. Turn right (northbound) on the A.T. It isn't long before you open onto the south side of the rock jumble that is Blackrock Summit. Hundreds, likely thousands, of broken stones rise in a pile prescribed by the hands of God. Views open to your south, then west. Paine Hollow creates a void below, while the forest and rock slopes of Trayfoot Mountain rise in the distance. The boulder stack of Blackrock rises to your right, coming together in a crown above. The stones of Blackrock are actually grayish, but a dark lichen known as rock tripe grows on them, lending a dark appearance from afar. It will be hard to keep active kids from scaling the boulders. Why stop the fun anyway? Maybe you should join them. The view spreads 270 degrees from the top!

Intersect the Blackrock Spur Trail at 0.6 mile. More interesting geological formations are down that trail, including mammoth boulder "gates" through which you walk. This loop stays with the A.T. as it continues circling around Blackrock. A more accessible rock outcrop—as opposed to the jumble above you—stretches left toward

Trayfoot Mountain. And as you turn north, a talus slope falls far down the mountain, hundreds of feet, revealing a wealth of national park beyond. Furnace Mountain forms a knob to the west. The talus slope drops to Madison Run below; the valley is also called Dundo Hollow. Austin Mountain constructs a wooded wall across Madison Run. More Shenandoah highlands meld into the horizon, while the Shenandoah Valley flanks the lowlands below. Pull up a boulder and soak in the vista.

Leave the open rock expanse for the shady, singletrack, fern-bordered A.T. The walking is easy and level. It isn't long before you meet the short spur to the wide Trayfoot Mountain Trail and complete your loop. From there, backtrack to the parking lot, finishing the walk.

Nearby Attractions

Hikers can increase this walk, find solitude, and grab a view from little-visited Furnace Mountain by taking the Trayfoot Mountain Trail then Furnace Mountain Trail for a 6.8-mile out-and-back hike from the Blackrock trailhead.

Directions

From Charlottesville, Virginia, take I-64 West to Exit 99 for US 250/Afton/Waynesboro. Turn right onto US 250, entering Shenandoah National Park, and immediately make a sharp left onto Skyline Drive. Follow Skyline Drive 20.6 miles north to Blackrock parking area on the west side of Skyline Drive at milepost 84.8. During winter, Skyline Drive may close. Call 540-999-3500 (option 1 then option 1 again) for the latest road conditions.

40

Falls Loop
from Browns Gap

LOWER DOYLES RIVER FALLS MAKES ITS NARROW FAUCET-LIKE WHITE PLUNGE.

GPS TRAILHEAD COORDINATES: N38° 14.427' W78° 42.634'

DISTANCE & CONFIGURATION: 7-mile loop

HIKING TIME: 4.5 hours

HIGHLIGHTS: Old-growth forest, waterfalls, history

ELEVATION: 2,575' at trailhead; 1,470' at low point

ACCESS: National park entrance fee required; Skyline Drive may close in winter; call 540-999-3500 for the latest road conditions.

MAPS: Potomac Appalachian Trail Club *Map 11 AT and other trails in Shenandoah National Park South District;* Trails Illustrated *Map #228 Shenandoah National Park;* USGS *Browns Cove*

FACILITIES: None

CONTACT: Shenandoah National Park: 540-999-3500, **nps.gov/shen**

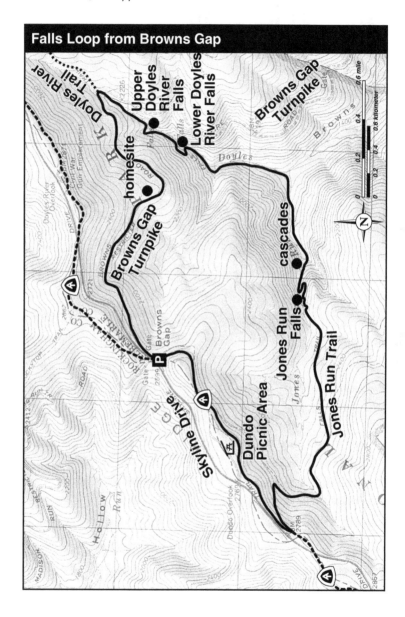

Falls Loop from Browns Gap

Overview

Water lovers will fall for this loop. The trail passes three major cataracts and numerous other cascades as it explores two boulder-strewn canyons connected by the Appalachian Trail (A.T.). The hike up Jones Run passes some old-growth tulip trees with impressive girths. This waterfall extravaganza is best in spring, with wildflowers and bold cataracts. Summer can be crowded. The streams will likely be low in autumn. Ice forms on the cascades during brisk winter days.

Route Details

Start your hike at Browns Gap, a location of historical significance. Confederate general Stonewall Jackson passed through here in early 1862 while outwitting Union forces in the mountains around the Shenandoah Valley. Jackson's local knowledge left the Northerners bamboozled time and again. Browns Gap was important because of the strategic turnpike that went through it. The turnpike linking Richmond and the Shenandoah Valley was built in 1805. You will walk the very same turnpike on the first leg of this hike. Think of all the farmers loaded with corn (and liquid corn, also known as moonshine), circuit-riding preachers, traveling hucksters, weary immigrants, and Civil War soldiers who walked this way. And now you come.

Cross Skyline Drive and immediately begin descending on the Browns Gap Fire Road, the current name of the turnpike (Madison Run Fire Road, which leaves west from the gap near the parking area,

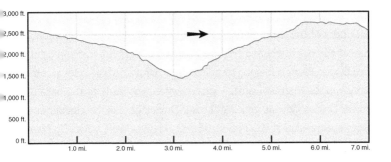

is the western relic of this turnpike). Look for a small path leaving the road to your left at mile 0.4. Scramble a few feet up this path to the grave of William H. Howard, Confederate States of America soldier. The carved stone slab marks his interment locale. Return to the fire road and continue down the trail on a gentle grade, passing through a stand of pines. Views open through the trees toward the Piedmont.

The wide track makes for easy walking. On your left at 0.9 mile, a brushy area contains relics indicating former human habitation, such as piled rocks. Imagine the forest as cleared and cultivated. As the trail swings to the left, the canopy of trees and oaks thickens. Watch for some large trailside trees, including a noteworthy tulip tree at 1.2 miles. Cross an iron bridge spanning sassy and shallow Doyles River. Reach a trail junction at 1.7 miles.

Turn right onto Doyles River Trail. Other hikers will be joining you, having come from Skyline Drive and the upper Doyles River Trailhead. The footpath descends along lively Doyles River. Cross the waterway—an easy rock hop—at mile 1.9. This vale was once full of hemlocks. They were attacked by an invasive insect known as the hemlock woolly adelgid, which killed these trees by sucking the sap out of them. The hemlock woolly adelgid is thought to have been introduced to the United States from Asia in 1924. Nearly all hemlocks in the Appalachians have succumbed to this deadly pest, save for ones the park has treated with an insecticide injected into the ground below the trees. The forest is now dominated by hardwoods. Wildflowers carpet the woodland floor.

Doyles River Trail continues along the watercourse but swings away before Upper Doyles Falls. At mile 2.1, a side trail leads to the dark pool of the three-tiered, 30-foot falls that spills into a bouldery glen at the point where a tributary feeds the river. The canyon tightens; Doyles River is making frenzied drops. Unnamed cascades accompany you downstream until a sharp switchback leads to the base of Lower Doyles Falls at mile 2.4. Lower Doyles Falls is the steeper and more spectacular of the two at 63 feet. It dives over a rock lip then spills in ribbons, strands and crashing channels over multiple tiers to finally land in a pool before charging on. The cataract will look different depending on flows. A rock wall extends across the far gorge.

The trail squeezes down the narrow, very rugged gorge, using a wooden bridge to span a cascading tributary spilling into Doyles River at 2.7 miles. At 2.9 miles, find a deep pool between fast-moving rapids. At 3.1 miles, in a small flat that would make a good lunch spot, come to a trail marker and the end of Doyles River Trail. Jones Run and Doyles River merge below the signpost. Note the sycamores in the lower valley—the climate is just too cold for them upstream on either branch.

Veer right on lesser-used Jones Run Trail and begin to climb, rock-hopping Jones Run at 3.3 miles. Tulip trees grow with such a diameter it would take several hikers to encircle them. Look up the slope. Jones Run gorge is littered with huge boulders. Keep an eye on the creek too, as many scenic cascades tumble down the relentless watercourse, including some long slide cascades. At 3.8 miles, step over a tributary. You'll arrive at Jones Run Falls, where water dives 45 feet over a solid rock wall. Large waterside rock slabs make for good observation points. Feel the cool air and mist from the cataract.

The trail turns sharply left, circumventing a rock rampart. Achieve the top of the falls. The path traces Jones Run past more cascades before veering away from the creek. Gently ascend through a cove-hardwood forest with an open understory of grass and ferns. At 5 miles, join an old wagon road. The path widens. Step over Jones Run, minute at this point at 5.2 miles. The Jones Run Trail makes a sharp left turn at 5.4 miles. Meet the Appalachian Trail at 5.7 miles. The Jones Run trailhead and parking area are just steps away. Turn right (northbound) on the Appalachian Trail toward Dundo Picnic Area. Dry species such as mountain laurel and chestnut oak straddle the grade back to Browns Gap. Pass spur trails to Dundo Picnic Area at 6.3 miles. Intermittent views of Cedar Mountain open. The A.T. descends before arriving at Browns Gap. Complete your loop at 7 miles.

Nearby Attractions

The South District of Shenandoah National Park is the quietest part of the preserve, with trails galore that visit other waterfalls and overlooks.

Directions

From Charlottesville, Virginia, take I-64 West to Exit 99 for US 250/Afton/Waynesboro. Turn right onto US 250, entering Shenandoah National Park, and immediately make a sharp left onto Skyline Drive. Follow Skyline Drive 22.4 miles, to Browns Gap parking area, milepost 83 on Skyline Drive, on your left. During winter, Skyline Drive may close. Call 540-999-3500 (option 1 then option 1 again) for the latest road conditions.

41

Rapidan Camp Loop

SCENERY: ★ ★ ★ ★
TRAIL CONDITION: ★ ★ ★ ★
CHILDREN: ★ ★
DIFFICULTY: ★ ★ ★
SOLITUDE: ★ ★ ★

THE CABIN WHERE HERBERT HOOVER RETREATED DURING HIS PRESIDENCY IS NOW IN THE SHADOW OF THE APPALACHIAN TRAIL.

GPS TRAILHEAD COORDINATES: N38° 30.010' W78° 26.752'

DISTANCE & CONFIGURATION: 7.2-mile loop

HIKING TIME: 6 hours (includes 1 hour at Rapidan Camp)

HIGHLIGHTS: High peak, historic presidential retreat, waterfall

ELEVATION: 3,265' at trailhead; 3,812' at high point

ACCESS: National park entrance fee required; Skyline Drive may close in winter; call 540-999-3500 for the latest road conditions.

MAPS: Potomac Appalachian Trail Club *Map 10 AT and other trails in Shenandoah National Park Central District;* Trails Illustrated *Map #228 Shenandoah National Park;* USGS *Big Meadows* and USGS *Fletcher*

FACILITIES: Big Meadows visitor center, campground, and wayside is a few miles north

CONTACT: Shenandoah National Park: 540-999-3500, **nps.gov/shen**

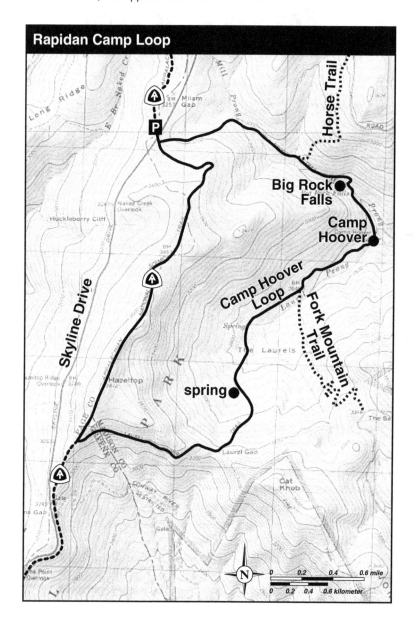

Rapidan Camp Loop

Big Rock Falls

Camp Hoover

Camp Hoover Loop

Fork Mountain Trail

Horse Trail

Skyline Drive

spring

Overview

Follow the Appalachian Trail (A.T.) over Hazeltop, the third-highest peak in Shenandoah National Park, and then trace attractive Laurel Prong Trail down to Rapidan Camp, the woodland getaway for President Herbert Hoover. The camp has much to see; you can even embark on a self-guided interpretive tour. Return to Milam Gap via Mill Prong Trail and view Big Rock Falls along the way.

Route Details

This loop takes you over Hazeltop, the third-highest peak in the park, and then traces attractive Laurel Prong Trail down to Camp Hoover, the woodland getaway for President Herbert Hoover (1929–33). The camp has much to see; you can even embark on a self-guided interpretive tour. Return to Milam Gap via Mill Prong Trail and view Big Rock Falls along the way.

Head southbound on the Appalachian Trail from the Milam Gap parking area. Note the preponderance of apple trees in this area. Bears gorge on them in fall. Cross Skyline Drive and come to a trail junction. To your left is Mill Prong Trail, your return route. Continue gently uphill, southbound on the A.T. through a forest shading fields of ferns, and reach a sharp right turn at mile 0.4. Now you are really going south as the A.T. heads toward Hazeltop. The trail grade is nearly level, but it rises slightly on a slowly narrowing ridge. At points, the A.T. is arrow straight. Note the trailside upthrust rocks. At 1.9 miles, a spur leads

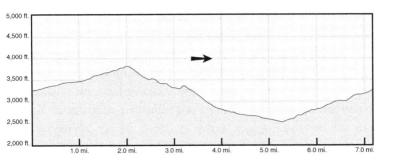

right to a rocky overlook. Here, you can enjoy an open view to the west, of the South Fork Shenandoah River valley and waves of mountains in the distance. Achieve the peak of Hazeltop (3,812 feet) at 2 miles. To your right is a gnarled oak next to a large embedded rock, the actual top of the summit. To the left of the trail is a small balsam fir, a survivor of the forests that now thrive much farther north in New England and Canada. Its needles are flat, fragrant, and friendly (not sharp). Leave the summit and come to a left turn. To your right are two red spruce trees, another member of the Canadian forest. Its needles are a darker green, rounded, and sharp. These trees grow only in a few locations in Shenandoah National Park.

The A.T. drops moderately and approaches the scenic Laurel Prong Trail at mile 2.4. Turn left on Laurel Prong Trail. Several springs flow over the boulder-laden slope. The going is slow on the irregular tread. The Conway River valley falls away to your right. The trail descends sharply, levels off, and then makes a final dip to arrive at Laurel Gap and a trail junction at 3.4 miles. Cat Knob looms to the east. This is a good place to take a break—if the winds aren't howling.

Turn left, staying on Laurel Prong Trail. It continues to drop sharply while snaking through The Laurels, a concentration of mountain laurel and likely the inspiration for the stream's name. Pass a spring at 3.9 miles, the first of several rills flowing off Hazeltop. Dead hemlocks have fallen, and the forest is in transition. Rock-hop Laurel Prong at 4.1 miles. Watch for stone fences from pioneer farming days. At 4.7 miles, Fork Mountain Trail leaves right, into a thicket of rhododendron that is perhaps yet another inspiration for the stream's name, as mountaineers often called rhododendron "laurel" and mountain laurel "ivy." Confusing, huh?

Continue straight on Laurel Prong Trail. Watch as a spur trail leads left to Five Tents, the original dwelling site for Herbert Hoover. When the president first came here, workmen built five tents on platforms, around which a cabin was ultimately constructed. You can still see the fireplace. Arrive at Camp Hoover, alternatively known as Rapidan Camp, at 5.3 miles. Situated at the confluence of Laurel Prong and Mill Creek, the camp lies in a lovely wooded setting. Check out the three buildings and interpretive information. There are short nature trails here too. This place is engaging, so give it at least an hour. During summer, park interpreters can take you on a tour of the retreat's interior. Imagine the president and his compadres strategizing on subjects of national import—trout fishing too. Back then, hemlocks shaded and cooled the flat.

Continue your loop hike on the Mill Prong Trail, which starts near the Creel Cabin. Climb along the steep valley, rife with wildflowers in spring. The trail now drops to Mill Prong, crossing it below Big Rock Falls at mile 5.7. Big Rock Falls slips 15 feet over a rock slide into a large, deep pool. Herbert Hoover surely slung a fly rod here.

The trail switchbacks, levels off in a rocky section, and intersects the Mill Prong Horse Trail at mile 6.1. Bear left, still on the Mill Prong Trail, crossing a side branch, and then rock-hop Mill Prong once more at 6.6 miles. The stream is now wide, shallow, and pocked with stones. The path leads into an open, ferny forest. Enter a grassy glade before intersecting the A.T. at mile 7.2. Turn right on the A.T., cross Skyline Drive, and return to the Milam Gap Trailhead.

Nearby Attractions

The greater Big Meadows area of Shenandoah National Park is a few miles north of this trailhead. Here, there's a visitor center, a lodge, a campground, and a camp store; ranger tours are offered.

Directions

From Harrisonburg, Virginia (an officially designated Appalachian Trail Community), take US 33 East 23.1 miles to Shenandoah National Park and Swift Run Gap. Turn north onto Skyline Drive and follow it 12.7 miles to the Milam Gap Trailhead, at milepost 52.8, on the west side of Skyline Drive. The Appalachian Trail is found behind the parking area. During winter, Skyline Drive may close. Call 540-999-3500 (option 1 then option 1 again) for the latest road conditions.

42

Lewis Spring Falls Loop

SCENERY: ★ ★ ★ ★ ★
TRAIL CONDITION: ★ ★ ★ ★
CHILDREN: ★ ★ ★
DIFFICULTY: ★ ★
SOLITUDE: ★ ★

LEWIS SPRING FALLS DASHES 81 FEET DOWN A NAKED CLIFF.

GPS TRAILHEAD COORDINATES: N38° 31.020' W78° 26.496'

DISTANCE & CONFIGURATION: 3.4-mile loop

HIKING TIME: 2.5 hours

HIGHLIGHTS: High-country waterfalls, high-country views

ELEVATION: 2,470' at trailhead; 3,685' at high point

ACCESS: National park entrance fee required; Skyline Drive may close in winter; call 540-999-3500 for the latest road conditions.

MAPS: Potomac Appalachian Trail Club *Map 10 AT and other trails in Shenandoah National Park Central District;* Trails Illustrated *Map #228 Shenandoah National Park;* USGS *Big Meadows*

FACILITIES: Big Meadows visitor center, campground, and wayside is nearby

CONTACT: Shenandoah National Park: 540-999-3500, **nps.gov/shen**

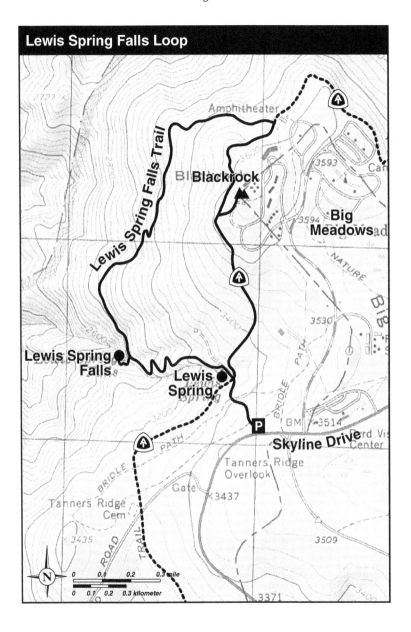

Lewis Spring Falls Loop

Overview

This popular high-country loop is in the Big Meadows area of Shenandoah National Park. Leave Skyline Drive and head northbound on the Appalachian Trail (A.T.), climbing to view-laden and geologically rich Blackrock (a different peak than Blackrock of the South District of the park, see page 224). From there, the hike passes more interesting rock features, then joins the Lewis Falls Trail, leading to a loud and dramatic cataract with its own views near and far.

Route Details

You will want to capture the visual features with your smartphone or camera along this hike that starts high and stays high. This loop takes place near the busy Big Meadows area, with its park lodge, visitor center, ranger station, and campground. Thus, this loop gets traffic, but deservedly so. Leave the parking area near Tanner Ridge Overlook, heading down Lewis Spring Service Road to reach the Appalachian Trail. Walk northbound on the A.T., climbing to Blackrock and its stellar views. From there, the hike passes more attention-grabbing rock features, then joins the Lewis Falls Trail. The path leads to a loud and dramatic cataract. Lewis Spring Falls is one of the highest elevation falls at Shenandoah. The distance is very doable, and the elevation changes aren't overly much, leaving you time to enjoy the other aspects of the greater Big Meadows area.

Leave the little parking area with several spots just north of the Tanner Ridge Overlook. Walk just a few yards north along Skyline

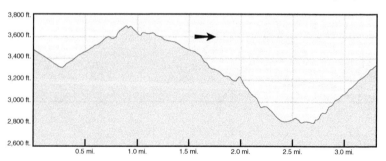

Drive to reach the Lewis Spring Service Road. Pass around a chain gate, then head downhill on a gravel track bordered by a stunted high-country forest of haw, fire cherry, and maple, reclaiming former fields. Look for apple, birch, and locust trees too. The blue-blazed track crosses the yellow-blazed Tanners Ridge Horse Trail and continues descending.

At 0.2 mile, reach the Appalachian Trail. Turn right (northbound) here, heading for Big Meadows Lodge. Lewis Spring is just below this intersection. Begin working uphill in hardwoods mixed with pines, even a preserved hemlock or two. Rocks and boulders of all sizes and descriptions are strewn about the forest floor. The well-used path features stonework to keep the trail from being sloped. At 0.7 mile, reach a spur trail leading right to Blackrock. Turn right here and make the 0.1-mile climb to the outcrop, at 3,720 feet. Along the way, see if you can find a few red spruce trees. In winter, they are easy to spot among the barren hardwoods. Mountain ash clings on the crags of Blackrock. The spiny rock protrusion opens to the west, where you can see the towns of Stanley and Luray in the Page Valley, amid the 180-degree view to the southwest and northwest, especially the high peaks of the park's North District. Luray has the distinction of being an officially designated Appalachian Trail Community. Below, the tops of oak trees seem close enough to touch. The A.T. can be seen below when the leaves are off.

Return to the A.T., curving below the stone massif of Blackrock. Another, smaller vista lies off the trail. Ahead, pass below the Big Meadows Lodge before meeting the Lewis Falls Trail at 1.3 miles. Here, turn acutely left on the Lewis Falls Trail amid lush woods with a ferny understory. Keep down slope, looking for a level grassy spot near the trail good for picnicking, at 1.6 miles. Keep south along the western escarpment of the mountain, which drops off to your right. At 1.9 miles, the trail skirts below a lichen-covered rock protrusion. Beyond here, the rocky trail steepens beneath the woods. Curve onto a southwest facing slope, with mountain laurel and pines joining the sturdy oaks. Outcrops along the trail provide views into the hollow of upper Hawksbill Creek, which becomes audible. Reach another junction at 2.5 miles. Here, a spur trail leads right to an outcrop and view into the valley below and lands beyond. Massanutten Mountain forms a backdrop. The main spur path crosses wide and rocky Hawksbill Creek then curves beyond a precipice. A guardrail guides you the last bit to a rock-walled observation point. Here, you can look down at the 81-foot falls spilling over the rock face, crashing into rocks and then splashing out of sight.

Backtrack to the Lewis Falls Trail and begin a switchback-filled ascent along Lewis Run, drifting into rich waterside woods and drier pine-oak forest away from the stream. Join an old roadbed, then pass the actual Lewis Spring, which is housed in a rock-and-wood structure with a visible outflow. Just ahead, reach the A.T. again at 3.2 miles. To your right is another boxed spring, and the site of the long-dismantled Lewis Spring trail shelter. From here, keep straight on the gravel road, backtracking to the trailhead.

Nearby Attractions

The greater Big Meadows area of Shenandoah National Park is just north of this trailhead. Here, you can go to the visitor center, overnight at a lodge, camp in a campground, take guided ranger tours, or head to a camp store.

Directions

From Luray, Virginia, take US 211 East 8.8 miles to the Thornton Gap entrance of Shenandoah National Park. Take Skyline Drive south 19.9 miles to the parking area for the Lewis Spring Service Road at milepost 51.4 on Skyline Drive. This parking area is sandwiched between Big Meadows south entrance and Tanners Ridge Overlook on the west side of the road. During winter, Skyline Drive may close. Call 540-999-3500 (option 1 then option 1 again) for the latest road conditions.

43

Stony Man Loop

SCENERY: ★ ★ ★ ★ ★
TRAIL CONDITION: ★ ★ ★ ★
CHILDREN: ★ ★ ★ ★
DIFFICULTY: ★ ★
SOLITUDE: ★

THE SHENANDOAH VALLEY AND WAVES OF RIDGES EXTENDING TO WEST VIRGINIA STRETCH OUT BEFORE THE CRAGS OF STONY MAN.

GPS TRAILHEAD COORDINATES: N38° 35.584' W78° 22.545'

DISTANCE & CONFIGURATION: 3.7-mile loop

HIKING TIME: 2.5 hours

HIGHLIGHTS: Fantastic views, national park history

ELEVATION: 3,700' at trailhead; 4,015' at high point

ACCESS: National park entrance fee required; Skyline Drive may close in winter; call 540-999-3500 for the latest road conditions.

MAPS: Potomac Appalachian Trail Club *Map 10 AT and other trails in Shenandoah National Park Central District;* Trails Illustrated *Map #228 Shenandoah National Park;* USGS *Big Meadows* and USGS *Old Rag Mountain*

FACILITIES: Skyland Resort is nearby

CONTACT: Shenandoah National Park: 540-999-3500, **nps.gov/shen**

Stony Man Loop

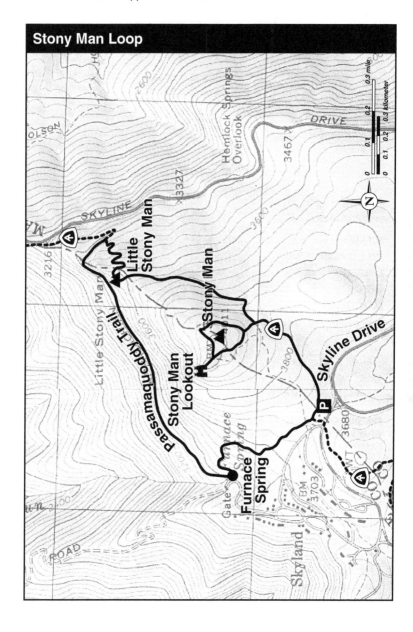

Overview

This hike traverses some of the highest terrain in Shenandoah National Park. First, you will cruise a high-country nature trail and make a side loop to the summit of Stony Man Mountain. You will then take Little Stony Man Trail to the peak of Little Stony Man, where more overlooks await. Your return trip is along the Passama-quoddy Trail, where vistas continue. Hike along the north slope of Stony Man Mountain to reach Furnace Spring, which once was used in a copper-mining operation. Climb through mixed evergreens and hardwoods back to the trailhead, completing this highlight-laden circuit. The first 0.4 mile of the trail is wheelchair accessible.

Route Details

The beginning can be a little confusing. Here a sign indicates the path as Stony Man Nature Trail; however, this is also the Appalachian Trail. They run in conjunction here. An interpretive booklet can be purchased at the trailhead to enhance your nature trail experience. Walk a pleasant pea gravel all-access path amid fern gardens overlain by hardwoods. Preserved hemlocks add a touch of evergreen to the woods. Later you will also see a few spruce trees.

At 0.4 mile, come to an intersection. This is the highest point on the Appalachian Trail in Shenandoah National Park—3,837 feet. However, you are about to go even higher. Turn left, still ascending to make the sub-loop to the summit of Stony Man, staying with the

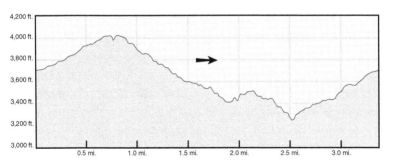

nature trail. Split right ahead, following the sequence of the interpretive posts. Note the squat, wind-sculpted haw trees as you climb. At 0.7 mile, reach a four-way trail intersection. Turn right toward the summit of Stony Man. Incredible panoramas open ahead. To your left, Skyland Resort stands on the shoulder of Stony Man. Ahead lie Shenandoah Valley and the town of Luray, Massanutten Mountain running parallel to the Blue Ridge, and beyond that North Mountain forms the Virginia–West Virginia state line. To your right (north), look below at the upthrust cliffs of Little Stony Man and at Skyline Drive and the park's North District. The name Stony Man derives from this peak— the park's second-highest point—looking like the face of a bearded man. This face can be clearly seen from the north on milepost 38.9 of Skyline Drive at Stony Man Mountain Overlook.

Return to the Appalachian Trail, then resume a northbound direction. The trail drops steadily through northern hardwoods, including cool-climate specialist yellow birch, on the east slope of the Blue Ridge. Reach the tan cliffs of Little Stony Man at 1.7 miles. More grand views open before you. Look up to Stony Man for little stick figures milling about. The jagged cliffs have an especially rugged appearance as they emerge from the surrounding forest. The squared-off fields of Shenandoah Valley below contrast with the craggy mountains to your right.

Return to woods beyond the cliff, switchbacking downhill to make another trail junction at 1.9 miles. Leave the white-blazed Appalachian Trail and turn left on the Passamaquoddy Trail, blazed in blue. Soon pass beneath the cliffs of Little Stony Man on a path constructed with considerable effort from native stones. Open onto a lower outcrop that avails yet another overlook from which the west side of the Blue Ridge and Lake Arrowhead opens below. The rising slope of Stony Man Mountain is especially impressive. Begin meandering the northwest side of the peak on a steep slope, yet the well-constructed trail makes hiking a breeze. Walk beneath cliffs. Come to a rock overhang and a dripping spring at 2.4 miles. At 2.5 miles, reach your low point of 3,200 feet, then begin a gentle uptick. Fire cherry trees are rising where hemlocks once stood. Pass beneath a transmission line at 2.8 miles.

Reach Furnace Spring at 2.9 miles. You can hear the water flowing behind a locked door. The old copper mine was in this vicinity and utilized the spring, but the shaft has since been filled in, and no trail leads to it. Come to an intersection with Skyland Fire Road and the Furnace Spring Trail. Make a hard left here, joining the yellow-blazed Furnace Spring Trail, passing directly above Furnace Spring on a doubletrack. The path then narrows and reenters deep woods. Snake your way uphill in rocky forest. The trail bed is fainter here. Look for yellow blazes on the trailside trees amid more preserved hemlocks. Meet the Stony Man Horse Trail and turn left, tracing it a short distance to reach the Stony Man Nature Trail parking area and the hike's conclusion.

Nearby Attractions

The Skyland Lodge area offers more hiking as well as lodging, horseback rides, casual food, and dining.

Directions

From Luray, Virginia, take US 211 East 8.8 miles to the Thornton Gap entrance of Shenandoah National Park. Take Skyline Drive south 10.5 miles to milepost 41.7. This is at the north entrance to Skyland Resort off Skyline Drive. At the turn, you will see a sign indicating that this is the highest point on Skyline Drive. Immediately after turning toward Skyland Resort, turn right into the parking for Stony Man Nature Trail. During winter, Skyline Drive may close. Call 540-999-3500 (option 1 then option 1 again) for the latest road conditions.

44

Marys Rock via The Pinnacle

SCENERY: ★ ★ ★ ★ ★
TRAIL CONDITION: ★ ★ ★ ★
CHILDREN: ★ ★
DIFFICULTY: ★ ★ ★
SOLITUDE: ★ ★ ★

HERE, THE A.T. STRETCHES OVER THE SPINE OF THE BLUE RIDGE, LEADING YOU TO THE WONDERFUL VIEWS ATOP MARYS ROCK.

GPS TRAILHEAD COORDINATES: N38° 37.484' W78° 20.537'

DISTANCE & CONFIGURATION: 7.2-mile out-and-back

HIKING TIME: 4 hours

HIGHLIGHTS: Multiple stunning views

ELEVATION: 3,360' at trailhead; 3,730' at high point

ACCESS: National park entrance fee required; Skyline Drive may close in winter; call 540-999-3500 for the latest road conditions.

MAPS: Potomac Appalachian Trail Club *Map 10 AT and other trails in Shenandoah National Park Central District;* Trails Illustrated *Map #228 Shenandoah National Park;* USGS *Old Rag Mountain* and USGS *Thornton Gap*

FACILITIES: Picnic area, restrooms, water

CONTACT: Shenandoah National Park: 540-999-3500, **nps.gov/shen**

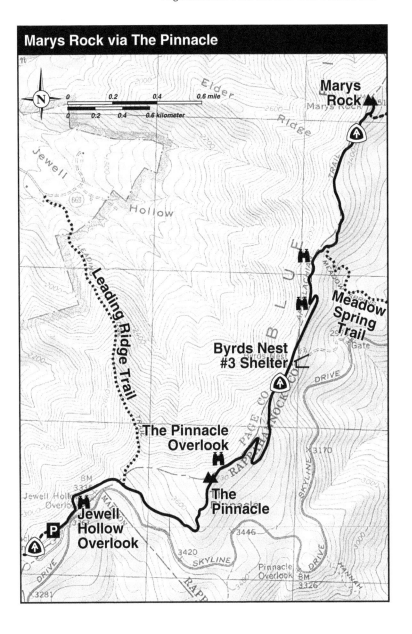

Marys Rock via The Pinnacle

Overview

This hike over The Pinnacle to Marys Rock is arguably the best of the Appalachian Trail (A.T.) in Shenandoah National Park. Views are expansive and frequent after leaving Pinnacles Picnic Grounds. A climb leads to The Pinnacle with an outstanding vista. Finally reach what Shenandoah old-timers believe is the best vista in the entire park—Marys Rock.

Route Details

The hike over The Pinnacle to Marys Rock will garner the attention of even the most jaded A.T. hiker. The views are constant and capacious. Nevertheless, hiking to a view is always more rewarding than driving to a view, and there are plenty of those along Skyline Drive. On the hike, panoramas open up shortly after leaving the Pinnacles Picnic Area. A climb leads you to The Pinnacle with an outstanding vista. Still more views keep your neck craning from the Blue Ridge before reaching what many Shenandoah old-timers feel is the best vista in the entire park—Marys Rock.

The rewards for these sceneries far outstrip the effort needed. Elevation changes only amount to climbs and drops of 450 feet each—not bad for the spine of the Shenandoah highlands. Pick up the Appalachian Trail in the grassy margin to the right of the picnic area entrance road. Head right (northbound) on the A.T. for Jewell Hollow Overlook. Pass some likely planted spruce trees. Immediate

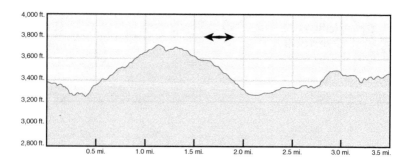

views open to your left as you travel along a stony upthrust escarpment. Dip to reach the Jewell Hollow Overlook at 0.2 mile. The A.T. actually goes south a short distance before making a switchback to head back north. Come to a small field below the overlook. Enjoy an unobstructed opening to the west. Lake Arrowhead lies below. Begin climbing beyond the field. Reenter woodland, coming to a trail junction at 0.5 mile. Pass the Leading Ridge Trail and continue north on the A.T.

The path tunnels through an understory of mountain laurel in dense woodland. At 0.9 mile, enter a forest area littered with massive gray boulders. The trees here are short. Thin soils and rough climatic conditions atop these mountains stunt their growth. Meander amid the boulders, watching for unusual stacked stones that seem likely to fall. Open onto The Pinnacle, elevation 3,730 feet, at 1.2 miles. The rock outcrop is fronted with a sheer drop-off. Be prepared for an incredible view of Virginia mountains and valleys from the west to the east, north too. You can see Luray below, and on a clear day look north at the balance of the park, including your destination—Marys Rock, a mere bump along the ridge from here. Be prudent on these jagged, uneven rocks.

The A.T. continues north and descends a series of switchbacks in very stony woods. Slip over to the southeast side of the mountain. In a gap, reach Byrds Nest Shelter 3 at 2.1 miles. The three-sided camping structure is open to Appalachian Trail thru-hikers, defined as three consecutive nights or longer on the A.T. This stone shelter has a picnic table and provides a respite from the elements, but do not expect the water fountain to work. A privy stands just ahead. Follow the service road that leads from Byrds Nest Shelter 3 to Skyline Drive for a short distance. Veer left at the intersection, staying on the A.T. The service road drops right to a spring.

Another westward view opens at mile 2.5, soon after a switchback to the left. You can also look back at The Pinnacle and its outcrops, where you were earlier. A grassy flat here beckons a rest. Ahead, a rock promontory offers more looks at 2.7 miles, including

Stony Man Mountain. The Meadow Spring Trail leaves right at mile 2.9. Begin climbing for 0.25 mile. The trail levels as it approaches the backside of Marys Rock. Continue downhill to the Marys Rock spur trail at 3.5 miles. Turn left on the spur trail and rise to Marys Rock, reaching it at 3.6 miles.

The panorama from the huge outcrop ranges—well, just about everywhere. Choose your viewing spot. To the north, easy views open of many Blue Ridge peaks. The town of Luray and the Shenandoah Valley stretch to the west. The Thornton Gap entrance station stands clearly below. Agile hikers can walk to the highest rock of the outcrop, due south from the main overlook. The top is marked with a pair of U.S. Geological Survey markers. From there, you can see in all four cardinal directions. Decide for yourself if Marys Rock has the best view in the park. Just be careful doing it. It is undeniably one of the best and a personal favorite of mine.

Nearby Attractions

The Skyland Lodge area is located south of the Pinnacles Picnic Area, and offers more hiking, lodging, horseback rides, casual food, and dining.

Directions

From Luray, Virginia, take US 211 East 8.8 miles to the Thornton Gap entrance of Shenandoah National Park. Take Skyline Drive south 5.2 miles to the Pinnacles Picnic Area, located at milepost 36.7. Pick up the Appalachian Trail on your right as you top out in the picnic area, before the road starts looping around. If the picnic area is closed (winter), simply start at Jewell Hollow Overlook, milepost 36.4. Go to the south end of the overlook and pick up the Appalachian Trail there. During winter, Skyline Drive may close. Call 540-999-3500 (option 1 then option 1 again) for the latest road conditions.

45

Sugarloaf Loop

SCENERY:	★ ★ ★ ★
TRAIL CONDITION:	★ ★ ★ ★ ★
CHILDREN:	★ ★ ★
DIFFICULTY:	★ ★
SOLITUDE:	★ ★ ★

AUTHOR JOHNNY MOLLOY CONTEMPLATES YET ANOTHER STELLAR PANORAMA
OF THE SHENANDOAH VALLEY FROM THE A.T.

GPS TRAILHEAD COORDINATES: N38° 45.594' W78° 16.955'

DISTANCE & CONFIGURATION: 4.7-mile loop

HIKING TIME: 3 hours

HIGHLIGHTS: Views, cascade, geology

ELEVATION: 3,385' at trailhead; 2,565' at low point

ACCESS: National park entrance fee required; Skyline Drive may close in winter;
call 540-999-3500 for the latest road conditions.

MAPS: Potomac Appalachian Trail Club *Map 9 AT and other trails in Shenandoah National
Park North District;* Trails Illustrated *Map #228 Shenandoah National Park;* USGS *Bentonville*
and USGS *Thornton Gap*

FACILITIES: None

CONTACT: Shenandoah National Park: 540-999-3500, **nps.gov/shen**

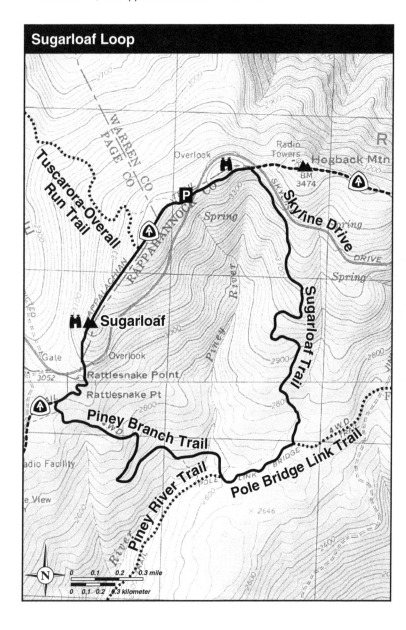

Sugarloaf Loop

Overview

This loop dips off the eastern side of Hogback Mountain into the upper Piney River valley. Relish far-reaching views on the Appalachian Trail (A.T.), then follow a moderate grade into the Piney River on the Sugarloaf Trail. A grassy flat beside the Piney River makes for a great resting spot. Head back to the high country, grabbing more panoramas from Hogback Mountain before completing the circuit.

Route Details

Spring–fall are the most rewarding times for this trek. Wildflowers will be showing in the valley during spring. Summer will offer a cool and shady respite. Enjoy views on clear fall days, and during this time you might even spot wildlife on the trail. From the parking area just south of Hogback Overlook, pick up the A.T., northbound, as it crosses over to the eastern side of Skyline Drive. Hike through fern-floored oak woods, shortly climbing to a rocky knob spiked with uptilted rock. Note the rock combination just to the right of the trail that resembles a chair. Many an A.T. hiker has had their picture taken in that oversized throne.

At 0.2 mile, a side trail leads left to a rock outcrop framed in mountain ash trees. The western vistas are extensive. Hogback Mountain Overlook is just below you. Overall Run cuts a chasm. Ridges rise around it. The Shenandoah Valley stretches out past the park.

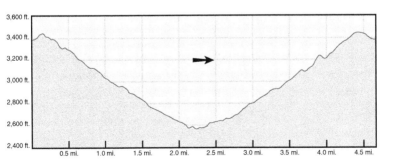

Beyond the valley, other mountains rise to frame the patchwork of farm, field, and town, a classic Shenandoah National Park panorama.

Descend among rocky woods. Notice the trees' wind-sculpted easterly tilt. Reach the slender Sugarloaf Trail at 0.3 mile. Here, turn right onto a singletrack path lined with mountain laurel beneath scattered oaks. Briefly run parallel to Skyline Drive, joining an old wagon road. The Sugarloaf Trail curves back to the right, winding on a slight sloped ridge, former pastureland. Descend to step over two rocky streamlets, wide but shallow feeder branches of the Piney River. Straight rock pioneer walls contrast the fluid shapes of nature. Backpackers find legal campsites off the trail in the next mile or so. This loop is a great break-in trip for the novice overnighter, and is a quick, quality one-night getaway for everyone.

Reach a trail junction at mile 1.7. Turn right onto the Pole Bridge Link Trail. The land is level in these parts—for mountain land. It was cultivated too, despite the rocks you see. Pass through a changing forest, where hardwoods such as black birch and yellow birch are vying to replace the fallen hemlocks that once colored the vale evergreen. The gradual descent leads to another trail junction at 2.1 miles. Stay right with the Piney Branch Trail. If you went left down the Piney River Trail, you would reach 25-foot Piney River Falls in 1.9 miles. Our hike takes the Piney Branch Trail. Step over the rocky branches you crossed earlier before reaching the upper Piney River in 0.1 mile. Large boulders and rocks line the watercourse. Cross the river to a grassy flat flanked by a large boulder. This locale makes a nice respite. A worth-a-look set of cascades falls downstream of this crossing.

Leave this low point of the loop—you are still over 2,500 feet—and start climbing toward the crest of the Blue Ridge on a gentle grade. Big rocks line the trail bed. At mile 3.2, pass through an open area with a tremendous rock face rising up the hill to your right. In September, bears converge and eat fruits of cherry trees that grow nearby. You will see much purple, seed-laden bear scat along this path in the fall. Curve uphill away from the roadbed to cross a second roadbed near a national park survey marker. The Appalachian Trail is just uphill, at 3.5 miles. Turn right onto the A.T., making northbound tracks through open woodland where large widespread oaks grow over grass. Younger trees vie for sunlight. Undulate over a rocky hill to reach Skyline Drive at 3.7 miles. Rattlesnake Point Overlook is just up the road. Keep northbound, crossing Skyline Drive, and ascend the south side of Hogback Mountain. A side trail at mile 4 leads left to an outcrop with views. The ridgeline that is Massanutten Mountain forms a backdrop to South Fork Shenandoah River valley. Range upon range of Shenandoah's mountains roll south. Rejoin the A.T., then dip into a pretty, grassy gap, then resume climbing to reach the Tuscarora–Overall Run Trail at mile 4.5. Pass a limited vista point on trail right before drifting into the parking area at mile 4.7, completing your circuit.

Nearby Attractions

Matthews Arm Campground is located a mile south from the trailhead. It offers drive-up camping and makes a great base for exploring the North District of Shenandoah National Park.

Directions

From Luray, Virginia, take US 211 East 8.8 miles to the Thornton Gap entrance of Shenandoah National Park. Take Skyline Drive north 10.2 miles to the parking area on the west side of Skyline Drive, just before Hogback Mountain Overlook, milepost 21.1. The loop hike starts on the eastern side of Skyline Drive where the A.T. crosses the road. During winter, Skyline Drive may close. Call 540-999-3500 (option 1 then option 1 again) for the latest road conditions.

Appendix A:

Contact Information

GEORGIA

CHATTAHOOCHEE NATIONAL FOREST
Blue Ridge Ranger District:
706-745-6928
Conasauga Ranger District:
706-695-6736
www.fs.usda.gov/conf

TENNESSEE

CHEROKEE NATIONAL FOREST
Watauga Ranger District:
423-735-1500
www.fs.usda.gov/cherokee

**GREAT SMOKY MOUNTAINS
NATIONAL PARK**
865-436-1200
nps.gov/grsm

NORTH CAROLINA

BLUE RIDGE PARKWAY
828-298-0398
nps.gov/blri

NANTAHALA NATIONAL FOREST
Nantahala Ranger District:
828-524-6441
www.fs.usda.gov/nfsnc

PISGAH NATIONAL FOREST
Appalachian Ranger District:
828-689-9694
www.fs.usda.gov/nfsnc

VIRGINIA

**GEORGE WASHINGTON AND
JEFFERSON NATIONAL FORESTS**
Glenwood–Pedlar Ranger District:
540-291-2188
Eastern Divide Ranger District:
540-552-4641
www.fs.usda.gov/gwj

**MOUNT ROGERS NATIONAL
RECREATION AREA**
276-783-5196
tinyurl.com/mtrogersnra

SHENANDOAH NATIONAL PARK
540-999-3500
nps.gov/shen

Appendix B:
Appalachian Trail Communities

THE APPALACHIAN TRAIL COMMUNITY program is an Appalachian Trail Conservancy initiative that seeks to develop mutually beneficial relationships with interested towns and counties along the Appalachian Trail to enhance their economies, further protect the trail, and engage a new generation of volunteers.

GEORGIA
Hiawassee/Towns County
Helen/White County
Union County (Blairsville, Suches)
Dahlonega
Ellijay/Gilmer County

TENNESSEE
Unicoi County (Erwin)

NORTH CAROLINA
Hot Springs
Fontana Dam
Franklin

VIRGINIA
Berryville/Clarke County
Front Royal/Warren County
Luray/Page County
Harrisonburg
Nelson County
Waynesboro
Buena Vista
Glasgow
Troutville
Narrows
Pearisburg
Bland
Marion/Smyth County
Abingdon
Damascus

Index

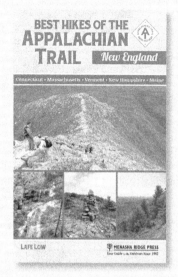

About the Author

JOHNNY MOLLOY is a writer and adventurer based in Johnson City, Tennessee. His outdoor passion ignited on a backpacking trip in Great Smoky Mountains National Park while attending the University of Tennessee. That first foray unleashed a love of the outdoors, which led the native Tennessean to spend more than 3,500 nights backpacking, canoe camping, and tent camping over the past three decades.

Friends enjoyed his outdoor adventure stories; one even suggested he write a book. He pursued his friend's idea and soon parlayed his love of the outdoors into an occupation. The results of his efforts are more than 60 books and guides. His writings include hiking guidebooks, camping guidebooks, paddling guidebooks, comprehensive guidebooks about a specific area, and true outdoor adventure books throughout the Eastern United States.

Though primarily involved with book publications, Molloy writes for varied magazines and websites and is a columnist and feature writer for his local paper, the *Johnson City Press*. He continues writing and traveling extensively throughout the United States, endeavoring in a variety of outdoor pursuits.

A Christian, Molloy is an active member of First Presbyterian Church in Johnson City. His wife, Keri Anne, accompanies Johnny on the trail and at home. Johnny's non-outdoor interests include reading, American history, and University of Tennessee sports. For the latest on Johnny, visit **johnnymolloy.com.**

About the Appalachian Trail Conservancy

THE APPALACHIAN TRAIL (A.T.) is incredibly well-known around the world, not just among the diverse hiking and backpacking communities. Less well-known is what put it on the ground in the 1920s and '30s and manages it to this day: the staff and more than 6,000 volunteers under the umbrella of the Appalachian Trail Conservancy, founded in 1925 by 22 pioneers.

Yes, the A.T. has been a part of the national park system since 1968, but part of the deal with Congress was that this small, private, nonprofit organization would continue to do the bulk of the work and raise most of the money to pay for that work—rather than have taxpayers underwrite what would be a typical national park staff to care for 250,000 acres of public land. (The National Park Service does have a small A.T. office of fewer than a dozen employees working with us on major legal issues of environmental and historic preservation compliance and law enforcement.)

What does "take care of" mean? It means keeping the footpath of more than 2,189 miles open and safe for outdoor recreation of most nonmotorized types (including hunting for about half the area). It means maintaining in good condition overnight shelters and tent sites, absolutely necessary bridges, and other facilities.

It means monitoring the health of more than 550 rare, threatened, or endangered species that call the trail lands home (we don't yet have a count on the animals)—more than almost any other national park. It means preserving more cultural artifacts still in place than in any other park. (Remember, these ridgelines were the Colonial frontier before the seas and the West, and they were the site of Underground Railroad stops and then dozens of Civil War battles, as well as farms taken over by freed slaves.)

It means working cooperatively with the National Park Service, U.S. Forest Service, and 14 states that hold title to those lands for the public—altogether almost 100 agency partners. It means bringing into the fold for mutual benefit 85 counties' officials and the governments and businesses for almost three dozen places officially designated as an Appalachian Trail Community. It means watching for and combating threats to all from incompatible development.

It means providing the public with timely, comprehensive, and useful information about the A.T.'s wealth of natural beauty and how best to enjoy it—for example, through books such as this, in which we are proud to have a role.

We consider it our job to conserve, promote, and enhance the Appalachian National Scenic Trail every day. We do all that for less than $6.75 in private funds per day per mile (and about $2.75 more in targeted federal contracts).

You can support that effort by going to **appalachiantrail.org** to learn more and/or become a member. Old school (like us)? You can write to Appalachian Trail Conservancy, P.O. Box 807, Harpers Ferry, WV 25425, or call 304-535-6331.

Most of all, we hope that you enjoy in some way the People's Path. It *is* yours, after all.

DEAR CUSTOMERS AND FRIENDS,

SUPPORTING YOUR INTEREST IN OUTDOOR ADVENTURE, travel, and an active lifestyle is central to our operations, from the authors we choose to the locations we detail to the way we design our books. Menasha Ridge Press was incorporated in 1982 by a group of veteran outdoorsmen and professional outfitters. For many years now, we've specialized in creating books that benefit the outdoors enthusiast.

Almost immediately, Menasha Ridge Press earned a reputation for revolutionizing outdoors- and travel-guidebook publishing. For such activities as canoeing, kayaking, hiking, backpacking, and mountain biking, we established new standards of quality that transformed the whole genre, resulting in outdoor-recreation guides of great sophistication and solid content. Menasha Ridge Press continues to be outdoor publishing's greatest innovator.

The folks at Menasha Ridge Press are as at home on a whitewater river or mountain trail as they are editing a manuscript. The books we build for you are the best they can be, because we're responding to your needs. Plus, we use and depend on them ourselves.

We look forward to seeing you on the river or the trail. If you'd like to contact us directly, visit us at menasharidge.com. We thank you for your interest in our books and the natural world around us all.

SAFE TRAVELS,

Bob Sehlinger

BOB SEHLINGER
PUBLISHER